British cinema of the 1950s:
a celebration

MANCHESTER
UNIVERSITY PRESS

British cinema of the 1950s: a celebration

edited by
IAN MACKILLOP AND NEIL SINYARD

Manchester University Press
Manchester and New York

distributed exclusively in the USA by Palgrave

Published by Manchester University Press
Oxford Road, Manchester M13 9NR, UK
and Room 400, 175 Fifth Avenue, New York, NY 10010, USA
http://www.manchesteruniversitypress.co.uk

Distributed exclusively in the USA
by Palgrave, 175 Fifth Avenue, New York, NY 10010, USA

Distributed exclusively in Canada
by UBC Press, University of British Columbia, 2029 West Mall,
Vancouver, BC, Canada V6T 1Z2

British Library Cataloguing-in-Publication Data
A catalogue record for this book is available from the British Library

Library of Congress Cataloging-in-Publication Data applied for

ISBN 0 7190 6488 0 *hardback*
    0 7190 6489 9 *paperback*

First published 2003

10 09 08 07 06 05 04 03   10 9 8 7 6 5 4 3 2 1

Typeset in Fournier and Fairfield Display
by Koinonia, Manchester

Printed in Great Britain
by Bell & Bain Ltd, Glasgow

Contents

Acknowledgements

We are very grateful for the patience of our contributors who have dealt with many queries. We have had indispensable editorial help from Hilary Barker, Rebecca Broadley, Rosie Ford, Helena Pinder and Sue Turton.

IAN MACKILLOP AND NEIL SINYARD

A 1950s timeline

Occasionally names of personnel are included in these lists ('d.' for director, 'p.' for performer/s) to point up a presence, e.g. John Schlesinger as director of *Starfish*. Non-British films which were nonetheless really important are asterisked and put out of the alphabetical sequence. The temptation to include five excellent films of 1960 could not be resisted.

Cinema	Theatre, writing, broadcasting	Events
1950		
Humphrey Jennings dies	Theatre: *Hamlet* (p. Michael	Labour Party elected:
Bitter Springs (music: Vaughan	Redgrave)	Clement Atlee PM
Williams)	Theatre: T. S. Eliot, *The*	Korean War
The Blue Lamp	*Cocktail Party*	'McCarthyism'
Dance Hall	Writing: George Orwell dies	
The Happiest Days of Your Life		
Odette		
Seven Days to Noon		
The Starfish (d. John		
Schlesinger and others)		
1951		
'X' certificates start	Theatre: *Richard II*	Festival of Britain
*South Pacific**	(p. Michael Redgrave)	Conservative Party elected:
The Browning Version (p.		Winston Churchill PM
Michael Redgrave)		
Festival in London		
The Galloping Major		
His Excellency		
The Lavender Hill Mob		
Life in Her Hands		
The Magic Box		
The Man in a White Suit		
Tales of Hoffman		
White Corridors		
1952		
National Film Theatre opens	Theatre: Agatha Christie,	Coronation of Elizabeth II
Sequence ends	*The Mousetrap*	Fog kills 4,000 Londoners
*This is Cinerama**	Writing: Angus Wilson,	Mau-Mau rebellion in Kenya
The Robe (in CinemaScope)*	*Hemlock and After*	First British atomic tests

Cinema	Theatre, writing, broadcasting	Events
1952		
High Noon*		
Frightened Man		
The Importance of Being Earnest		
Long Memory		
Mandy		
Outcast of the Islands		
Voice of Merill (Tempean Films)		
Wakefield Express (d. Lindsay Anderson)		
Women of Twilight		
1953		
Richard Winnington dies (film critic of *News Chronicle*)	Writing: L.P. Hartley, *The Go-Between*	Soviet Union uses hydrogen bomb
Ripening Seed (d. Claude Autant-Lara)*		Alfred C. Kinsey, *Sexual Behaviour in the Human Female*
The Cruel Sea		
Genevieve		Smoking connected to lung cancer
Hobson's Choice		
The Titfield Thunderbolt		
World Without End		
1954		
The Belles of St Trinians	Theatre: Kenneth Tynan becomes drama critic for the *Observer*	British troops withdraw from Egypt
The Divided Heart		Stanley Kauffmann's *The Philanderer* prosecuted for obscene libel
Doctor in the House		
Father Brown	Theatre: Terence Rattigan, *Separate Tables*	
A Kid for Two Farthings (p. Diana Dors)	Writing: Kingsley Amis, *Lucky Jim*	
The Maggie	Broadcasting: Dylan Thomas, *Under Milk Wood* (BBC radio)	
The Sea Shall Not Have Them	Broadcasting: *Dixon of Dock Green* (BBC TV)	
1955		
Films and Filming starts	Theatre: *Titus Andronicus* (d. Peter Brook, p. Laurence Olivier)	Conservative Party elected: Anthony Eden PM
1984		
Animal Farm (d. Halas and Batchelor)	Writing: F. R. Leavis, *D. H. Lawrence: Novelist*	
The Deep Blue Sea (p. Vivien Leigh, Kenneth More)	Broadcasting: Nikolaus Pevnser, *The Englishness of English Art* (BBC Reith Lectures)	
Escapade		
Foot and Mouth (d. Lindsay Anderson for Central Office of Information)		

Cinema	Theatre, writing, broadcasting	Events
1955		
I am a Camera (p. Laurence Harvey)		
Impulse (Tempean Films)		
The Ladykillers		
The Quatermass Xperiment		
1956		
Sir Alexander Korda dies	Theatre: Angus Wilson, *The Mulberry Bush* (first English Stage Company production)	Hungarian revolution Anglo-French invasion of Suez
The Good Companions		
Jacqueline		
My Teenage Daughter		
Richard III (d./p. Laurence Olivier)	Theatre: John Osborne, *Look Back in Anger*	
The Spanish Gardener		
A Town Like Alice		
Who Done It? (Benny Hill)		
Yield to the Night		
1957		
The Archers productions stop	Theatre: John Osborne, *The Entertainer*	Soviet satellite Sputnik I launched
Happy Road (p. Michael Redgrave)*	Writing: John Braine, *Room at the Top*	Anthony Eden resigns, Harold Macmillan becomes PM
Across the Bridge	Writing: Evelyn Waugh, *The Ordeal of Gilbert Pinfold*	Wolfenden report on homosexuality
Admirable Crichton		
The Bridge on the River Kwai		
Every Day Except Christmas (d. Lindsay Anderson)	Writing: Richard Hoggart, *The Uses of Literacy*	European Economic Community founded
The Running Jumping and Standing Still Film	Broadcasting: BBC reduces hours of the Third Programme	
Shiralee		
The Smallest Show on Earth		
Time Without Pity	Broadcasting: *Emergency Ward – 10* (ITV)	
Woman in a Dressing Gown		
1958		
Tempean starts its 'A' films	Theatre: Harold Pinter, *The Dumb Waiter*	Commercial stereo recording begins
Carry On Sergeant		
Dracula (Hammer: d. Terence Fisher, p. Peter Cushing)	Theatre: Ann Jellicoe, *The Sport of My Mad Mother*	Campaign for Nuclear Disarmament launched
The Duke Wore Jeans	Writing: Raymond Williams, *Culture and Society*	Race riots in Nottingham and Notting Hill, London
Horse's Mouth		
A Night to Remember		
1959		
Ealing Studios closes	Theatre: Arnold Wesker, *Roots*	Labour Party pamphlet, *Leisure for Living*
*Hiroshima Mon Amour**		
Carry On Nurse	Theatre: John Arden, *Sergeant Musgrave's Dance*	Obscene Publications Act
Dangerous Age (d. Sidney J. Furie)		

Cinema	Theatre, writing, broadcasting	Events
1959		
I'm All Right Jack	Theatre: Willis Hall, *The*	
Look Back in Anger	*Long and the Short and*	
Make Mine a Million	*the Tall* (d. Lindsay	
Sapphire	Anderson)	
The Scapegoat		
Separate Tables		
Tiger Bay		
1960		
The League of Gentlemen		Harold Macmillan
Our Man in Havana		acknowledges African
Peeping Tom		nationalism
The Siege of Sidney Street		Independence of Nigeria

Celebrating British cinema of the 1950s

IAN MACKILLOP AND NEIL SINYARD

To counterbalance the rather tepid humanism of our cinema, it might also be said that it is snobbish, anti-intelligent, emotionally inhibited, willfully blind to the conditions and problems of the present, dedicated to an out of date, exhausted national idea. (Lindsay Anderson)

Who will ever forget those days at Iver when, cloistered in the fumed oak dining room (reminiscent of the golf club where no one ever paid his subscription), frightened producers blanched at the mere idea of any film that contained the smallest tincture of reality? (Frederic Raphael)

THE ORIGIN OF this book is an event which took place on Saturday, 5 December 1998 at the British Library in London. It was a study day consisting of lectures about British cinema in the 1950s: most of these are printed here, with an equal number of new essays which have been written since. In the evenings of the week preceding the study day, seven films were screened. They appeared under the headings of 'Festive Fifties' (*The Importance of Being Earnest*, in a sparkling new print), 'Community Fifties' (*John and Julie* and *The Browning Version*), 'Tough Fifties' (*Women of Twilight* and *Hell Drivers*) and 'Women's Fifties' (*My Teenage Daughter* and *Yield to the Night*).

I am Professor of English Literature at the University of Sheffield. I am the author of two books on British intellectual life: *F. R. Leavis: A Life in Criticism* (Allan Lane, 1995) and *The British Ethical Societies* (Cambridge University Press, 1985), and a book about François Truffaut and Henri Pierre Roché, author of *Jules and Jim* and *Two English Girls and the Continent. Ian MacKillop*

I have written over twenty books on film, including studies of Richard Lester, Nicolas Roeg and Jack Clayton. I am the co-editor of the ongoing series of monographs, 'British Film Makers', published by Manchester University Press. I grew up in the 1950s and my love of cinema dates from a childhood which has left indelible filmgoing memories: of a cinema within walking distance of seemingly everyone's home, of copies of *Picturegoer* and the *ABC Film Review*, of usherettes, and choc ices before the main feature, of continuous programmes that permitted you to stay in the cinema all day and see the main feature more than once, of the undignified scramble at the end to get out before the striking up of the National Anthem. *Neil Sinyard*

Why the 1950s? After all, as the prefatory remarks of Anderson and Raphael show, this is perhaps the most derided decade in British film history. It is commonly characterised as the era in which the national cinema retreated into quaintly comic evocations of community or into nostalgic recollections of the war. (It was Brian McFarlane who suggested that Lewis Gilbert's stereotypical war film of 1953, *The Sea Shall Not Have Them*, could be more aptly retitled *The Sea is Welcome to Them*.) Coming after the golden period of the immediate post-war years (with Olivier's rousing Shakespeare, Lean's compelling Dickens, the passionate opuses of Powell and Pressburger, a trilogy of masterpieces from Carol Reed and much else besides) and before the mould-breaking New Wave of the early 1960s (Richardson, Reisz, Schlesinger and others), British cinema of the 1950s has commonly been stigmatised as conservative and dull. It is a judgment ripe for reappraisal, and the films of the decade invite a closer consideration not simply as social documents (which hitherto has generally been the approach, apologetically undertaken) but also as aesthetic artefacts.

It would not do to over-state the achievement: after all, it is a period in which directors such as Alberto Cavalcanti, Thorold Dickinson, Carol Reed and Robert Hamer (as Philip Kemp persuasively demonstrates in this collection) for the most part failed to deliver on the promise they had shown in the late 1940s. It is also a period which sees a migration to Hollywood of some of its most luminous acting talent: James Mason, Deborah Kerr, Stewart Granger, the inimitable Audrey Hepburn and the irreplaceable Jean Simmons. At the same time, this is a period in which British cinema was connecting with its home audience more successfully than at any time in its history, culminating in the quite extraordinary statistic (almost inconceivable today) that the top twelve box-office films of 1959 in Britain were all actually made in Britain. The legacy of the 1950s is being felt to this day. The modest and genial mayhem of comedies like *The Parole Officer* (2001) and *Lucky Break* (2001) recall the filmic material of stars like Norman Wisdom, Tony Hancock and Peter Sellars in their 1950s heyday, just as Hugh Grant's bumbling comic hero in *Four Weddings and a Funeral* (1994) is essentially the Ian Carmichael 'silly ass' transmogrified for a more permissive era. It might be recalled that two of the most progressive directors of the modern cinema, Mike Figgis and David Mamet, have seen fit to remake Terence Rattigan classics of around that era, respectively, *The Browning Version* (1994) and *The Winslow Boy* (1999); and who could really argue that either made a better fist of it than the Anthony Asquith versions of half a century ago? (The chapter by Dominic Shellard in this volume offers a powerful contribution to the continuing re-evaluation of Rattigan.)

In the recent edition of the *Journal of Popular British Cinema* (Flicks Books 2001), Roy Stafford quotes some representative views of British cinema of the 1950s: 'timid', 'complacent', 'safe', 'dim', 'anodyne' are the adjectives used, with the judgment being that this is the 'doldrums era'. British cinema at this time consists of parochial comedy – what one might compositely call the 'Carry On Doctor at St Trinian's' school of mirth – weary transpositions of West End successes, and bland World War II heroics designed to steel us against the loss of the Empire. But is this really true? For example, Anthony Asquith's stage adaptations have often been dismissed as unimaginative filmed theatre, but to see his version of *The Importance of Being Earnest* (1952) with an appreciative audience is to recognise how meticulously it has been edited, with every cut timed to the second to ensure that each laugh is given its due, but without covering the following line and therefore without disrupting the verbal flow. Similarly with the war films, as Fred Inglis argues passionately in his chapter, there is a lot more going on than nostalgia. What home audiences might have been responding to in these films was a proud but restrained Englishness that made a welcome contrast to American brashness. (There is a separate book to be written about the depiction of Americans in British films of that time: some way from a special relationship.) In any case, is it not an oversimplifiation to recall the service portrayal of, say, Jack Hawkins, Richard Todd and Kenneth More as icons of wartime heroism, and imply that the evocations of World War II were always offered in a spirit of nostalgia and as demonstrations of national cohesion where everyone knew his place? This hardly fits the madness of David Lean's *The Bridge on the River Kwai* (1957) or the cruelties of Asquith's *Orders to Kill* (1958) and Jack Lee's *Circle of Deception* (1960). John Mills's justly famous performance of masculinity in crisis in *Ice Cold in Alex* (1958) is the absolute reverse of stiff upper-lip: he is as tremulous, sulky, simpering and vulnerable as James Stewart on a bad day, and indeed foreshadows Stewart's performance nearly a decade later in *The Flight of the Phoenix* (1965), where, like Mills, he almost cracks up at the indignity of being bested by German superiority. Nor does nostalgia and nobility fit the impudent opening of a war film like Don Chaffey's *Danger Within* (1958), when what at first looks like a dead body tragically stretched out on the ground after battle is actually revealed to be a sunbathing prisoner of war. (The deception is exposed when he begins to scratch his behind.) 'What do you think this place is, a holiday camp?' asks Bernard Lee of Dennis Price, and it is a fair question: as well as its extended homage to the plot situation of Billy Wilder's 1953 hit, *Stalag 17* ('Who is the traitor in our midst?'), *Danger Within* is also not afraid to seek an emulation of that film's wicked and sometimes transgressive comedy. Dennis

Price (as Hamlet!), Michael Wilding and Peter Jones have a whale of a time. The film seems less about war than an extended metaphor on the concept, in all its forms, of camp.

British film of this period is not often credited with that kind of audacity or comic cheek. The comedy is often characterised as postcard or parochial, with the likeable but limited registers of, say, Henry Cornelius's *Genevieve* (1953) or Basil Dearden's *The Smallest Show on Earth* (1957) being typical of the range. Actually there is a surreal quality to the latter film, exemplified by Margaret Rutherford's imperious observation, as the person in charge of the of the Bijou cinema's finances, that 'you could hardly send a third of a chicken to the Chancellor of the Exchequer!' (The context of such a statement seems quite superfluous.) It also has its cutting edge, as when someone remarks that 'she was as pretty as a picture' before adding the mortifying modification, 'a B-picture, mind you'. In his contribution to this book, Dave Rolinson, particularly in his recovery of the neglected *The Horse's Mouth* (Ronald Neame, 1958), aptly draws attention to a sharper edge to 1950s British film comedy than is always acknowledged. This edge sometimes comes through in a performance like Peter Sellers's hatchet job on Wilfred Pickles in *The Naked Truth* (Mario Zampi, 1957), or even in Sellers's plaintive last line in Alexander Mackendrick's *The Ladykillers* (1955) when confronted by a former friend, now frenzied assailant (Danny Green), who is about to kill him: 'Where's your sense of humour?' The darkness of that film has been generally recognised and celebrated, but this is not the case with Mackendrick's previous and most underrated comedy, *The Maggie* (1954), about an American businessman (Paul Douglas) who, trying to transport some cargo to a nearby Scottish island, has the misfortune to run into the crew of an old puffer who offer to help him – at a price. Often characterised as a light piece of Scottish whimsy, *The Maggie* is actually closer to the ferocity of something like *The Wicker Man* in its study of the progressive humiliation and torture by wily locals of its naive, outsider hero. After a series of adventures more harrowing than humorous and where the hero is almost killed by the young boy in the crew, the film builds to an extraordinary moment when the American decides to sacrifice his cargo (symbolically, materialism) in order to save the boat (symbolically, tradition). At this point, Douglas turns to the old skipper, who has given him such grief, and, with the utmost logic and sincerity, utters what must be one of the most remarkable lines of any screen comedy. 'I want you to understand something – I'm serious,' he says. 'If you laugh at me for this, I'll kill you with my bare hands.'

The screenplay for *The Maggie* was the work of the American, William Rose, one of the best screenwriters of this (or any other) period. His contribution is a reminder of the truism that one of the limitations of British film at this time was that it was a writer's and an actor's cinema: the director's presence was nebulous to the point of invisibility and there was a poverty of visual style. The point tended to be underlined by the curious statistic that, during the 1950s, no fewer than eleven British films were Oscar-nominated in the writing categories, which was by far its best representation in any Oscar category. Between the Oscar-winning writing successes of *Seven Days to Noon* (1950), *The Lavender Hill Mob* (1951) and *Room at the Top* (1959) came nominations for *The Man in the White Suit* (1951), *The Sound Barrier* (1952), *Genevieve* (1953), *The Cruel Sea* (1953), *The Captain's Paradise* (1953), *The Ladykillers* (1955), *The Horse's Mouth* (1958) and *Separate Tables* (1958). These remind us that the literateness of British film of the decade is something to be treasured, but pictorial skill must be recognised too. After all, visual reticence is an appropriate correlative to a reticence of temperament: when Anthony Asquith shoots the emotional breakdown of the repressed schoolmaster Crocker-Harris (Michael Redgrave) in *The Browning Version* from behind his back, one senses a perfectly appropriate visual respect for the character's private pain, for the man's sense of shame at this ungentlemanly release of tears that must be hidden from view. (Corin Redgrave discusses this moment sensitively in his moving recollection of his father in this book.) In a different vein, J. Lee Thompson's heightened style can also be absolutely in harmony with its subject: Melanie Williams's discussion in this volume of the expressive appropriateness of his *mise-en-scène* in *Woman in a Dressing Gown* (1957) silences forever Jean-Luc Godard's vituperation against its so-called excrescences.

Indeed there is more visual bravura in the British cinema of this time than is often recognised. Think of the virtuoso scene in Lean's *Hobson's Choice* (1953) when a drunken Charles Laughton is mesmerised by the reflection of the moon in a gleaming Manchester puddle; or, in the same film, the wonderful Victorian self-parody of the opening, the grim atmosphere deflated when the dark shadow of Laughton appears at the doorway, wobbles and then emits a rotund belch. The stricken close-up of Claire Bloom in Carol Reed's *The Man Between* (1953), as she sees her lover shot in the snow, resonates long after the film is over: it affected Andrew Sarris more deeply, he said, than the whole of *The Spy Who Came in from the Cold*. Charles Frend's *The Long Arm* (1957) has a teasingly deceptive flashback in the manner of Hitchcock, and a poignant use of subjective fades to black to suggest the 'dying of the light' as a mortally injured Ian Bannen tries unavailingly to attend to what a policeman is saying to him. In Charles Crichton's *Dance Hall* (1950), the crosscutting between dance hall and train station as the heroine (Natasha Parry) is taken almost to the point of suicide eloquently forges a connection between the deceptive illusions of the former setting ('You're Only Dreaming' is its theme song) and the heroine's current desperation: considering the film thirty years later in the December 1981 issue of *Films Illustrated*, the critic Brian Baxter had no hesitation in declaring Crichton, on this evidence, as a greater director than Bernardo Bertolucci. No less memorable is a begrimed and tormented Rod Steiger finally destroyed by his one human weakness – his love of his dog – as he tries to cross the border in Ken Annakin's extraordinary *Across the Bridge* (1957). This is one of the finest of all Graham Greene adaptations, a masterpiece in Mike Leigh's eyes (see his foreword to Annakin's autobiography, *So You Wanna be a Film Director*), one of Quentin Tarantino's top ten films, and a British film that, in theme, ambience and atmosphere, even looks ahead to Orson Welles's noir masterpiece of a year later, *Touch of Evil*. No visual impoverishment there.

Far from being cinematically backward, 1950s British film had dashes of imagination that outdid more famous or prestigious examples from the cinematic canon. Lewis Gilbert's *The Good Die Young* (1954) has a doomed fatalistic narration over a planned crime that becomes a rendezvous with death which anticipates the similar mode of narrative presentation in Stanley Kubrick's *The Killing* (1956). For shock effect, the star heroine of *The Ship that Died of Shame* (Basil Dearden, 1956), played by Virginia McKenna, is killed off even sooner than Janet Leigh in *Psycho*. The wail of a car horn in Seth Holt's *Nowhere to Go* (1958), in its context, is an imaginative trope of tragedy and death in a manner that looks forward to *Chinatown* (1974). Even Guy Hamilton's film of J.B. Priestley's *An Inspector Calls* (1954) makes one think ahead to Luis Buñuel's *The Discreet Charm of the Bourgeoisie* (1972) with its similar ingredients of interrupted meals and ghosts, and its critique of a self-serving, uncaring bourgeoisie who believe there is no such thing as society. Of course, one is not chauvinistically arguing that these British films are on the same level of artistic accomplishment as the films they recall: in some cases, far from it. But it does suggest that British cinema of the time was more formally and thematically adventurous than it is sometimes given credit for.

The national cinema of the decade was, then, shot through with sometimes unexpected variety and interesting contradictions. It has been described as insular and parochial, but, in fact, a number of foreign voices added a more complex colouration. The case of Joseph Losey is discussed elsewhere in these pages, but one might also cite Jacques Tourneur, whose British horror film *Night of the Demon* (1957) has the spooky suggestiveness of his best work for Val Lewton, or Hugo Fregonese, whose *Harry Black and the Tiger*

(1958) is one of the finest safari movies ever made, or Robert Parrish, whose film *The Purple Plain* (1954) is a war film with a difference, pitting a quest for survival alongside a fascination with death and featuring the finest ever screen performance of one of our most dependable supporting actors, Maurice Denham. A special case is the blacklisted Cy Endfield, who, like Losey, came to England from Hollywood to restart his career, and who was to find his alter ego in Stanley Baker and fulfil his promise in *Zulu* (1964). *Hell Drivers* (1957) is particularly interesting for the way Endfield uses the material to suggest an allegory of his own situation (a hero trying to shake off his past and make a new start) and injects an unashamed melodrama into the action that is redolent of the radical American cinema of the late 1940s. Patrick McGoohan's black-leather villainy in the film seems almost like a conscious aping of Marlon Brando's performance in *The Wild One* (1954), which, for many of us at that time, would have been the nearest we could get to seeing it: *The Wild One* had been banned from public exhibition for alleged excessive violence by the British Board of Film Censors, whose operation then is astutely discussed below by Tony Aldgate.

Again a classic image from 1950s British cinema would be Jack Hawkins in *The Cruel Sea*, the epitome of quiet English integrity. But during this decade, Hawkins is also the permanently irascible Police Inspector Gideon of *Gideon's Day* (John Ford, 1958), possibly a forerunner of David Jason's Frost; or the Hentzau-like suave political villain in Sidney Gilliat's *State Secret* (1950) who, having made a hurried getaway, even has the cheek to pop back and enquire of the hero if he knows of any good vacant Chair of Political Science. Dirk Bogarde is, archetypally, Simon Sparrow of the Doctor films and Rank's resident self-sacrificing romantic of *The Wind Cannot Read* (1956) and *A Tale of Two Cities* (1958); see Robert Giddings's piece for a careful historical placing of the latter film in the British film history of the decade. But Bogarde is also the exotic ('homoerotic'?) Spanish hero of *The Spanish Gardener* (Philip Leacock, 1956) and the notorious bandit in *The Singer not the Song* (Roy Baker, 1960), which is the closest the British cinema has got – or might want to get – to *Duel in the Sun*. A dual role in *Libel* (Anthony Asquith, 1959) allows Bogarde to give his screen image a thorough going over, as if he is already looking forward to *The Servant*: he does a hilarious, mocking impression of his 'good' self and even makes the simple phrase 'in Darlington' sound like the height of decadence and degeneracy.

If the British cinema of the decade has been characterised as a complacent cinema, then the cracks in that complacency are discernible some time before the appearance of the New Wave, with its new priorities, its new order of things, its new social configurations. The old class hierarchies are breaking down along with the remembered comradeship of the war. 'Gentle-man's agreement, old boy?' says Roland Culver's peacetime Major (a superb performance) to Richard Attenborough's post-war spiv in *The Ship that Died of Shame* (1955), to which Attenborough replies: 'Don't be silly'. It seems a logical progression from that to *The League of Gentlemen* (Basil Dearden, 1960), where the kind of military expertise that was formerly put to the service of the nation is now applied to bank robbery, the ultimate statement of post-war disillusionment. And, as Alison Platt argues later in these pages about *The Spanish Gardener*, if the moral health of the country can be gauged by the way it treats its children, then the British cinema of the time was giving off some quite ambiguous signals. Films like Alexander Mackendrick's *Mandy* (1952) and J. Lee Thompson's *The Yellow Balloon* (1952) both con-vey a troubled sense of the vulnerability of children in an era of post-war demoralisation where the scars of battle are still visible on the landscape.

In his essay on Raymond Durgnat Robert Murphy points out how film criticism can become outdated and its authors be time-bound. The academic manner aspires to a universality which time will show to be pitiful. As editors we do not think we can escape being locked into the period in which these essay were written and we freely confess it. We have tried to admit our time-determined nature by the small device of giving biographical notes on contributors which are more personal than is customary, pointing up the generations (several) to which we belong. Just as criticism and commentary belong in time, so do the films themselves on which we write: for them exist-ence in time implies deterioration. Of course film is prolifically available in the theatres, not to mention TV, video and DVD, but there is actually no reason to be optimistic about the survival and preservation of the medium, a subject dealt with here by Bryony Dixon. Even landmark films are not reliably available. One such is the subject of Dave Rolinson's essay: *The Horse's Mouth* (Ronald Neame, 1958), with Alec Guinness who partly wrote it. Dixon tells us that it is held at the British Film Institute, but only in a colour positive acquired from a major American distributor which was clearing out its vaults. As this is the only element archivally existing, it is unavailable for screening or research in the United Kingdom. There *may* be 16mm prints somewhere, dating from the time when many films were reprinted for non-theatrical use and there is an American VHS tape available, but it cannot be said that there is a proper original-format 35mm print preserved in any UK collection. We hope this book will draw attention to such problems.

Although not intended as a comprehensive survey of the decade (film historians such as David Pirie and Peter Hutchings, for example, have dealt with the 1950s phenomenon of Hammer horror in some detail), this collection tries to give new perspectives on areas and personalities hitherto neglected: for example, Charles Barr's investigation of the post-*Western Approaches* work of Pat Jackson; Brian McFarlane's heartening tribute to that staple diet of the double bill, the British B-movie; Stephen Lacey's analysis of the close interaction between theatre and film in the British cinema of this decade; Kerry Kidd's reading of *Women of Twilight* that fascinatingly reconstructs the sexual politics of the time. As well as revaluing large areas of British cinema, the book offers surveys of other cinematic features of the decade. Archivist Bryony Dixon shows her expertise on how these films are preserved; Sarah Easen recalls the impact of the Festival of Britain on the British film industry; Eric Hedling and Robert Murphy pay homage to two of the most valuable film commentators of the period, Lindsay Anderson and Raymond Durgnat. Isabel Quigly sharply evokes the life of the national film critic during this time, in so doing recovering something of the quality of the whole cinema-going experience in the 1950s, which, memory tells us, is so different from our present multiplex days. (As Terence Davies's films lovingly show, there was still a magic and an innocence attached to the cinema in those days, which one can rediscover in reading through fan magazines and old film annuals: a reader wins 10s 6d from *Picturegoer* for observing that 'no screen actor has whiter teeth than Audie Murphy'; a *Preview* film annual (1960) has an article by Rock Hudson with a title that would now take on a retrospective irony: 'Leave My Private Life Alone'.)

We would have liked to include more. We have Isabel Quigly, Erik Hedling and Robert Murphy on film criticism of the 1950s, but we would have liked something on Paul Dehn, on Kenneth Tynan as film critic and on the underrated Richard Mallett of *Punch*, admirably disinterred by Richard Chatten in a 2001 essay in the *Journal of British Cinema*. We would have liked reference to foreign views of British cinema, say, Stanley Kauffmann's from New York. We are always hearing that Truffaut said 'Britain' and 'cinema' are incompatible terms. But less known is his clear-sighted appraisal of *Doctor in the House*.

> This is a historical documentary – hardly romanticized – about British medical schools. It has no plot, no suspense, no drama, but a series of gags and of charac-ters, calm good humour, and excellent actors – especially Kenneth More, one of the drivers in *Genevieve*, playing the role of a student who deliberately fails his exams because his grandmother has bequeathed him £1000 a year for as long as his studies last. All lovers of English humour have to see this movie. It has lots of spirit. (*Arts*, December 1954)

Every word of this is true. The first 'Doctor' film has some of the quality of the first 'Carry On' film; an accuracy in showing what an actual work situation is like (medical school, army national service), which in any case is a particular strength of British cinema. Of course, the 'Doctors' and the 'Carry Ons' degenerated into raucousness and camp, but at the beginning they were unpretentious observant comedy – and *Doctor in the House* is actually observant in an area in which the 'Doctors' are supposed to be weak (or, worse, 'misogynist'): note the place of Muriel Pavlow in it. Following through Truffaut's review, we might have had something to say about *Genevieve* with its enchanting score, and about Kenneth More, who was indeed an interesting actor, as realised by Peter Hall when he offered More the part of Claudius in *Hamlet* (More modestly declined). We would have liked more on cinemas themselves (the multiples like the emerging Granadas and State movie theatres, the aptly named Classics, and the best London cinemas, like the Curzon and the Academy). We are aware that we have nothing on the Film Society movement or on the *avant garde*, or on art films (though Sarah Easen mentions the 'Poet and Painter' films made for the Festival of Britain).

Nonetheless our contributors give unprecedented coverage to the decade and help us understand interrelationships between past and present, two in particular. First: a past period can help us see the present more clearly, by supplying a standard for judging the new. If we know X of the past, we are less likely to be bowled over by Y in the present. So Alison Platt's essay about the old *Spanish Gardener* makes the new *Billy Elliot* look less than impressive. Second: our present can alert us to unrecognised felicities of the past. Thus, Platt also shows that we who have *The Sixth Sense* now are the better placed for observing how good the 1950s was at showing children, especially children old before their time (whatever that is).

Our contributors also show what it was like to see films in the 1950s, by trying to account for the experience of a generation of filmgoers whose enduring fondness for the films is bound up with recollections of the circumstances and conditions under which they were shown. A new era was undoubtedly coming. 'Change was the keyword for the end of the fifties,' said Patricia Warren, seeing on the horizon the films of the British New Wave and first-rate movies like *Room at the Top* (Jack Clayton, 1959), *Peeping Tom* (Michael Powell, 1960) and *Tunes of Glory* (Ronald Neame, 1960) which portended a different direction. We hope this book demonstrates that these later achievements came out of the rich soil of the 1950s.

Critics

Raymond Durgnat and
A Mirror for England

ROBERT MURPHY

If clearly marked personal style is one's criterion of interest, then few British films reward the concern given to such directors as, say, Dreyer, Buñuel, Franju and Renoir. But other criteria of interest exist, whereby many of the subtlest meanings behind a personal style may be related to the collective vision of a particular tradition, period, background or 'school'. It's logical and usual to consider even impersonal and anonymous artworks as an expression of a general consensus (*A Mirror for England*, p. 4).[1]

RAYMOND DURGNAT'S *A Mirror for England: British Movies from Austerity to Affluence*, which deals extensively with British films of the 1950s, was written in the mid-1960s and was published in 1970. Given the shifts in attitudes over the past thirty years – in society generally as well as in the little world of film studies – one might expect the judgments expressed there, the choices of what is important, to have become dated and irrelevant. If one reads Roy Armes's *A Critical History of British Cinema*, which was published in 1978, one is propelled into a time warp where academics with long hair wore tank tops and flared jeans, and had posters of *La Hora de los Hornos* on their walls. Armes draws inspiration from a deadly cocktail of Althusserian Marxism and the languid snobbery of C. A. Lejeune to take to task an industry which 'has never created an adequate working

---

Raymond Durgnat died in June 2002 at the age of 69. The Australian online journal *Senses of Cinema* devoted a substantial part of its June issue to a Festschrift planned to honour his seventieth birthday <www.sensesofcinema. com>.

I am Professor in Film Studies at De Montfort University. My first teaching experience was a one-term class at Morley College in Lambeth on British cinema in the 1940s. The students were refreshingly enthusiastic and most of them enrolled for a second term on British cinema in the 1950s. Unfortunately this was a period I was weak on and I will remain eternally grateful to one of the students – Richard Dacre, who runs the Flashbacks shop in Soho – who agreed to teach it with me; and to Raymond Durgnat's *A Mirror for England* which proved to be a mine of useful and inspiring information about a period of British cinema no one else seemed to take seriously. My most recent book is *British Cinema and the Second World War* (Continuum, 2000). *Robert Murphy.*

context for those who wish to question the dominant stylistic approaches or provide stimulus for social change, with the result that there has been virtually no avant-garde film-making and no effective militant cinema in Britain'.[2] Durgnat is much less time-bound and his analysis of British cinema has proved remarkably prescient. *A Mirror for England* deals with topics such as national identity and the decline of empire, realism and romanticism, politics, class, masculinity, sexuality and social problems. Durgnat writes appreciatively about Hammer and Gainsborough, purveyors of despised melodramas and horror films; he takes Powell and Pressburger seriously and gives sympathetic consideration to directors like Val Guest, Roy Baker, J. Lee Thompson, Basil Dearden, Roy and John Boulting and John Guillermin who were regarded as irredeemably mediocre by other critics.[3] Thirty years before the James Bond films found an intellectual champion in James Chapman and Andrew Spicer made a detailed study of British male types, Durgnat divided the cads from the cadets, the gentlemen from the players and argued 'it's only natural to like Ian Fleming's naughty hero better than the male nannies of sweetness and light who deprecate him' (pp. 152–3).[4]

A Mirror for England was popular and well reviewed – by David Pirie in *Time Out* (10–17 June 1973) and Charles Barr in *Monogram* (issue 3 in 1972), for example – but it was never afforded the academic respectability granted Pirie's *A Heritage of Horror* (1973) and Barr's *Ealing Studios* (1977). This was partly a matter of timing. In 1970 when film theory was young and determined to embrace the *avant garde*, *A Mirror for England*, with its patriotic red, white and blue cover, its presumptuous claims for directors whose careers seemed to have slipped into terminal decline and its focus on the stuffily conservative 1950s, seemed to dwell unnecessarily on a best-forgotten past.[5]

For those unfamiliar with the field and unwilling to devote the time and attention to learning about it which *A Mirror for England* demands, it is not an easy book to penetrate. The film enthusiasts who read *Films and Filming*, where Durgnat tried out many of his ideas and subjects for the book, would have seen most of the films he discusses on their original cinema release and were sophisticated enough to appreciate his mischievous juxtapositions – such as that comparing Pat Jackson's masterpiece of wartime realism, *Western Approaches* (1944), with Don Chaffey's pre-Roman epic, *Jason and the Argonauts* (1963). But this was an ageing and shrinking readership, and for the academic mind unprepared to follow the convoluted logic of Durgnat's method, the book must have seemed inexcusably haphazard and untidy.

Durgnat warns us in his introduction that he intends to concentrate 'less on evaluating the texture of films than on critical exegesis of certain themes, undercurrents and overtones' (p. 3) This is a book which dispenses with narrative or chronological progression. There are no neat divisions into directors or writers or studios or genres. Instead of histories of Ealing and Gainsborough, career profiles of John Mills and Richard Attenborough, assessments of the achievements of Asquith and Cavalcanti, there are chapters with headings like 'Points of View' and 'Our Glorious Heritage' divided into mystifying sub-headings such as 'Gangrene-British Style' and 'The Impotence of Being Earnest'. *The Dam Busters* (1954) and *Carve Her Name With Pride* (1958) disconcertingly rub shoulders with *They Can't Hang Me* (1955), *Violent Playground* (1958) and *Beat Girl* (1960) ('System as Stalemate'). Most of Powell and Pressburger's wartime films appear along-side Asquith's *The Demi-Paradise* (1943), Hitchcock's *The Skin Game* (1931) and Lean's *Great Expectations* (1946) in 'The Nine Lives of Colonel Blimp'; the post-war films turn up in 'Between Two Worlds' where Powell is classified as a romantic alongside Lean, Cavalcanti and John Guillermin. For Durgnat's views on World War II films one has to flit between 'Tunes of Bogey', 'The Lukewarm Life', 'System as Stalemate', 'The Doctored Documentary', 'Stresses and Strains', 'The Glum and the Guilty', 'Gangrene – British Style' and 'The British Constitution'. What one finds is valuable and interesting and uncontaminated by the prevailing prejudices of the time but it requires a degree of diligence to extract it.

In the 1980s as the revival of interest in British cinema began to gather momentum, the value of *A Mirror for England* (then still widely available in second-hand bookshops and the shelves of public libraries) began to be recognised. In 1986 Julian Petley wrote about an unmapped British cinema beyond the small canon of culturally respectable realist films and expressed the hope that in time the films he discusses 'would look less like isolated islands revealing themselves, and more like the peaks of a long submerged lost continent'.[6] *A Mirror for England*, with its passages on morbid thrillers, gothic horror films and exotic melodramas, was one of the few sources one could turn to as a guide to this legacy of lost films. But Durgnat's enthusiasm for forgotten films from the realist mainstream such as Anthony Asquith's *Orders to Kill* (1958) and Jack Lee's *Circle of Deception* (1960), Val Guest's *80,000 Suspects* (1963), J. Lee Thompson's *Woman in a Dressing Gown* (1957) and *No Trees in the Street* (1958), and Roy Baker's *Passage Home* (1955) and *A Night to Remember* (1958), troubles and contradicts the idea that the most exciting and valuable part of British cinema was that which defied the realist ethos.

Durgnat emerges, despite his enthusiasm for Terence Fisher's gothic horror films and the artistically extravagant work of Michael Powell and Emeric Pressburger, as a rationalist rather than a romantic. He had described himself seven years earlier as 'a Socialist Freudian Epicurean stoic scientific humanist critic' and his experience of growing up during the war and undergoing national service left him with a tough-minded resistance to mystical evocations of English society.[7] This can be seen in his somewhat harsh treatment of Humphrey Jennings, where his empathy is held firmly in check by his suspicion of the underlying ideology. In *A Diary for Timothy* (1945), for example, 'A scattering of faces, of observations extremely beautiful in themselves, and, to this writer, tearingly nostalgic of some intense childhood moments, are pressed into the service of a quiet near-jingoism which altogether understandable in war, cannot achieve more than second-rate artistic status' (p. 15).

One of Durgnat's strengths is his awareness of the world beyond the film and his concern with how well or how distortedly it has been represented, of 'how far to match a film's picture of reality against other evidence as to the real nature of this reality' (p. 9). In analysing *I Believe in You* (1951), for example, a classic 'do-gooding' social-problem film, he illustrates how the integrity of the film-makers (Basil Dearden and Michael Relph) and the conviction of the actors give it a rewarding and satisfying complexity. The film's simplistic ethos displays a 'paternalism more marked than that of the probation service itself' and 'subsists in the supposition that what lads need is relationships with firm and responsible father- and mother-figures from the upper-classes'. In the real world, Durgnat argues, 'Much delinquency isn't the product of personal misfits at all but of emotionally quite normal attachments to a sub-society poorly integrated with the sub-society from which the judiciary springs'. It's unlikely that Dearden and Relph shared such a view, but in the performance of the young Joan Collins, whose 'grace, vigour and insolent savoir-vivre validate her character's subversive attitudes', the expression of this contradictory interpretation of delinquency finds a powerful and persuasive voice (p. 138).

Durgnat claims that he wants to 'underline unnoticed ambivalences' in films he 'would like to promote from the ranks of mediocrity to the status of interesting or poignant films, and even, occasionally, a minor classic' (p. 9). But he also offers new ways of looking at well-established films. David Lean's *Great Expectations*, for example, 'trembles on the brink of being a classic Marxist fable about bourgeois "confusionism" with Miss Havisham as the vampire of upper-middle-class snobbery and frigidity, accepting gratitude, giving nothing' (pp. 22–3). He challenges the view that 'run-of-the-mill movies never say anything, that vivid or insightful remarks or situations are a monopoly of a few prestigious individuals' (p. 4). But he is no iconoclastic cultist casting out false idols from the temple of British cinema and installing new gods. His 'First Draft Pantheon' of British films is stuffed with worthy theatrical adaptations like *The Browning Version* (1951) and *The Long and the Short and the Tall* (1960), artistically fashionable films such as Antonioni's *Blow Up* (1966) and Losey's *King and Country* (1964) and established classics like *Brief Encounter* (1945) and *Odd Man Out* (1946). Lower down, *Black Narcissus* (1947) and *Tiger in the Smoke* (1956) make their appearances but there are notable omissions – *A Canterbury Tale* (1944) and *The Small Back Room* (1949), *The Cruel Sea* (1952) and *A Town Like Alice* (1956) – and the only costume melodramas to make it into the top one hundred are Losey's *The Gypsy and the Gentleman* (1957) and Dickinson's *Queen of Spades* (1948) and *Gaslight* (1940).

The high estimate put on the English films of Joseph Losey, the determination to disrupt the aura of reverence around the British Documentary Movement, the questioning of the importance of Free Cinema and scepticism about the status of *The Third Man* (1949) as a masterpiece, were shared by other young critics, particularly the auteurists clustered around the journal *Movie*. In the early 1960s auteurism provided a battering ram to shatter the hallowed portals of the critical establishment and Durgnat was intent on attacking the British Film Institute and its house journal *Sight and Sound*. In a wide-ranging polemic against prevailing cultural attitudes he complained that: 'The trouble with the S & S non-theory is that it is an assortment of prejudices and habits which thinks it is the broadest possible, the biggest and best, range of tastes. Actually, its scope, minimal in the first place, is not increased but diminished by the play of the contradictions beneath the mask of tolerant eclecticism'.[8]

But Durgnat's relationship with auteurism is a complex one. He was influenced more by the left-wing populism of *Positif* than the *politique des auteurs* espoused by *Cahiers du Cinéma*, and was sceptical of the over-emphasis on style and the over-valuing of Hollywood directors by English auteurists, but he was even more dubious about the opposite camp of 'commitment' critics who wanted an openly political cinema and retained the Documentary Movement's hostility to popular commercial cinema. He argues for an auteurism capable of coming to terms with British cinema: 'Even within the assumptions of auteur theory, I would suggest that it's absurd to notice such Hollywood conformists as Hawks, McCarey and Walsh, yet deny equally high honours to, say, Roy Baker, Michael Powell and Terence Fisher' (p. 4). Indeed, the final chapter of the book, 'Romantics and Moralists', makes a convincing auteurist case not only for Fisher, Powell and Baker, but for Basil Dearden, Val Guest, J. Lee Thompson, Roy and John Boulting, David Lean, Launder and Gilliatt, Alberto Cavalcanti, John Guillermin, Anthony

Asquith and Thorold Dickinson. (Other directors, notably the 'pessimists' Carol Reed and Robert Hamer, are given their due elsewhere in the book.) He is robust in favourably contrasting denigrated British directors with their fondly indulged Hollywood counterparts, but makes no attempt to disguise the thin soil of British film culture. While restoring Powell and Pressburger's *The Tales of Hoffmann* (1951) to its rightful place as a minor classic, and acknowledging the brilliance of Heckroth's designs, he exposes the wobbly philosophical underpinning upon which it is constructed.

> One need only compare the awkward way in which humans and puppets mingle in a symbolic quadrille with the similar mixture in the night club scene in L' Herbier's *La Nuit fantastique*. L' Herbier, however academic, had grown up within a climate infected by Surrealism, by the sombre, toughly Marxist poetry of Prévert-Carné, by Delluc, by Vigo. Powell-Heckroth have as inspirational trampoline the visual culture of Ye Olde Junke Shoppe. (p. 211)

Though he went on to write books on Jean Renoir, Alfred Hitchcock, Georges Franju, Luis Buñuel and King Vidor, who would now be acknowledged as film artists, Durgnat shared the same enthusiasm for popular culture and scepticism about the relevance of high-art criteria which Lawrence Alloway had expressed in 'The Long Front of Culture' back in 1959: 'Mass production techniques, applied to accurately repeatable words, pictures and music, have resulted in an expendable multitude of signs and symbols. To approach this exploding field with Renaissance-based ideas of the uniqueness of art is crippling. Acceptance of the mass media entails a shift in our notion of what culture is.'[9] *A Mirror for England* attempts the ambitious task of dealing with the cultural significance of a whole tradition of film-making. In 1947 when Siegfried Kracauer had attempted to examine a period of German cinema in *From Caligari to Hitler*, he had constructed an over-arching theory – that German films of the 1920s manifested the internal sickness of German society and presaged the rise of Hitler – to link together the disparate films he discusses.[10] Durgnat sets himself looser parameters, offering 'a survey of some major recurring themes in British movies between 1945 – being the end of the war and the election of the post-war Labour government – and 1958, when the success of *Room at the Top* marks the breakthrough of a new cinema'.

In *From Caligari to Hitler*, Kracauer's analysis is distorted by his need to strong-arm films into becoming symbols of the zeitgeist. Durgnat's mosaic of essays is held together by more tenable and durable principles:

1   that films don't have to be masterpieces to be worth writing about;
2   that national cinema is intrinsically interesting as a window onto the society from which it emerges;

3 that auteurism could be a useful concept for analysing films made by the same director even when they did not reflect a coherent world view and a personal vision;

4 that it is possible to discern patterns across groups of films which did not necessarily share the same director, or the same production company or even the same genre.

They are principles which continue to be useful for the study of British cinema.

In *Films and Feelings* Durgnat admits that 'It is surprisingly easy to deploy certain exegetical techniques as to make extremely simple and dreary works of art sound interesting'.[11] He vows to abstain from such specious intellectualism, but in *A Mirror for England*, where he seeks to prove 'that artworks not of the highest textual quality' nevertheless deserve thematic exegesis, and that 'many fascinating moments occur in generally mediocre films', the temptation is sometimes too great (p. 4). In summing up the work of his mentor, Thorold Dickinson, for example, he makes claims for a depth and complexity which is not obviously apparent:

> Dickinson's films, baroque in their diversity, in their volatile mixture of strength and adaptability, are baroque also in a deeper sense. Superficially, the rationale of the style would seem to be its conjuncture of sensitivity and showmanship. One deploys one's effects to render nuances of feeling and to move the spectator. But their mercuriality is such that, sensed as one would a painter's or a poet's style, the cinematographic quality becomes that of an imperious form overlying assertions and contradictions whose synthesis must be radical uncertainty. We are led straight towards the existentialist paradox, of being as not-being, of life's discontinuities as freedom fraught with anguish and, curiously, a sense of fate. (p. 233)[12]

On the other hand, Durgnat's comment on a still neglected director, Roy Baker – 'The barbed force of Baker's films lies in his feeling for evil as both result of injustice, and an impersonal force which, lurking in the nature of man, takes him over' – is eloquent and persuasive (p. 241).[13] While even Dickinson's admirers might balk at *Men of Two Worlds* (1946) being included among the top fifty British films, Durgnat's comparison of Cavalcanti's *They Made Me a Fugitive* (1947) with Howard Hawks's *The Big Sleep* (1946) and his praise for David MacDonald's *The Brothers* (1947) for dealing effectively with issues explored in American Westerns seems judicious, and his claims for the films of Powell and Pressburger now look surprisingly modest.

A Mirror for England has acquired an unjustified reputation for plot and character errors. It tends to be assumed that, prior to the widespread availability of video, books were written from dimly remembered cinema screenings. But Durgnat, as one of the small group of students under Thorold Dickinson's tutelage at the Slade School of Art, had privileged access to National Film Archive prints and, particularly for those films he analyses in detail, characters, plot and meaning are accurately and perceptively dealt with. Inevitably, in covering some 750 films, there are a few mistakes: it was Googie Withers herself, not the character she plays in *The Loves of Joanna Godden* (1947), who upped sticks and emigrated to Australia; in *They Came to a City* (1944) not all the representatives of society turn their back on the utopian city; James Mason in *The Man in Grey* (1943), beats his mistress (Margaret Lockwood) to death, not his wife (Phyllis Calvert); Rosamund John is mistaken for Joy Shelton in *Waterloo Road* (1944), Phyllis Calvert for Anne Crawford in *Millions Like Us* (1943); *The Proud Valley* (1939) metamorphoses into *Pastor Hall* (1940), and the list of illustrations turns Donald Sinden into Denholm Elliott. But these are the sort of mistakes which should have been picked up and corrected by a good editor and, irritating though they might be, they rarely invalidate Durgnat's analyses.

In an editorial for the stimulating but short-lived journal *Motion*, Durgnat argues that 'At its best, the thoroughly efficient, apersonal commercial film attains the eloquence and beauty of a myth. It is the sentiments of a group crystallized into dramatic terms, and shared'.[14] But he is always aware that commercial films are the imperfect products of a system designed to make money not to create art, and at times his frustration with the way in which some of his chosen films miss their chances sometimes breaks out into an alternative scenario (as with Roy Baker's *Flame in the Streets* (1961)) where contradictions and complexities are resolved in a more creative, adventurous and satisfying way. This sense of cinema as fluid and unfixed runs counter to the idea of cinema as an unchanging arena of masterpieces and failures and is considerably more liberating for the historian. Though most of the films, the directors, the issues and concerns Durgnat excavates have subsequently been dealt with in more detail elsewhere, *A Mirror for England* remains relevant because it views the past not as a drab catalogue of mistakes which must be erased or corrected by the creation of a more rigorous type of cinema, but as a cornucopia of riches to be enjoyed and shared and drawn upon as a way of illuminating life and art.

Notes

1   All page references are to *A Mirror for England* unless otherwise stated.
2   Roy Armes, *A Critical History of British Cinema* (Secker & Warburg, 1978), pp. 3–4 .
3   *Mirror*'s treatment of Powell and Pressburger predates the collections of interviews and essays edited by Kevin Gough Yates in 1971 as *Michael Powell in Collaboration with Emeric*

Pressburger (British Film Institute) and by Ian Christie in 1978 (*Powell, Pressburger and Others*, British Film Institute), though it is preceded by Ian Johnston's 'A Pin to See the Peepshow' in *Motion* 4 (February 1963), and *Midi-Minuit Fantastique*, 'Dossier Michael Powell' (October 1968). There is a seminal essay on Powell in *Movie* by O.O. Green (Autumn 1965); 'Green' is Durgnat under another name.

4   James Chapman, *Licence to Thrill: A Cultural History of the James Bond Film* (I.B. Tauris, 1999) and Andrew Spicer, *Typical Men: The Representation of Masculinity in Popular British Cinema* (I. B. Tauris, 2001).

5   The idea that British cinema is too dull to be worth the serious consideration of intellectuals lives on. See, for example, Gilbert Adair, 'One of those Films Destined to be Forgotten', *Independent on Sunday* (12 November 2000).

6   Julian Petley, 'The Lost Continent', in Charles Barr (ed.), *All Our Yesterdays* (British Film Institute, 1986), p. 118.

7   ' Standing Up for Jesus', *Motion* 6 (Autumn 1963), p. 41.

8   'Standing Up for Jesus', p. 39. For Durgnat's relationship to other critics of his generation, see Jonathan Rosenbaum,'Raymond Durgnat', and Raymond Durgnat, 'Apologia and Auto-Critique', *Film Comment* (May 1973), pp. 65–9; and 'Critical Debates', ch. 3 of Robert Murphy's *Sixties British Cinema* (British Film Institute, 1992).

9   Lawrence Alloway, 'The Long Front of Culture', *Cambridge Opinion* 17 (1959), reprinted in Suzy Gablik and John Russell (eds), *Pop Art Redefined* (Thames & Hudson, 1982).

10   Siegfried Kracauer, *From Caligari to Hitler: A Psychological History of the German Film* (Princeton University Press, 1947).

11   *Films and Feelings* (Faber & Faber, 1967), p. 15.

12   See also Jeffrey Richards, *Thorold Dickinson* (Croom Helm, 1986). Richards shares Durgnat's high regard for Dickinson, but in a book-length study has the space to discuss his weaknesses, too.

13   See Peter Hutchings, 'Roy Ward Baker and Authorship', in Justine Ashby and Andrew Higson (eds), *British Cinema, Past and Present* (Routledge, 2000). Baker changed his name to Roy Ward Baker in 1967.

14   'Editorial', *Motion* 3 (November 1962), p. 4.

Durgnat on British cinema: a select bibliography

Durgnat's publishing range is vast – from Marilyn Monroe to Georges Franju, from animation to film noir: I have included here only his essays and articles on British cinema.

'A Salute to Slaughter', *Ark: Journal of the Royal College of Art* 30, 1961–62.
'Puritans Anonymous', *Motion* 6 (Autumn 1963), p. 3.
'Standing Up for Jesus', *Motion* 6 (Autumn 1963), pp. 25–42.
'Old Wine in New Bottles', *Film* 39 (Spring 1964), pp. 32–3.
'The Mass-Media – A Highbrow Illiteracy?', *Views* 4 (Spring 1964), pp. 49–59.
'Vote for Britain: A Cinemagoer's Guide to the General Election', Part 1, *Films and Filming* (April 1964), pp. 9–14; Part 2, *Films and Filming* (May 1964), pp. 10–15; Part 3, *Films and Filming* (June 1964), pp. 38–43.
'Horror is My Business', *Films and Filming* (July 1964), pp. 7–8 (with John Cutts).
'Ten Years That Shook an Art', *Film* 40 (September 1964), pp. 22–3 (with Peter Armitage).
'The Impotence of Being Ernest', *Views* 8 (Summer 1965), pp. 76–80.
'Michael Powell', *Movie* 14 (Autumn 1965), pp. 17–20 (as O. O. Green).
'Loved One', *Films and Filming* (February 1966, April 1966), pp. 19–23; March 1966, pp. 37–40.
'Losey: Modesty and Eve', *Films and Filming* (April 1966), pp. 26–33.
'Losey: Puritan Maids', *Films and Filming* (May 1966), pp. 28–33.
'Two on a Tandem', *Films and Filming* (July 1966), pp. 26–33.

'Brain Drains: Drifters, Avant-Gardes and Kitchen Sinks', *Cinema* 3 (June 1969), pp. 48–53.

A Mirror for England: British Movies from Austerity to Affluence (Faber & Faber, 1970).

'Shoot Out in Dean Street', *Films and Filming* (February 1972), pp. 41–2.

'Swinging London: Canes and Guitars', ch. 3 in *Sexual Alienation in the Cinema* (Studio Vista, 1972).

'O Lucky Man or the Advantages of a Clockwork Cheese', *Film Comment* (January–February 1973), pp. 38–40.

'Britannia Waives the Rules', *Film Comment* (July–August 1976), pp. 50–8.

'The Great British Phantasmagoria', *Film Comment* (May–June 1977), pp. 48–53.

'Aiming at the Archers', *Positif* (February 1981), pp. 22–3.

'History Man Bites Lucky Jim', *Films* (November 1981), p. 24.

'On the Alternative Options of Burning an Illusion', *Films* (November 1982), p. 37.

'A Skeleton Key to Stephen Dwoskin – Outline for a Text Not Written', *Monthly Film Bulletin* (November 1982), pp. 252–3.

'Out of the Looking Glass or a Phantasmagoric Mirror for England', *Monthly Film Bulletin* (February 1984), pp. 39–40.

'Black Narcissus (... and in Theory: Towards a Superficial Structuralism)', *Monthly Film Bulletin* (October 1984), pp. 313–16.

'Gainsborough: the Times of its Time', *Monthly Film Bulletin* (August 1985), pp. 259–61.

'The Ploughman's Just Desserts', *American Film* (November 1985), pp. 48–54, 80.

'The Pre-war Bs: Rewards and Fairies', *Film Comment* (May–June 1990), pp. 28–30.

'The Powell and Pressburger Mystery', *Cineaste* (December 1997), pp. 16–19.

Lindsay Anderson: *Sequence* and the rise of auteurism in 1950s Britain

ERIK HEDLING

THE 1950S REPRESENTS an upheaval in European film history. The financial losses of the Europeans, as compared to the Americans on the popular market, caused drastic changes within the European film industries, leading up to the continental government-subsidised film industries of the present. Even if the historical reasons for the changes in European film policies were mainly socio-economic, they were at the time mostly discussed and dealt with in aesthetic terms, and we saw eventually the emergence of the European art cinema, a new kind of film, specifically aimed at the literate and professional middle classes.

One of the most important European contributions to the film history of the 1950s was, thus, undoubtedly the sudden rise of the auteur, the film director extraordinaire and the notion of the authored art film. Sweden had Ingmar Bergman, Italy had, for instance, Fellini, Rossellini, Visconti, and Antonioni, France had the *Cahiers du Cinéma* generation, towards the end of decade represented by the breakthrough of the *nouvelle vague*, with Truffaut, Godard, Rohmer and Chabrol. Traditionally, Britain has been said to have missed out on the development of auteurism and art cinema in the 1950s, instead clinging to its traditional industrial policies of trying to (albeit unsuccessfully) compete with the Americans on the popular market. (Peter Wollen's essay on 1980s British films as 'The Last New Wave' is a good illustration of this attitude.)[1] Even if this was true for the film industry, it is not entirely so for film culture as a whole, since Britain was at least intellectually at the very core of the foundation of the European art cinema in the 1950s, even if the art films as such – in the Bordwellian sense of personal vision, loose narrative structure, ambiguity and various levels of heightened realism – were not really to emerge until the 1960s (perhaps with the exception

---

I was born in the mid-1950s and had my first overwhelming experience of the cinema watching Lindsay Anderson's *If* ... in 1969. My training in England and Sweden (Lund University) as an academic in film and literature eventually led to my writing my book *Lindsay Anderson: Maverick Film-Maker* (Cassell, 1998). *Erik Hedling*

of Jack Clayton's *Room at the Top* in 1959).[2] The seeds for an art cinema and auteurist policies were to a large extent sown in 1950s Britain, not least by the journal *Sequence*, founded in 1947 and in 1952, when its critics joined *Sight and Sound*, the most prestigious British film periodical, and there pursued similar ideological concerns.

In one of the original art cinema manifestos, Alexandre Astruc's famous *caméra stylo* essay of 1948, the writer pleaded for a cinema in which the camera is handled like a pen, that is, the author/film director employs his personal instrument, the pen/camera, to express a personal vision and create a work of art.[3] Unsurprisingly, most of the would-be European authors were writers before entering cinema, eventually exchanging their pens for cameras. Antonioni was a highbrow film critic for the Italian journal *Cinema* during the war, Truffaut and his contemporaries all wrote sophisticated film criticism for *Cahiers du Cinéma* in the 1950s, in which Truffaut formulated the intellectual basis for auteurism, 'La politique des auteurs' in 1954, and Ingmar Bergman was an aspiring author of dramas, short stories and film scripts in Sweden in the early 1940s.[4]

Britain and *Sequence* had, among others, Lindsay Anderson, the writer who would most eloquently formulate the art cinema credo, even before Truffaut did so, and who would later become something of an auteur himself, even if he was only to direct six feature films between 1963 and 1987, from *This Sporting Life* to *The Whales of August*. He was also to be a central intellectual figure within the European art cinema, among other things organising the famous 'Free Cinema' screenings at the National Film Theatre in London in between 1956 and 1959, where many of the most well-known future European auteurs (Claude Goretta, Alain Tanner, Truffaut, Claude Chabrol, Roman Polanski) were first presented to an international audience.

Lindsay Anderson joined the university film society at Oxford, where he was an English literature student, at the age of 23 in 1946. In his seminal book *About John Ford* (1981) he describes his keen interest in the cinema from an early age.[5] From the autumn of 1947, Anderson was one of the editors of the journal *Sequence*, a continuation of the Oxford University Film Society magazine, along with, from time to time, for instance, Gavin Lambert, Penelope Houston and Karel Reisz.[6] All of them would later become prominent film critics, and in the case of Reisz, along with Anderson himself, a successful director of films, both in Britain and America, of works such as *Saturday Night and Sunday Morning* (1960) and *The French Lieutenant's Woman* (1981). When Anderson graduated in 1948, he and his friends continued to publish the journal from London until the beginning of 1952.

Sequence was specialist, small-circulation (never more than 5,000 copies) and not very well known – when Charles Barr and his friends started writing in *Movie* at the beginning of the 1960s, they had never heard of it although they, of course, knew of Anderson and his writings for *Sight and Sound*. But it became a force behind a British art cinema aesthetic and an intellectual venture to be reckoned with. Two major British auteurs, Anderson and Reisz, eventually emerged from its pages, and also two later editors of *Sight and Sound*, Gavin Lambert and Penelope Houston. It also acquired a certain cult status. In the words of Brian McFarlane, 'considering how short-lived it was – a mere fourteen issues between 1947 and 1952 – it acquired a firm niche in the history of British cinema criticism. Across the intervening decades, one found tantalizing references to it in the writing about cinema, suggesting how influential it had been among those who took cinema seriously'.[7]

Paul Schrader, scriptwriter and film director, has expressed his reverence for the writings in *Sequence*, claiming that he used to keep 'all sorts of rare things, like every issue of *Sequence*' in the back of the car in which he lived in Los Angeles towards the end of the 1960s, when he was the editor of the journal *Cinema* before himself entering the film industry in the mid–1970s.[8] Not many have studied *Sequence* for its historical importance to the 1950s film debates, particularly its auteurist philosophy, or for the radical art cinema doctrine that it taught.[9] The *Sequence* writers were influenced by Romantic philosophy, such as the writings of the German poet Novalis, and by the tendencies of literary New Criticism at the time: they were, after all, students of English literature. It is easy to compare the concerns of *Sequence* to Leavisite conceptions of the author – in *Sequence*'s version the film directors – whose works of art create a fusion of form and content. Thus, they were among the first European writers to create systematically a cult of the film director, or in other words, some of the initiators of the highly influential auteurist philosophy of the 1950s. This took place without the *Sequence* writers themselves really being aware of it, as is illustrated by Anderson's own introduction, written in the 1980s, for a planned reprint of *Sequence* material. In it he states that *Sequence* 'was quite untouched by French influence and the aesthetics of *Cahiers du Cinéma*. We certainly had no time for the auteur theory. From the start we knew that the film director was the essential artist of cinema – but we also knew that films have to be written, designed, acted, photographed, edited and given sound'.[10]

The writings themselves, however, do not entirely justify this, since those of Anderson's articles that deal exclusively with personalities mainly focus on individual directors like Alfred Hitchcock, John Ford and Vincente Minnelli. In a kind of generational rebellion, the *Sequence* writers quickly wrote off most of the British cinema of the 1940s, particularly the influential documentary doctrines of John Grierson, and his belief in the utilitarian aspects of film, which had permeated much of British film criticism up to that date. In a 1947 article called 'Angles of Approach' Anderson delivered a fierce attack on contemporary British film culture, outlining a model for a devoted politics of creation, well in line with what we would later understand as auteurism and art cinema aesthetics.[11] On the role of film criticism, Anderson wrote: 'It is the critic's first duty (and in this sense we are all critics) to perceive the object of a film and to judge its success in achieving that object. This does not mean accepting every film at its own valuation; it means allowing every film to justify itself by its own standards, not by our preconceptions'.[12] Anderson was thus advocating a basically aesthetic approach to the art of film. In a later article, 'A Possible Solution' (1948), Anderson was enthusiastic about Italian neorealism, the first real art cinema movement to emerge after World War II.[13] On the same lines he praised little-known independent British film productions, such as Clive Brook's *On Approval* (1944), summing up his argument for a creative, non-industrially based cinema like this: 'what is required is a cinema in which people can make films with as much freedom as if they were writing poems, painting pictures or composing string quartets'. He is close to Alexandre Astruc's idea of the camera-pen.[14] Cinema, then, was an art form, and not a Griersonian institution of social propaganda, and it was particularly not supposed to be a commercial industry, producing popular entertainment for the masses. Anderson's favoured metaphors were 'poetry' and 'poet', used as a way of describing great cinematic art as well as the cinematic artist: he believed that the real poets of the cinema were to be found in countries such as France and America. In this, Anderson and *Sequence* differed dramatically from the bulk of British cinema criticism of the late 1940s and early 1950s in which the realism and narrative unity of British films was generally applauded.[15]

Even if Anderson's polemic was directed at the documentarists, he shared with them certain values and also gave them some credit. He supported their realist aesthetic, the creative use of spatial verisimilitude, but generally spurned what he thought of as the use of realism as an 'excuse' for bad films. In a review of Rossellini's *Paisa* (1946) Anderson said that

> the so-called 'Documentary approach' has no doubt its very considerable virtues. It makes for realism, for authenticity of atmosphere, for sincere if unpolished acting. But to the extent that it inhibits the artist (in this case the director) from imposing his ideas on his raw material, from exercising his right to shape and to exclude, it is not conducive to the making of masterpieces. Most directors would be all the better for a spell in the open-air (provided it didn't kill them); Rossellini one would like to see take an enforced vacation in a studio.[16]

Accordingly, the director (or poet) must shape his work according to artistic patterns, whatever the raw material. This view of realism was most clearly articulated in Anderson's article 'British Cinema: The Descending Spiral' (1949).[17] (The title alluded to a piece in *Vogue* by George Stonier, 'British Cinema: The Ascending Spiral'.)[18] In this piece, Anderson denied the documentary tradition the weight it had been given by several of his fellow critics. 'It was inevitable that British features should become more realistic as a result of the war, but whether as a result it is legitimate to associate them with the movement which started with *Drifters*, and during the war gave us many feature-influenced documentaries, is questionable.'[19] He vigorously attacked some recent British films, among them Charles Crichton's *Another Shore* (1948), Charles Frend's *Scott of the Antarctic* (1948) – the caption for the accompanying illustration sarcastically read 'The Frozen Limit' – and Harry Watt's *Eureka Stockade* (1948). All were condemned in spite of their realist pretensions.[20]

> It is ironic that, for all their determination to avoid hokum, and their sense of social and artistic responsibility, these directors end up making films whose predominant characteristic is their unreality. It is not that they lack an eye for realism, but that through inexperience or incapacity each shows inadequate grasp of what is even more important – the technique of drama. In varying degrees, particularly, their ability to characterize is weak.[21]

The ability to handle drama as well as the realistic environment – to be a poet – was to be found elsewhere.

Anderson also discussed at length the question of cinematic authorship, presenting a strong argument for the validity of the concept of director in articles such as 'Creative Elements' (1948) and 'The Director's Cinema' (1950).[22] In them Anderson outlined precisely the various contributors to cinema, ending up with a plea for the director as the primary artist of the cinema. In 'Creative Elements', Anderson says this:

> So, in this gathering together, this fusion, there must be a central figure, one man conscious of the relative significance of every shot, the shape and flow of every sequence. But he cannot stand alone; he stands with, dependent on, his author and his cameraman. No doubt in an ideal world the same man would fulfill each function, but it is no use writing criticism for an ideal world.[23]

Anderson's auteurist argument was sometimes more subtle than that of his French colleagues: compare, for instance, Truffaut's bold rhetoric in 'Une certaine tendence du cinéma français' where he frankly pronounces 'Long live audacity. You will have understood that these audacities are those of the cinema [like Renoir, Clouzot or Bresson] and no longer of scenarists, directors and litterateurs'.[24] Although Anderson, like Truffaut and *Cahiers du Cinéma*, expressed deep admiration for European directors like the Italian neorealists, the surrealist Jean Vigo, and other auteurs canonised during the 1950s, like Renoir and Cocteau, his first directorial study, his first piece of auteur criticism proper, was the later often-quoted article 'Alfred Hitchcock', published in 1949.[25] Anderson's deep concern and search for a unique directorial style, in this case the 'Hitchcock touch', for instance in *The Lodger* (1926), is obvious: 'Most remarkable ... is the rapid, ingenious style of narration. From the opening – the close-up of a man's pale hand sliding down the banister-rail as he slips quietly out of a dark house – the camera seizes on the significant details which convey the narrative point of the scene. The result is a compression which gives the film continuous excitement'.[26] This to Anderson highly original approach signified a true filmmaker, a 'poet', even if that metaphor was never used to describe Hitchcock. (Anderson would later in his own films often 'quote' the films he had written about in *Sequence*. The most obvious Hitchcock allusion was significantly taken from *The Lodger*, which also provided the main still illustration for the original article. In *If...* (1968), the hero Mick Travis (Malcolm McDowell) makes his entrance dressed exactly like Ivor Novello in *The Lodger*.)

Anderson's preferred director, or auteur, however, was John Ford. In his writings on Ford, Anderson particularly stressed exactly the aspects of Ford's film-making which could be connected to what was later identified as formal properties in European art cinema. Accordingly, Anderson 'close-read' Ford's *They Were Expendable* (1945). He was convinced the film dismantled traditional narrative, and that it was also an expression of a personal vision.[27] In Ford's films Anderson notes that

> close-ups, noble or affectionate, are held at leisure; long-shots are sustained long after their narrative function is performed, a marginal figure is suddenly dwelt on, lovingly enlarged to fill the centre of the screen. Informed with this heightened emotion, a single shot, abruptly interposed – a ragged line of men marching into nowhere, one of them playing a jaunty bugle-call on his harmonica – assumes a deeper significance than is given by its position in the story.[28]

Anderson concludes his essay by claiming that some of Ford's films 'stand among the truly noble works of art of our time'.[29] (Anderson would make it into one of his own artistic trademarks to employ the same loose narrative structure, as in *If...* and *O Lucky Man*, a mode typical also of the European art cinema.) In 1952 his final piece for *Sequence* was a review article about Ford's *The Quiet Man*, released that year, giving also an interview with the director. Anderson famously concluded that a good deal would seem to hang on *The Quiet Man*, for its success or failure must affect Ford's attitude towards film-making in the future. In any event it is difficult to believe that he will not continue at it for a while yet. 'I want to be a tug-boat captain,' he says. But God made him a poet, and he must make the best of that.[30]

Besides the refinement of the notion of cinematic authorship, the apology for American cinema was the most important contribution to the discourse of criticism made by *Sequence* (which in this regard places it with *Cahiers du Cinéma*), a reappraisal which was part of critical debate about cinema in the 1950s.[31] It is interesting to note that the Ford films most admired by Anderson and *Sequence* were hardly ever the ones canonised by earlier criticism.

After its fourteenth issue *Sequence* ceased to function for financial reasons. In March 1952 Anderson wrote to Ford personally that 'my magazine has had finally to close down' and he also humbly asked the American director for work. He did not receive a reply.[32] The critical aesthetic introduced by *Sequence* at the end of the 1940s and after (objective realism; cinema as art; harmonic relationship between form and substance; critical affirmation of American cinema; and – particularly – auteurism) became established within British as well as European highbrow film criticism in the 1950s. This was partly a consequence of the recession at the British cinemas in 1948–49 and the general decline of critical support for British films in that period, and at least partly the fact that the *Sequence* critics became regular contributors to *Sight and Sound* which had a comparatively large circulation and was very much a trend-setter in British cinema criticism of the 1950s.[33]

Anderson would later become an auteur, very much in the style he had advocated in *Sequence*, trying to exert control over his own films, handling the camera as his own pen. Even if Anderson was to become a known film-maker in the 1950s, with widely circulated documentaries like the Venice prize winner *Every Day Except Christmas* (1957), he never did adopt entirely the Fordian poetics he had himself hailed, instead turning to more theatrical means – particularly in the Brechtian vein – for films like *If...* and *O Lucky Man*. When Anderson's late, elegiac film *The Whales of August* (1987) was released, Richard Combs claimed that Anderson in it for once fulfilled the promises of *Sequence*.[34] He did occasionally work in the *Sequence* mode – never more so than in a film that was never actually released, *Wham in China* (1986), originally a feature-length documentary. Anderson was hired by George Michael to direct a film about the pop group Wham's tour of China in 1984. In it Anderson tried to create a poetic film utilising the *Sequence* aesthetic, down-playing the role of the band performances and focusing instead on images of modern China. In his original cut, called 'If You Were There!' Anderson included, for instance, an extended poetic montage of images of the river in Canton, with boats, people on bicycles, close-ups and long shots against the background of a magnificent sunset. Anderson called this montage the 'river of life' sequence, according to his editor, Peter West.[35] Never in his career was Anderson closer to the concept of 'close-ups, noble or affectionate, held at leisure, long-shots sustained long after their narrative function is performed [or] a marginal figure suddenly dwelt on lovingly enlarged to fill the centre of the screen', to reprise his eloquent words about Ford in *Sequence*. It was hardly surprising, taking into account the style of mainstream commercial pop film-making in the 1980s, that Anderson was fired and his film completely recut.

In his final work, the 'farewell' film *Is That All There Is?* (1992), Anderson included the occasional '*Sequence* touch', not least in his initial quotation from the Free Cinema manifesto, 'Perfection is not an aim'. As to the upshot of Anderson's mission, *Sequence* was possibly more influential on film-makers and critics than Anderson himself. Auteurism and art cinema, for good and for bad, came to dominate the European cinema after the 1950s. For bad, it possibly caused, as Angus Finney claims in *The State of European Cinema*, disastrous financial decline in comparison to the American cinema. For good, it created some of the greatest cinematic masterpieces.[36]

Notes

1   Peter Wollen, 'The Last New Wave: Modernism in British Films of the Thatcher Era', in *British Cinema and Thatcherism: Fires Were Started*, ed. Lester Friedman (UCL Press, 1993), pp. 36–7.
2   David Bordwell, *Narration in the Fiction Film* (Methuen, 1985), pp. 205–33.
3   Alexandre Astruc, 'Naissance d'une nouvelle avant-garde: le caméra stylo', *L'Écran français* 144 (30 January 1948), p. 588.
4   See François Truffaut, 'Une certaine tendance du cinéma français', *Cahiers du Cinéma* 31 (January 1954), pp. 15–29.
5   Anderson, *About John Ford* (Plexus, 1981), pp. 13–17.
6   Among the contributors were Peter Ericsson, Lotte Eisner, Alan Cooke, Derek Grigs, Satyajit Ray and Siriol Hugh Jones.
7   Brian McFarlane, 'Sequence: Saying Exactly What We Liked', *Filmviews* (Autumn 1988), p. 31.
8   Kevin Jackson (ed.), *Schrader on Schrader and Other Writings* (Faber & Faber, 1990), p. 19. It would not be very difficult to relate the *Sequence* aesthetic to the narrative progression and style of some of Schrader's own works, like his script for *Taxi Driver* (1976) or his aesthetically influential film *Hardcore* (1979).
9   My book, *Lindsay Anderson: Maverick Film-Maker* (Cassell, 1998) contains a chapter on Anderson's film criticism.
10 Anderson, '*Sequence*: Introduction to a Reprint', p. 8 in the Lindsay Anderson manuscript collection kept at the British Council, but later removed and location now uncertain. It is also interesting to note how critically Anderson would handle the *Cahiers du Cinéma* form of directorial worship, as in a *Sight and Sound* piece in which he calls the journal's adulation of directors such as Hawks and Preminger 'a perverse cultivation of the meretricious'. See 'French Critical Writing', *Sight and Sound* 24, 2 (October–December 1954), p. 105.

11 Anderson, 'Angles of Approach', *Sequence* 2 (Winter 1947), pp. 5–8.
12 Anderson, 'Angles of Approach', p. 7.
13 Anderson, 'A Possible Solution', *Sequence* 3 (Spring 1948), pp. 7–11.
14 Anderson, 'A Possible Solution', p. 9.
15 See John Ellis, 'Art, Culture and Quality: Terms for a Cinema in the Forties and Seventies', *Screen* 19, 3 (Autumn 1978), pp. 15–20.
16 Anderson, '*Paisa*', *Sequence* 2 (Winter 1947), p. 31.
17 Anderson, 'British Cinema: The Descending Spiral', *Sequence* 7 (Spring 1949).
18 Anderson, '*Sequence*: an Introduction to a Reprint', p. 7.
19 Anderson, 'British Cinema', p. 6.
20 Anderson, 'British Cinema', p. 7.
21 Anderson, 'British Cinema', p. 8.
22 Anderson, 'Creative Elements', *Sequence* 5 (Autumn 1948), pp. 8–12 and 'The Director's Cinema', *Sequence* 12 (Autumn 1950), pp. 6–11, 37.
23 Anderson, 'Creative Elements', p. 12.
24 François Truffaut, 'A Certain Tendency of the French Cinema' [1954] in *Movies and Methods*, ed. Bill Nichols (University of California Press, 1976), p. 234.
25 Anderson, 'Alfred Hitchcock', *Sequence* 9 (Autumn 1949), pp. 113–24.
26 Anderson, 'Alfred Hitchcock', p. 115.
27 Anderson, 'John Ford and *They Were Expendable*', *Sequence* 11 (Summer 1950), pp. 18–31.
28 Anderson, 'John Ford', p. 115.
29 Anderson, 'John Ford', p. 31.
30 Anderson, '*The Quiet Man*', *Sequence* 14 (New Year 1952), pp. 18–31.
31 John Ellis, 'Art, Culture and Quality', p. 46.
32 Anderson letter to John Ford, 12 March 1952, John Ford manuscript collection, Lily Library, Indiana University.
33 See John Ellis, 'Art, Culture and Quality', p. 46.
34 Richard Combs, '*The Whales of August*', *Monthly Film Bulletin* 652 (May 1988), p. 154.
35 I was given a tape of Anderson's original cut by the director in the late 1980s.
36 See Angus Finney, *The State of European Cinema: A New Dose of Reality* (Cassell, 1966).

Mirroring England

National snapshots: fixing the past in English war films

FRED INGLIS

$\mathbf{A}$T THE VERY end of *Saving Private Ryan* (1998), Steven Spielberg presents us with a screen-filling view of the Stars and Stripes. The flag is huge, well-travelled, loved and faded, like a Jasper Johns painting. It is held out bravely by the wind, which blows it rollingly across the full screen. It is now unthinkable that a British film would end in such a strong, big-hearted and perfectly unironic way. Even British Airways took the flag off their tail fins, though it is to the point of my argument that a surprising number of people noticed the erasure and expostulated.

In addressing myself to the English and their Englishness I intend no offence, these neurotically offendable days, either to Scots, Welsh or Irish still ambivalently gathered under the heading 'British' (and still formally recognising the Union Jack as their national flag), still less to the 5 per cent of the population whose parents left the old empire some time between 1950 and 1970 or so for the promise of life, liberty and the pursuit of happiness as held out in Birmingham, Bradford, Liverpool, East London and elsewhere. In part, indeed, I am addressing that smallish diaspora, since they came to what was thought of, not inaccurately, as the parent-nation in expectation of what parents should give, and that parent in particular: comfort, support, shelter, justice, authority, steadiness, love, trustworthiness. These were qualities which, it was alleged, the British at large and the English as dominant had contrived into the practices of a culture and the formations of a state. Those practices and formations were no doubt spotted and disfigured also by the usual bloody cold of the English as well as their mildish racism, but they would nonetheless pass liberal muster in most historical reviews. Englishness had for a season an honourable moral content and a

I am Professor of Cultural Studies at the University of Sheffield and author, most recently, of *People's Witness: The Journalist in Modern Politics* (Yale University Press, 2002). My immediate interest in the war films of the 1950s was prompted by my national service as a 2nd Lieutenant in the Parachute Regiment and the Middle East during and after the disgraceful Suez campaign of 1956. *Fred Inglis*

place to which it belonged. That place was home, a term as absent from the indexes of the official classics of political science as it is central to the political values each of us instinctively invokes if we want to talk about politics in everyday life.

Englishness, however, has taken a bit of a pasting these past thirty or so years, and the kind that I am talking about was only embarrassed by the efforts of Mrs Thatcher and her cronies to reassert a fatuous Great Britishness, which turned out to be in truth a merely shop-keeping little Englandism. Those same efforts of hers compounded the derision of Englishness so cordially expressed over the borders of Scotland, Ireland and Wales, and concentrated at home by critics flying on the queasy, internationalist wings of academic leftism. Given that politics is now so completely dissolved into culture, those same critics on the left, friends and comrades of mine, found the Englishness of their malediction in every turn of the country's popular narratives. In the poetry of Ted Hughes and Philip Larkin, the novels of John Fowles and Penelope Lively, the music of Benjamin Britten and William Walton, the architecture of Leslie Martin and Colin St-John Wilson and above all in the films of Michael Powell, David Lean, Anthony Asquith, Humphrey Jennings, the Brothers Boulting and company, this small, malevolent church detected a threnody sung over the loss of empire and the decline of British (which is to say English) imperial power.

No one can doubt the facts of that decline, nor regret what was, for many English men and women, the happy evaporation of empire. At the same time, I suggest that 'decline' itself became a reflex rhetorical weapon with which to describe the veerings of English cultural life from the time of the Festival of Britain onwards. Those with plenty to lose from the tidal wavelets of egalitarian change which rippled mildly over England after 1945 not only scoffed at the little surge of modernist culture which flowered at the Festival, but announced the advent of general decline in a way that gripped much of the London literary imagination for the next half-century. The moral and emotional distance from Evelyn Waugh's ugly contempt as expressed for the Sword of Stalingrad on display in Westminster Abbey as well as for the long, shabby and reverent queues of visitors who trooped around it, to the Isle of Wight theme park in Julian Barnes's *England, England* of 1998 is quite short. The ethics of decline, like the tropes of disappointed love, are less a matter of moral vision and more a matter of fashion as compelled by social structures than most writers and art house film-makers would like to believe. There seems to me, however, something solid to rest on in these historical glimpses, and something solid to say about the relations between the English at war and the films the English made about themselves being at war immediately after the war ended, and for thirty or so years after that.

In affirming a detectable solidity in the relations of history and more-or-less historical films, there is implied a no-nonsense theory of representation in which a flat screen, black-and-white photography, a family parade of extremely familiar and gloriously indistinguishable theatrical heroes and stars playing unknown warrior-heroes, and the direct gaze of unselfconsciously English directors combine to tell true enough stories about real enough events.

Such a task can only be brought off, of course, at those few historically privileged moments since the invention of film at which popular sentiment, technological recording systems, and the forced march of quotidian eventuality can be made to fit together with comparatively little interpretative play or slippage. These conditions held pretty tightly in the 1950s. War itself had provided a comprehensive account of eventuality, not only one in which the mere facts of life could be rendered immediately intelligible by surrounding them with strategic explanations, but also one in which conduct itself, whether admirable or not, rarely provided a moral puzzle. The deadly sins and the cardinal virtues assumed significance in terms dictated by the plot of the anti-fascist war, its compulsory conception of duty and what Conrad called, in *The Shadow Line*, 'the blessed simplicity of its ... point of view on life'.

That perspective was commonly tightened upon the facts by the addition of news photography. In the century or so since Daguerre's amazing invention, the establishment of the news photograph both as incontrovertible testament and cherished revocation of the irrevocable past went unquestioned. Moreover, and in spite of widespread recognition that the same black-and-white photography once it had electrified into motion lent itself to all sorts of unreal mockeries and delirious fantasy, the *authority* of black-and-white images lent likelihood to fairy tale and certified headline and ticker-tape with the stamp of truth.

Finally, in this happy coincidence of camera, fact and feeling, that elusive historical necessity, popular sentiment, was keenly actualised in the forms of contemporary narrative in the 1950s. Men and women in their thirties and forties (and more: the period is also striking for the common lack of distinction in the dominant structure of feeling as between the generations) looked back on their shared experience of wartime as it began to come into an always provisional and evaluative balance. That is to say, they were in a position to judge the films for truthfulness as picturing a people's experience of what Angus Calder called 'The People's War'. For the first time in cultural history a huge and historic sequence of events was narrated and represented not on behalf of a powerful elite and as redounding to its credit, but on behalf of a whole population, permitting them to judge for themselves whether they came out of it well or badly. Our family of directors, writers and performers contrived a common, popular aesthetic within whose polished, intensely organised styles the criteria of plainness and accessibility, of trust in the truths of feeling, domestic beauty, and in the reassuring factuality of *things*, came together in a noble declaration of unironic faith in some great romantic simples: love, 'solidarity', 'character', home.

Sixty or so subsequent years have corroded this innocence. Consumer capitalism and the absence of war have together worked to underfeed 'solidarity' until it has become so thin we can see through it, and placed the values of radical individualism (identity, fulfilment, self-discovery and so forth) at the centre of the board. But the war films of the 1950s will none-theless be represented by me here, in the face of supreme unction on the part of all-knowing postmodernism, as themselves representing pretty faithfully the feelings of a full generation as its members looked back ten or fifteen years to a time in which they belonged to an inclusive and acknowledged narrative, a time during which this generation could be said to have had the chance to live well, as well as watching others die, on the whole, to the point and with credit.

I am offering a snatch of a history of the feelings, and an account of the representation of those feelings as being more or less faithful to the facts. I shall also suggest that the feelings in question may not only turn out to be longer-lived than the rhetoric of decline would permit under any heading other than that of nostalgia, but persist as part of a still animated version of English identity not altogether irrelevant to a medium-sized state in the European Union. I shall start with some signs of the times around 1944, beginning with an exemplary tale.

The English historian Edward Thompson, professionally known as E.P. Thompson, had a brother, Frank. Frank was a big, handsome young man, born in 1920, who won scholarships to Winchester and Oxford as a result not only of his quite amazing facility for learning foreign languages – at his death he spoke and read eleven – but of his luminous intelligence, his gifts as a poet, his striking high-mindedness and idealism, his strong sense of the comic. At Oxford in 1938, with Iris Murdoch as his sweetheart, he was, like all generous-hearted and public-spirited young men and women of his class, a communist because communism taught the righteousness of anger at all that capitalism, especially in fsascist uniform, did so cruelly to the wretched of the earth.

In 1939 he quit his degree and joined up. His amazing command of languages and his quiet courage took him by way of long-distance radio patrols to volunteer for parachute training and membership of the Special Operations Executive. He was assigned to Yugoslavia to liaise with the Bulgarian communist partisans then in operation against their own collaborationist-fascist government. In a series of desperate forays and retreats – so nearly starved to death that they ate raw snails – the partisans being gradually picked off by betrayal, by exhaustion, by bitter cold as well as in hand-to-hand fighting, Thompson and his men faithfully supported their depleted allies until they were all captured, Thompson and his sergeant of course in British Army uniform. It was 1 June 1944.

Five days later the terrible carnage re-enacted by Spielberg in *Saving Private Ryan* had its first performance on Omaha Beach. The fascist police chief in Sofia responsible for Frank Thompson knew that his government, dreading the arrival in Bulgaria of the Red Army, was soliciting for peace. Edward Thompson's view was always that the Allied authorities had left the Bulgarians to do what they liked with his brother; neither they nor the victorious Red Army wanted the help of idealistic young democrats in the way of the forthcoming European carve-up. For a little earlier, in his Christmas letter home in 1943, Frank Thompson had written to his family that

> there is a spirit abroad in Europe which is finer and braver than anything that tired continent has known for centuries, and which cannot be withstood. You can, if you like, think of it in terms of politics, but it is broader and more generous than any dogma. It is the confident will of whole peoples, who have known the utmost humiliation and suffering, and have triumphed over it, to build their own life once and for all.[1]

This the voice of a member of one of the greatest English traditions: that well-educated, internationalist-minded, generous-hearted and courteous fraction of the non-exploitative bourgeoisie which is one recruiting ground for the best of dissenting English socialism. The two brothers were young officers in what Edward called 'a resolute and ingenious civilian army' and Frank, who fought through the campaign in the Western Desert as well as the Sicily landings, praised as 'the best ambassadors and gentlest conquerors the world has produced'.

On 10 June 1944, the repatriation officers having done nothing about him and after a ridiculous show trial, Frank Thompson was taken to a little grass-topped hill above the village of Litakovo and shot. In the last letter anyone ever received from him, he wrote:

> I've been working hard, I hope to some purpose, and keeping brave company – some of the best in the world. Next to this comradeship, my greatest pleasure has been rediscovering things like violets, cowslips, and plum-blossom after three

lost springs [in the desert] . . . All this makes me more homesick than ever before, because England, when you've said all you like about Greece or Italy or the Lebanon, is the only place where they know how to organise spring.[2]

The last small scrap of evidence I want to produce by way of indicating something of the actualities of general and popular feeling in 1945 is also taken from Edward Thompson's scattered memoirs of war. While his brother was in Bulgaria, Edward, aged barely twenty, was a tank squadron commander in the unbelievably arduous advance of the Allied forces up and down the vertiginous hills and valleys of the spine of Italy, from Anzio to Monte Cassino, and north through the Apennines.

On 19 June 1944 at 6.30 p.m. his tank was trundling and squealing toward the outskirts of Perugia, second in a troop reduced by battle damage to two. He might have been in the first tank but for army protocol about the troop commander not risking himself in the lead. It was blazingly hot. When the front tank was directly hit, two of its men got out and ran to safe cover in the narrow street with its high-walled gardens; the other three were killed. Thompson broke protocol by running forward to the Sherman under rifle fire, to call down into the turret. He received no answer.

It was a tiny exploit in that formal operation, the liberation of Perugia, itself part of the larger victory in Italy and, ultimately, the victory in Europe. But Thompson's memoir goes beyond the leggy boy running through bullets to check on his men and later finding half of one burned to ashes in the driver's seat. It includes the letters sent to him when, in spite of the certainty of the troopers' deaths, the army had only posted them as 'missing' and their families were being put through the mutual strain of hope and anguish for impossibly long. Here are some extracts from the letters quoted by Thompson. They break one's heart. 'My brother was all I had in the world we had lived together the last ten years since losing our mother and I would like to know a few more details, if the spot where he is buried is marked or did an explosion make this impossible?' 'Please did one of his friends pick some wild flowers and place them on his grave?' (Thompson said that whenever he 'sent the least scrap of news, this was received with pitiful expressions of gratitude from the kin of these troopers. They seemed to be astonished to receive any attention from anyone on authority'.) 'Hope I am not taking too much of your time I am so sorry to trouble you.' 'Will you try and do me a kindness and see that his personal belongings are sent back to me and if you really could get a photo of his grave it would set my wife's mind at rest as she is greatly grieved.'[3]

Perhaps this glimpse into the lives of the two Thompson brothers (and the lives and deaths which touched theirs) will serve sufficiently to support

my claim about the framework of sentiments which made the war intelligible to those who fought it, as soldiers or civilians. These were the
sentiments which served to give structure and value to the extraordinary
films which, as it were, 'explained' the moral inheritance of war and peace to
its children. The Thompson brothers were of much the same class as directors such as Anthony Asquith, Michael Powell and David Lean. Idealistic
and honourable young men of that moment had to be on the political left;
they shared a class education with at its centre those principles of national
solidarity, hope for international fraternity and modest social emancipation
and a strong public-spiritedness which found honest and piercing embodi-
ments in their films.

Powell's and Pressburger's wonderful inauguration of a small cinematic
epoch of war films is, of course, *A Matter of Life and Death* (1946). It anticipated the 1950s by four years, starting its action in May 1945, only a day or
two before Germany surrendered. It opens with a young poet (David Niven),
commanding a doomed Lancaster, frantically quoting Andrew Marvell and
Walter Raleigh to the young American woman checking the bombers home
from a coastline control tower. Niven jumps out into the night with no
parachute rather than be burned to death, misses his guardian angel in the
dark, hits the sea, survives to meet and fall in love with the American. He is
then tried in heaven for his life with the defence that because he has fallen in
love *after* the official moment of his death, heavenly bureaucracy is at fault
and his death revocable.

His prosecutor, ally and friend of Paul Revere, keeps up his nation's old
enmity against the English. The jury, appealed against as being all-
American citizens, is promptly replaced by exactly the same people in their
world-historical guises, all of them victims and judges of empire: Irish, Indian,
Chinese and so on. God is, naturally, an Englishman, but more importantly
he is the surgeon who repairs the lesions in the hero's brain, restoring him to
poetry and to a long and happy marriage with the American. The vision of
an all-powerful, just world order whose finally reconciled citizens are
apotheosised in the benignity of a hospitable United States was simple,
rousing and as the Marshall Plan opened its coffers the following year,
plausible as well. Fifty years later that strong vein of feeling which Frank
Thompson felt opening as a new spirit abroad in Europe retains its power.
For all her faults, America, as Noam Chomsky surprisingly put it, remains
'the freest society the world has ever seen'. Michael Powell's vision of fair
play as shared by Anglo-Americans, and domestic love and happiness as
cherished by everybody, retains the right kind of big sentimentality, the
kind politics now needs.

This noble film is an overture to the epoch. Thereafter, what one finds in the remarkable succession of honestly made, well-built and tightly told war films is not at all a threnody to empire or an aesthetics of decline, but rather a winning story about the necessity of duty, its visible fulfilment in modestly efficacious action, and the confirmation of its significance in the bonds of trust.

The classics of this tight articulation of form, feeling and meaning include in its heartening roll-call the following:

1945	*The Way to the Stars*
1946	*A Matter of Life and Death*
	The Captive Heart
1949	*The Small Back Room*
1950	*The Wooden Horse*
1952	*Angels One Five*
	Appointment in London
1954	*Carrington V.C.*
	The Colditz Story
	The Dam Busters
	The Sea Shall Not Have Them
1955	*Above Us the Waves*
1956	*Ill Met by Moonlight*
	Battle of the River Plate
1958	*Carve her Name with Pride*
	Ice Cold in Alex

The line was carried on in the 1960s by such workmanlike films as *The Battle of Britain* (1958) and comes to a sort of gentle finale with Richard Attenborough's careful and competent *A Bridge too Far* (1977) and John Boorman's endearing *Hope and Glory* (1987). *Henry V* (1944), you might say, was its holy book.

The 1960s and 1970s films are, of course, in colour and it is a commonplace, but a telling one, that the black-and-white film has its authority stiffened by the authenticity of black-and-white newsreel footage and of propaganda masterpieces like *Nine Men* (1943). However that may be, these films and many more like them gradually matched their ideal but not, I think, idealised narratives to the social map of England. That is to say, each social and combat group was provided with a story within which it could find an adequate reflection of its war. Gender, social class, region and division of labour together found a spot on the map, service by service, and within the services, to each according to his or her need: a film about bombers, a film about fighters; a film about infantrymen, a film about trucks, a film about the civilian bomb disposal teams; a film about battleships, about E-Boats, about the Merchant Navy; a film about prisoners and resistance fighters.

In each case, there being a war on and this being England, the officer class got the best parts, but that class as vastly enlarged and therefore as having learned civility from itself – as Edward Thompson says – by way of the necessities of conscription. When the working class does appear, justice is done to that terrific self-confidence, the political settledness which, uniquely in the world, effected an honourable class compromise held in place by high mutual respect, until at last the treaty was dissolved by Mrs Thatcher's short, murderous and victorious class war.

The Cruel Sea (1952) stands as one eponymous masterpiece at the head of all these films. What is striking about the film is the deliberately prosaic nature of its epic poetry. As the two senior officers on the little ship, so unobtrusively played by Jack Hawkins and Donald Sinden, close in friendship and shared hardship, held apart by rank, say at the end, there were only two enemy vessels sunk. Five years are concentrated into less than two hours, but such are the demands of the form; that form must hold in the tension of art the large frame (or structure) of feeling within which the English told themselves, not untruthfully, the story of the war.

This is *not* the story, on the one hand, of inane, improbable and repetitious heroics, as in *Where Eagles Dare* (1969); nor is it the story of *Catch 22* (1970), where greed, lust, cowardice and ineptitude combine to dissolve virtue into chaos (as it is the *point* of farce to do); still less is it the vapid and preposterous hokum of *Pearl Harbor* (2000).

In form and feeling, *The Cruel Sea* looks at first blush like a remake of *In Which We Serve* (1942). Made, of course, as pretty well a piece of straight propaganda, Noël Coward's film is in any case based on the unmistakably heroic but redolently regal early wartime caveats of the Lord Louis Mountbatten and his ship HMS *Kelly*. One can therefore scrape off its surface a slight but sugary glutinousness permissible in the circumstances but quite absent in the successor film. Jack Hawkins aboard *Compass Rose* is given no domestic life at all; Donald Sinden takes up, in a series of mere glimpses, with the formidably intelligent as well as beautiful Virginia McKenna, but it is the tacit and taciturn friendship with his captain that counts. Friendship, for sure – Sinden turns down a command in order to stay as Hawkins's Number One – but friendship defined as the faithful discharge of mutual obligations to the crew, to the service and – though no one would ever put it like that – to the country and the necessity to defeat fascism.

Much more, however, is made of saving lives and losing them than of cutting down or up the enemy. *Compass Rose* rescues sailors (including Scandinavian merchantmen), their lungs clotted with machine oil; in pursuit of a U-boat which they fail to catch they run down their own shipwrecked comrades struggling in the water; when the second of the two ships in the story comes finally home in 1945 the last word of the film is the bare order: 'Shut down main engines'. Meiosis is its stylistic trope, and that seems to square with the record. The chance of a second marriage for the plump, wholesome and widowed sister of one petty officer with another of his messmates goes down without a comment and with the ship. The beautiful Wren isn't waiting on the quayside. One trivially unpleasant officer (Stanley Baker) malingers his way to a cowardly shore job; another, unimportantly courageous and drily ironic volunteer officer, previously a barrister (Denholm Elliot), is first cuckolded and then drowned. It is the surprisingly domestic story of duty confirmed by significant action and set off by an upright courtesy towards death. The action is held within a polyphony of the sentiments still active in English society and, it may be, still giving a bit of spine and substance to Englishness.

Another half-dozen films on my list, less good than *The Cruel Sea*, but never less than strongly made, cleanly edited, vividly told, would sit easily in its company. One could identify, without recourse to irony, Marxism or psychoanalysis, as their structural constants and, in doing so, I believe, map them on to that structure of feeling within which the English and, give or take a nationalist adjustment or two, the Scots, Welsh and Irish, accommodated their experience of the war behind them. That is the moral point of those films and this essay. They provide accommodation in the social memory for a whole vast, disfiguring and – human history being what it is – emancipatory tableau.

The war films of the 1950s together constitute the assented-to record of the emotions and moral judgments called upon to set in order those disorderly events. Absolutely true to the feelings of the 1950s, sufficiently true to the facts of 1939 to 1945, they now serve as an extraordinarily detailed as well as compact encyclopaedia of these facts and feelings.

One test of this would be to consider the remarkable success of Thames TV's famous twenty-six parter of 1973, *The World at War*. Jeremy Isaacs and Phillip Whitehead, it will be recalled, were the two devoutly Labour-voting, Oxford-educated, unassertively English, extremely talented programme-makers of thirty-something who persuaded Thames to sink £3,000,000 and three years' research into a quite new kind of national-history-as-told-by-documentary-television. In spite of misgivings, Thames acquiesced, and found to their amazement that they had a world-beater on their hands, saleable in every corner of television's geography, still on show well past the millennium's end.

The form of the thing was simple and immediate. The producers picked first-class journalists of their own political persuasion to write the script (Neal Ascherson, Stuart Hood among them), and paid for the golden voice of the king of national theatre, Laurence Olivier, to speak the words and for the brilliant young composer-arranger Carl Davis to set the words to background music (with an unforgettably haunting signature tune). They then intercut black-and-white news footage with talking heads shot in colour and in sequences of spontaneously poetic reminiscence.

The relevance of this twenty-four-hour masterpiece to the theme in hand is that Isaacs and his men completed and expanded the work of those great 1950s films. Together they matched significant event to its democratic representation. That is, each arm and combat force had its footage and its impromptu historians: fighter pilots from 1940; air-raid wardens from the Blitz; Chindits from Burma; truck drivers from the Western Desert; submariners and merchantmen from the Atlantic. Beside them, the directors placed the grand strategists and commanders whose fatal decisions enfolded the everyday lives in triumph or disaster. Finally the whole picture was turned back to front by doing exactly the same for and with the people and the leaders not only of non-Anglophone allies – French, Soviets, Greeks – but of the Axis powers: Hitler's adjutant and his secretary, Albert Speer the Führer's minister of production, Hirohito's chief negotiator after Nagasaki, and a throng of junior officers to match the laconic, poetic, British petty officers from the Malta convoys, American infantrymen from Iwo Jima, Jewish doctors from Duchan, widows from Dresden and Stalingrad.

The 1950s films, with remarkable grace and celerity, dramatised and taught the same lessons within the family frame of the English at war. In that wonderful meditation upon the meaning of history, *Little Gidding* (written, it should be remembered, during and under the London *Blitzkrieg*), T.S. Eliot spoke of the mutual opponents in the English Civil War as afterwards 'accepting the constitution of silence' and as being 'enfolded in a single symbol'. This is the necessary, not-always-accomplished restoration and reparation at the heart of narrative history. One might say that such reparation remains uneffected for the 1917 revolution and civil war in Russia – Pasternak's *Dr Zhivago* and Paustorsky's *Scenes of a Life* were the first flutterings of a doomed attempt at healing; it is similarly unachieved for the American war in Vietnam. These hideous moments were aberrations, and the art of narrative history can find them no commemorative accommodation.

From the vantage point not only of the victors but of human emancipation at large, the retelling of the defeat of fascism makes for stories with plot, point, moral grip and a powerful ending. Its constituents are to be found in the English war films of the 1950s. There we see narrative becoming history, biography turning into myth. It is important to add, at a time when much of a putting-down kind is levelled against present British society for its nostalgic attachment to myths of a self-bolstering kind, that by 'myth' I here intend no more and no less than stories common to the social memory which embody principles to live by and ideals to live for. If we look to two formative essays which defined early and simply a provident mythopoeia for the English at war, we shall find the moral outline of a national fable which shaped the great reforms of the 1945 Attlee government and survives today as a necessary recollection of a social order in which solidarity is more important than status, and where dutiful self-sacrifice is vindicated by future liberations and fulfilments.

George Orwell in his great essay *The Lion and the Unicorn: Socialism and the English Genius* (1941) and William Connor, writing under his *Daily Mirror* professional name as 'Cassandra', in his parallel effort, *The English at War* (1941), alike emphasised that the country had discovered something about itself at war: that its army, navy and air force had best be as much civilian as military; that in the anti-fascist struggle the honours were (as Edward Thompson noted) evenly distributed between old-fashioned English Toryism and the different idealism of the left; that in any case the poisonous old snobberies and murderous old inequalities of the past *must* and would be transcended in the settlement of the peace; that the point of present privation and sacrifice would find commemoration in a just and happy society when the war was over and won.[4]

These noble lies and dignified desires were given ardent and classical expression in the films to hand. They remained a believable account of what people *felt* it had all been for, and they offered a feasible vision of a past surpassed but mythologised. In a small novella of a film, *The Sea Shall Not Have Them* (1954), virtually the whole action takes place in the company of four airmen in a dinghy in the North Sea. The film was made in honour, one can simply say, of the air–sea rescue boats and indeed, after a little straightforward suspense caused by bad weather and fog, the men are duly rescued from under the coastline guns of the enemy as they drift towards the Belgian shore. The substance of the film, however, is the little class struggle played out by the four men as, drenched, bitter cold, thirsty and wounded, they cling to hope of safety while at the same time bracing themselves to disappointment by keeping hope down.

Michael Redgrave, a wounded wing-commander carrying secret and urgent papers in a briefcase, discloses in irreproachably upper-class tones his own irreproachably working-class origins to Dirk Bogarde, a worthy enough sergeant-pilot bearing up only intermittently well under cold, fear and misery, but desperately keen to win a commission if and when he gets home. A sort of kindly class compromise is come to; promotion is worth aspiring for; scientific distinction (Redgrave) is rewarded by danger and paid for by disinterested courage; the rescue boat brings off its routine, precarious task with the usual grumblers and the bravery enjoined by discipline.

Many of the films follow that emotional shape and its factual isomorph. In *The Way to the Stars*, *Above Us the Waves*, *The Dam Busters*, *Angels One Five* and a dozen others, a fictional or real adventure picks its way from the hesitant beginnings and initiation of lost and gauche newcomers into the rites of the service and the mysteries of its technology until they can launch themselves with varying competence and uncertain temper into that concentration of action in which both character and efficacy coincide. The key actions are rarely epic: 'two U-boats in five years' in *The Cruel Sea*; the triviality of escape for three men from POW camp in *The Wooden Horse*; the utter anti-climax when the disgraced Captain Langsdorff (Peter Finch) scuttles the *Graf Spee* (and commits suicide) in *The Battle of the River Plate*. They are also rarely failures. Rather, they fix significance as the dramatic culmination of difficult and disciplined preparations during which human ardour may burst out but must be reconstrained, private love and longings will have their say but must be postponed and all intensities of utterance are compressed into understatement and excision. In the service of rendering the reassuring and blessed simplicity of such short passion plays, word and (black-and-white) image are superimposed upon one another with exceptional tautness and brevity. There are few long shots and, at least as now understood, even fewer close-ups. The frame of the shabby office, the cockpit, the seat of the truck, the ship's bridge, the railway compartment, silhouette the male and uniformed body and give it at once statuesque ease and domestic bulk. Thus and thus the heroes of a new Homeric order put on the lineaments of democracy.

Two films must serve finally to illustrate this high achievement. The two – *Ice Cold in Alex* and *The Small Back Room* – are mere indications of the line of my argument. Several others would serve, as would such almost-war films as *Whisky Galore* (1948) and *Passport to Pimlico* (1949), or such a robustly internationalist example as *The Captive Heart*, or the bitterly anti-war, even anti-British and little-known *Yesterday's Enemy* (1959).

Ice Cold in Alex comes towards the end of the 1950s and, it may be, at a moment when, having faithfully recorded as a duty to the documentary record the everyday lives of wartime, the movie-makers could pause a little and open up the narrative frame fitting so tightly over the facts of history and observe the recalcitrant tumult of feelings shimmering at the edges where people learned a style. The film seems to me to sustain much more careful consideration than David Lean's celebrated *Bridge On the River Kwai* (1957), partly because Lean's indulgence of the picturesque fairly runs away with him into the lusciousness of Burmese travelogue, but mostly because the exigencies of co-production made for sentimental anti-war clichés and utter confusion as to the plot.

Ice Cold in Alex has an exemplarily taut line to its tale; history, passion and actuality are exactly matched to our period aesthetics of fact, fiction and photography. It starts with John Mills, an RASC captain (decidedly *not* an elite corps), his sergeant-major (Harry Andrews) and a couple of nurses being waved down for a lift at the ignominious retreat from Tobruk in 1941. The hitcher is a purported South African, in fact a German spy, played by Anthony Quayle, stripped to waist and ankle, bronzed like a Greek hero, huge-chested, rangy, his wireless set slung across one massive shoulder in his haversack.

The truck is shot up escaping; one nurse is wounded and dies slowly and tidily. Mills is on the gin but strikes an anxious, motherly chord in Sylvia Syms (nobly revealing the first bare bosoms in British cinema). They rumble Quayle's ruse but say nothing. Quayle tries to lose his radio in the quicksands of Umm al Samim and, in a thrilling sequence, has his life saved as the others winch him out on a line hauled in by the truck. Gradually, human sympathy and a subdued gallantry unite the quartet against the terrible desert and in allegiance to the indomitable wagon. In a wonderful scene, Quayle saves the irreplaceable suspension and axles by taking the weight of the vehicle for a tense minute on his terrific shoulders when it starts suddenly to settle on its jack.

The truck finally bowls into Alexandria and they all drink the iced beers they had promised themselves during the hundreds of miles under the implacable sun. The three Britishers break it to Quayle that they have seen through his disguise and – since he is in British uniform and liable to be shot as the spy he is – save his life by telling the Military Police he is prisoner wearing kit loaned for the epic journey across the sands.

Spies in 1958 were conventionally villains. But spies in fact must be as exceptionally brave, resourceful and intelligent as the character played by Quayle. The film finds, in the generous accommodation made between those at war, a quite new drama of reconciliation even at the moment at which, in history, Rommel was at the gates of Alexandria. The emblems of this victory are a battered three-ton truck, a deep unspoken affection between officer and warrant officer, a nurse, a courageous enemy indispensable to their mutual survival, and four foaming beers in thickly frosted glasses. The RASC doesn't kill anybody; it brings up the supplies, and nurses are only women. Such winners are born losers. So it is a happy touch to contrive such a delicate and affecting moral only thirteen years after the gates of the death camps were opened.

The Small Back Room, adapted from a novel by Nigel Balchin, is a comparably stripped-down piece of work and, as befits its august writer-directors, makes its evaluations of war and the pity it distils in unexpected places. The film follows David Farrar as a civilian bomb-disposal specialist who has already had a foot blown off, taken to the whisky, as well he might, and been partially rehabilitated by the long-suffering Kathleen Byron. Powell and Pressburger note with a characteristic and laconic eye the active maintenance of status-competition and ineffable vanity (by, in an unexpected cameo, Jack Hawkins) even in the exigencies of war and rationing. They render, fondly and sardonically, the evasions, the self-servingness and severe purity of serious science in the research committees of Whitehall. Their bleakly understanding camera (the cameraman was Christopher Challis, a pupil of Humphrey Jennings) watches Farrar struggle against the seductions of the giant bottle of VAT 69 left deliberately visible in his grim flat.

The Germans have dropped little sprinklings of a trial anti-personnel mine with a carefully concealed second trigger. Farrar and Leslie Banks have to discover its mechanism. They question a victim on the point of death (with necessary brutality) for vital details. Banks is killed by the mine. Farrar hits the bottle and, hung over, is called out to defuse the next deadly delivery. This being the work of Powell and Pressburger, there is no promise that he will get away with it and, in any case, the character calls to our natural sympathy for his mutilation, but decidedly not to our liking.

In a fine sequence, reporting on his progress by walkie-talkie to a young engineer-colonel in a sandbagged redoubt, Farrar defuses the mine and falls back on the shingle. Torn by anxiety, the young colonel breaks cover and runs to his side. He runs well and all's well. He offers no praise, but as he bids goodbye and shakes Farrar's hand, he gazes at the civilian with profound admiration. Another smallish space in the frame of feelings built, taught and moralised by World War II is filled not with killing but with saving lives.

There is of course no shortage of death-dealing in the great films of this decade. But their scale, the very size and monochrome of their cameras, let alone the moral vision of their makers, keep death personal and saving life preferable. They cut the field of action down to the size of domestic homes and private gardens. The cup of tea, so standard a joke in war films because so standard a succour in war, is eloquent of that customary decency and exchange. The pieties of a teacup will hardly do to enclose a world at war, but the war itself can hardly be comprehended and brought within a manageable frame of popular sentiment as contrived by those who did the fighting to show themselves and their children what it meant, without the aid of that mighty midget of a symbol.

These sentiments join, in a habitable structure, the key values of the polity: love, in a rather low-key, rinsed-out form, mostly caught in moments of kindness and domestic affection, most intensely acted as tenderness; trust, where trust is in others to be faithful to what is known to be shared (trust *in*, therefore, as well as trust *of*); solidarity, the canonical value of the working class, but also of patriotism and of regiment or ship or squadron, nonetheless the principal virtue to have grown out of opposition to that militant capitalism of which fascism was the most monstrous embodiment; lastly, innocence. 'Never such innocence again,' Larkin said of 1914, but Edward Thompson, writing angrily and many years after his brother's death, spoke of the foul lies perpetrated by Thatcher's state upon the best values and sentiments of the old left, and remarked of those young men and women and their bravery that 'they were too innocent by half ... too bloody innocent to live'. That innocence nonetheless survived beyond 1945, nor was it dissolved by the end of the Cold War, nor in the quiet, unheralded victory of the petit-bourgeoisie in the two-hundred-year class war of old England.

The dead go on before us, larger than in life they seemed, as Larkin also said, never more so than in these films. As we heed them, in our history books and in our cinemas, their energies flow again down the reopened channels of feeling and imagination. The ghosts walk, inspiring us with new possibilities. That is what ghost stories are *for*.

Notes

1   E.P. and T.J. Thompson (eds), *Frank Thompson, There is a Spirit in Europe* (Gollancz, 1947), p. 169.
2   Edward Thompson, *Writing by Candlelight* (Merlin Press, 1980), p. 132.
3   E.P. and T.J. Thompson, *Frank Thompson*, p. 43.
4   Edward Thompson, *The Heavy Dancers* (Merlin Press, 1985), p. 188.

Film and the Festival of Britain

SARAH EASEN

THE FESTIVAL OF Britain, from 3 May to 30 September 1951, aimed to provide respite from the effects of World War II by celebrating the nation's past achievements in the arts, industry and science, as well as looking hopefully to a future of progress and prosperity. It marked the halfway point of the century, a natural moment at which to take stock and examine advances in British society. The Director General of the Festival, Gerald Barry, promised 'a year of fun, fantasy and colour', an interlude of 'fun and games' after the long run of wartime austerity.[1]

Film was integral to the Festival of Britain. It related to the Festival's three main areas of concern, the arts, industry and science. Britain's role in international film culture had already been established by the growth of the British documentary movement since the 1930s. The Festival of Britain therefore seemed a natural place to demonstrate the fruits of British film production. The Festival of Britain site in London on the South Bank featured a purpose-built film theatre, the Telekinema, for big-screen public television broadcasts and the showing of specially commissioned Festival films.[2] The Television Pavilion also displayed a brief history of the new medium. Cinemas around the nation featured seasons of classic British film-making. The exhibitions themselves also used film as a tool for expressing concepts and processes that could not easily be displayed. So film was not only a medium for the exposition of ideas within the Festival of Britain exhibitions, it also contributed to the entertainment on offer.

Originally the plan for a 1951 festival derived from the centenary of the Great Exhibition of 1851 which showcased the achievements of newly industrialised Victorian society and its global empire. Gerald Barry, editor

I work for the British Universities Film and Video Council on their British Newsreels Project. I am currently researching British women non-fiction film-makers. My interest in the post-war modernisation of Britain led me to programme a season of films and curate an exhibition at the National Film Theatre for May 2001 celebrating the fiftieth anniversary of the 1951 Festival of Britain. *Sarah Easen*

of the left-wing *News Chronicle*, had championed the idea in 1945. The government decided to set up the Ramsden Committee to investigate the idea of a
'Universal International Exhibition'. This was eventually downsized to a
national exhibition and by 1948 the structures were in place to begin the
planning phase by the Festival of Britain Office. On 5 May 1948 the head of
the Festival Council, Herbert Morrison, requested that the British Film
Institute (BFI) organise the film side of the Festival. Jack Ralph, previously
of the National Film Board of Canada, was appointed by the BFI in January
1949 as its representative responsible for all Festival film arrangements. To
discuss the role of film in the Festival he established the BFI Festival of Britain
1951 Panel consisting of prominent members of the British film industry,
including Michael Balcon, Anthony Asquith, John Grierson, Harry Watt
and Arthur Elton.

Initial plans were ambitious and many ideas had to be dropped due to
logistical problems and financial restrictions. A proposed international con-
ference of producers, directors and technicians was abandoned in June 1949
after it was decided that 1951 should only be a celebration of national achievements. A two-week festival of British films for June 1951 to be organised by
the BFI at the New Gallery cinema in London was cancelled because the BFI
was ineligible for exemption from Entertainments Duty and so could not
afford the undertaking. During 1949 and 1950 the press reported that several
of the large studios were making films for the Festival.[3] Frank Launder was
to make a Korda-produced film with action set during the Great Exhibition
of 1851. A non-profit making co-operative called Festival Film Productions
was making *The Magic Box*, a biography of the British cinema pioneer,
William Friese-Greene. Elstree was making *The Elstree Story* – a compila-
tion of films made at the studio over the previous twenty-five years, as well
as an adaptation of Thomas Hardy's *The Mayor of Casterbridge* starring
Richard Todd. Powell and Pressburger were shooting *Tales of Hoffman* and
Carol Reed was also rumoured to have something in the pipeline. In the
event, many of these films never made it past pre-production in time for the
Festival and only one was designated a Festival film, *The Magic Box*.

Documentary and experimental film-making initially fared better as the
Festival Executive provided a £120,000 budget for documentary film production. This was to be the seed for an idea that became the BFI's Experimental Film Fund, established in 1952. A sub-committee of the BFI Panel
selected six themes for Festival-sponsored films: 'The Sea', 'The Land', 'The
People', 'Royalty' (which included tradition and ceremony), 'Sport', 'The
Great Road' (a study of one of Britain's arterial highways) and 'The River'
(about the River Severn).[4] Unfortunately the Festival Office withdrew this

funding and in December 1949 the BFI Panel sub-committee metamorphosed into a new Committee of Sponsorship and Distribution to set about finding private and public sponsorship. Several established documentary units came to the rescue. The Shell Film Unit sponsored *Air Parade*. Humphrey Jennings's company, Wessex Film Productions, made *Family Portrait*. World Wide Pictures in conjunction with the Welsh Committee for the Festival of Britain financed *David*. International Realist made *Waters of Time*, which was sponsored by the Port of London Authority, and the Petroleum Films Bureau sponsored *Forward a Century*.[5] However, there is evidence to suggest that the Festival Office later restored £11,000 worth of funding to the BFI, for producing several experimental films for screening at the Telekinema.[6] These included four stereoscopic (3-D) and stereophonic films made under the guidance of Raymond Spottiswoode as well as the *Painter and Poet* series.

Not only were there problems with the pre-production of the films. Throughout 1949, the Festival Office and the BFI Panel could not agree on a suitable exhibition venue. When it was agreed that projection facilities should be included on the South Bank site, the panel complained that plans for a 450-seat cinema were 'thoroughly inadequate'.[7] However, the Festival Office duly appointed an architect, Dr W. Wells Coates, to design a building to accommodate the showing of 35mm film, stereoscopic (3-D) and stereophonic film and large-screen television. By October 1950 a grey oblong building, constructed from light steel and soundproofed, in a 'fly-away linear design [with a] gay façade and bold modern stare', was nestled next to the railway arches between the Royal Festival Hall and Waterloo Station.[8] This was the Telekinema. The seating capacity was 410, that is, 252 in the stalls and 158 in the balcony. The projection booth, situated between the balcony and the stalls, was behind glass. Visitors could see the film and television operating equipment as they entered the foyer, which also doubled as a television studio. Here celebrities were interviewed and these interviews were later broadcast as part of the special Telekinema programme along with selected material from the BBC. The remainder of the one hour and ten minute programme was made up with showings of the sponsored documentaries and four stereophonic films. The Telekinema was a great success: 458,693 visitors paid the separate admission charge of 2s and many people had to be turned away.[9] When the Festival ended in the autumn, there were calls from the press and the public to retain several landmarks, of which the Telekinema was one. After much wrangling with the LCC and the film industry, the building was formally handed over to the BFI for use as a members-only repertory cinema club. It was re-equipped with four hundred seats and projection facilities for both 16mm and 35mm, and was re-opened in October 1952 as the National Film Theatre. Five years later, the Telekinema building was closed when the BFI built its new cinema under Waterloo Bridge within a stone's throw of the old site.

The BFI Panel had strong ideas about using film in the displays. It was adamant that 'there should be facilities for continuous 16mm showings in as many sections of the Exhibition as possible, the film in this case being treated as an integral and functional part of the particular exhibit concerned'.[10] The panel minutes note that this recommendation should be taken up with the Festival Executive, suggesting that the executive did not realise the potential of film as a tool for instruction and education. However, 16mm film replaced the stagnant display of manufactured products, the impracticality of working models and the static wall displays that were frequently used in exhibitions. The centrepiece of the Land of Britain pavilion was a pillar of rock representing geological evolution, which concealed a 16mm projector showing a continuous film loop. This was projected on to a rubber screen, which transformed itself into a giant relief map every few seconds to show the birth of the nation.[11] The Dome of Discovery made extensive use of 16mm film including the use of a micro-projector to show an enlarged image of the working parts of a watch. The New Schools Pavilion displayed a film-strip projector and a 16mm sound projector as invaluable teaching tools in the primary and secondary classroom exhibits.[12] Educational films, a genre British film-makers had excelled in since the 1930s, were screened at the Exhibition of Science in South Kensington. Their specially constructed one-hundred-seat cinema showed a free continuous forty-minute programme of scientific films from 1.00 p.m. every day for the duration of the festival.

Those concerned with the Festival's film arrangements wanted British cinematic achievements to be celebrated by the whole nation not just those who visited the London sites. A travelling Festival Exhibition visited Manchester, Leeds, Birmingham and Nottingham during the Festival period. It had a 'People at Play' section with a small cinema which featured seven-minute film shows every fifteen minutes: it was regularly packed out. The fifth Edinburgh International Film Festival devoted its annual retrospective to British documentary, which included screenings of *Industrial Britain* (1931) and *Night Mail* (1936). Special screenings of Festival films were also programmed and 16mm prints of the stereoscopic films were shown twice nightly for the run of the film festival. Bath held an International Film Festival for children in May, and Glasgow hosted the 13th International Amateur Film Festival during August. Less formal evaluations of British film-making were also taking place such as film festivals organised by local authorities. Newcastle-upon-Tyne screened a season of British scientific, documentary and industrial films in early June.[13] The Barrow Arts Club sponsored a Festival of British Cinema which concluded with Paul Rotha's film *A City Speaks* (1948) and a session analysing *Odd Man Out* (1948).[14] The commercial Circuits Management Association (CMA) was also eager to participate in the celebrations. Their Gaumont and Odeon cinema chains programmed festivals of British films, held foyer exhibitions relating to the Festival, began a nationwide search for a 'Festival Girl' and organised the broadcast of King George VI's opening speech in many of their cinemas.[15] Independent cinemas also entered into the spirit of the Festival. A typical example was a Festival week at the Regal Cinema in Evesham, Worcestershire. The manager showed, among others, *Great Expectations* (1946), *Whisky Galore!* (1948) and *The Red Shoes* (1948).[16] The BFI attempted to fill the gaps left by local arts festivals, national cinema chains and independent exhibitors by mobilising film societies and education institutes to put on film shows during the Festival period. To this end, the BFI sent out a pamphlet called *How To Put on a Film Show* suggesting the sort of films that could be shown, the distribution libraries that stocked them and places to obtain equipment for projecting them. They also issued three lists of recommended films for screening during the five-month Festival period which included classic British documentaries such as *North Sea* (1938), sturdy educational films such as Gaumont-British Instructional's *Downlands* (1936) and, of course, the Festival films *Forward a Century* and *Family Portrait.*[17] Finally, if Festival visitors had not tired of the medium, they could purchase colour 16mm film of Britain's historic buildings and pageantry and filmstrips of the Festival of Britain and London as souvenirs.

The main attraction at the Telekinema was the showcasing of new cinematic technology – stereoscopic films. This was not the first time 3-D films had been shown to the public; in 1924 a programme of films had been shown in London and the USSR had already perfected stereoscopic projection without the need for the audience to wear special glasses.[18] Of the four films produced for the Festival, the Norman McLaren and National Film Board of Canada's animated Technicolor films *Now is the Time* and *Around is Around* garnered the most praise. Both films used McLaren's trademark technique of direct drawing on to 35mm film. The former was designed to introduce the viewer to the concept of 3-D using shapes and sound and the latter depicted patterns made by an oscilloscope set to specially composed music. It seemed the medium was better suited to abstract form as the two live action films, Pathé Documentary Unit's *A Solid Explanation* and International Realist's Technicolor *Royal River* were not well received by the critics. *A Solid*

Explanation suffered from 'an assured style but inadequate material' and only two things about the film (literally!) stood out – the handshake into the audience and the giraffe's neck at London Zoo.[19] *Royal River*, a trip down the River Thames, fared little better, the same critic pronouncing it 'very tame and stodgy' and a failure of content over form. Another critic went further, proclaiming it a 'handsome bore'.[20]

Nevertheless, the idea of a purpose-built cinema for 3-D sound and vision created a buzz among film enthusiasts all over the country. On the whole, the industry also responded favourably, but the prohibitive costs of producing the films and the need to re-equip theatres meant that many saw it as having very little immediate commercial impact. Oddly, the trade decided that the less said about stereophonic sound the better and treated it as little more than a novelty.[21]

The *Painter and Poet* series of four black and white art films, each under ten minutes long, was produced by the British animators John Halas and Joy Batchelor. Artists including Mervyn Peake, Henry Moore and Ronald Searle created visual impressions of eight poems, narrated by performers such as Michael Redgrave, John Laurie, Eric Portman and Stanley Holloway. It was recognised that the films were 'agreeable and enterprising [and that] they illustrate some of the possibilities of the technique even if, occasionally, they fail to realize them'.[22] The most liked was Ronald Searle's interpretation of the William Cowper poem *The Story of John Gilpin*. One critic referred to Searle's drawing as 'so dynamic, it is difficult to realize that no picture on the screen is moving'.[23]

Over a dozen sponsored documentary films were made for the Festival. Unfortunately there is not room here to discuss them all, so I will concentrate on five of the more high-profile productions: *Forward a Century*, *Air Parade*, *Waters of Time*, *Family Portrait* and *David*.

Forward a Century depicted the century between the Great Exhibition of 1851 and the Festival of Britain. Critics thought it 'well photographed and edited, and written with honesty and sincerity [as well as being] unusual and imaginative'.[24] After its screening at Edinburgh it was noted that 'the film as a whole is one of the most accomplished seen during the [film] Festival'.[25] Britain's realist documentary tradition was represented by *Air Parade*. A straightforward but patriotic exposition of the history of aviation, the film concentrates on Britain's recovery since the war to become a world leader in the civil aircraft industry. The other side of the documentary tradition – aesthetic as opposed to the more propagandist intentions of *Air Parade* – was represented by two films: Basil Wright's return to documentary directing, *Waters of Time*, and Humphrey Jennings's penultimate film, *Family Portrait*.

Basil Wright had been an original member of the British documentary movement in the 1930s. His film took a journey up the River Thames showing the
activities of the Port of London by means of the narrative of a ship docking,
unloading and reloading. Its images were accompanied by a complex soundtrack consisting of factual commentaries spoken by the dock master and a
docker, poeticised prose and a specially composed music score. The critical
press responded well to the film: the May issues of *Monthly Film Bulletin* and
Sight and Sound thought it a 'notable film'. The former added that it was
made with a range and technical finish rare in present-day documentary
while the latter praised its eloquent photography, the richness of texture in
the music and the care and complexity of the editing.

Humphrey Jennings's contribution, the quietly patriotic *Family Portrait*,
related more directly to the Festival than any other film. It is subtitled 'A
Film on the Theme of the Festival of Britain 1951' in approved Festival type-
face over the Festival logo. The film is constructed between the opening and
closing shots of a family photograph album; the family representing Britain.
It proceeds to celebrate British achievements in the arts (Shakespeare),
science (Darwin others) and industry (Stephenson), echoing the displays of
the festival exhibitions. Jennings regards these heroes of British life with
warmth. He refers to them as 'local lads who used their wits and had a good
laugh, and then, like Shakespeare and Newton and Watts started something
at home that went right around the globe'. The film acknowledges the
contradictions of the British character: an admiration for invention versus a
love of tradition, eccentricity versus practicality, domesticity versus pageantry. Overlying these paradoxes is Jennings's concept of Britain as a nation
where the need for innovation (prose) meets the creative mind (poetry).

Family Portrait is a poetic but overly literal film: the evolution of British
tradition, particularly democracy, is discussed over images of Runnymede,
the Houses of Parliament and council committee meetings. It was well
received by the press and Jennings's fellow documentarists. In retrospect it
is difficult to say just how much of this praise was a result of Jennings's
accidental death at the end of 1950. Many of the film's notices read like
obituary eulogies. Writing in the Edinburgh Film Festival publication, *Film
Festival: Third Week*, Edgar Anstey pronounced it to be the most important
documentary film made since the war. The *Monthly Film Bulletin* thought it
perhaps the most polished in style of all Jennings's films, adding that all the
elements of the film – camerawork, editing, voice-over and music – were
finely balanced, making it continuously fascinating, sharp and evocative.
Today's Cinema thought it a 'lovely, lingering experience' that should 'stand
as a yardstick for contemporary documentary'. Three years later in an

article for *Sight and Sound*, Lindsay Anderson wrote that *Family Portrait* could stand beside Jennings's wartime films, but that it lacked the passion of his earlier ones. However, in a 1981 revaluation, Anderson decided that *Family Portrait*, although distinctive and compositionally distinguished, was 'sentimental fiction'. He berated Jennings for his 'fantasy of the Empire' and his resort to 'The Past as a refuge'.[26] Although the film's patriotism is very much of its time, it closes with the realisation that Britain belongs 'to a communion across the Atlantic and the South Seas ... [and] to the family of Europe'. While acknowledging the influence of Britain's imperial past, Jennings was well aware that its future was reliant on wider global alliances.

In contrast to the national observation of *Family Portrait*, Paul Dickson's film *David* sought to embody the spirit of Welsh society through the small south Wales community of Ammanford. Dickson had won a British Film Award in 1950 for his first film *The Undefeated* (1950) and used the same technique of combining drama and documentary in *David*.[27] The film has a complex flashback narrative structure and a cast of local people, often playing their real-life roles. The local school caretaker, on whose life the film is based, plays the protagonist, Dafydd. The first flashback through the eyes of Ifor, a young villager who has returned for a visit, shows how the caretaker was an inspiration to him. The second flashback takes us through the caretaker's life beginning with his first job in the mine, which ends when he is injured in a pit accident. As he says, his life parallels that of the Welsh nation: 'most men of my age in Wales can tell the same story, getting coal was the thing, it was our wealth and in a way our destiny'. The people of Ammanford bear their hardships stoically; again, the character of Dafydd represents this. A poem he has written after the death of his son from tuberculosis is entered for the national Eisteddfod. It receives an honourable mention but does not win. The theme of the Eisteddfod, 'He who suffers conquers', is an equally fitting epithet for Dafydd, his community and the nation of Wales. The film ends with an ex-pupil from Dafydd's school, now a nationally respected scholar, returning as guest of honour to the school prize giving. Although he is a now a well-known figure, the scholar is still a part of the smaller community he was nurtured in. The most important factor, as the voice-over states, is being 'worthy of our heritage, our country, Wales'. *David* was uniformly praised for its naturalism and humanism. The *Monthly Film Bulletin* said it combined 'intelligent shaping of the narrative with an unrestrained realism'. Gavin Lambert, writing in *Sight and Sound*, thought it a 'success for all concerned' and it was listed as one of the magazine's 'Films of the Month'. *Today's Cinema* described it as 'the first really live and human film made for the Festival', adding that it was 'always restrained, dignified and extremely moving'. *Variety* commented that despite 'some too-evident artiness in the production technique, this short film registers with a moving sincerity'. *Kinematograph Weekly* thought it a 'charming and efficiently presented authentic life story of a Welshman'. In Wales itself *The Amman Valley and East Carmarthen News* concurred, stating that the caretaker's 'life story is [a] true reflection of the integrity of character that is a feature of the Welsh nation'.

The only feature officially nominated as a Festival film, *The Magic Box*, did not play at the Telekinema. It premièred on 18 September at the Odeon, Leicester Square, barely two weeks before the Festival closed. The cast was an extraordinary parade of British actors, many with only walk-on parts, including Laurence Olivier, Michael Redgrave, Richard Attenborough, Stanley Holloway, Eric Portman, Margaret Rutherford and Sybil Thorndike. Robert Donat played the central role of William Friese-Greene, the British inventor working on the patent for the first film camera in 1889, whose story tied in neatly with the Festival theme of celebrating the arts, industry and science. The story of his struggle to perfect an instrument capable of photographing and projecting movement involved engineering, physics, chemistry and ultimately entertainment. Eric Ambler adapted the script from Ray Allister's 1948 biography. When published the biography had resulted in a questioning of Friese-Greene's role in the invention of cinematography. The argument continued with the production of the film, mainly between an American historian, Terry Ramsaye, and the film's producers.[28] Although *The Magic Box* acknowledges the contribution of other cinema pioneers in its credit sequence, it portrays Friese-Greene as the true originary pioneer of cinematography. When his son returns from school with cuts to his face it transpires he has been in a fight defending his father's reputation as the inventor of moving pictures. Friese-Greene reassures the boy, but the scene ends with a melancholic Friese-Greene lamenting that the encyclopedia which his son's school friend consulted 'could have just mentioned my name. It wouldn't have hurt anybody'. The film illustrates the inventor's craving for recognition, but at the same time his possession of the English virtues of modesty, restraint and dignity. Unfortunately this was not an altogether accurate reading of the real Friese-Greene, who up until the moment of his death was still seeking acknowledgement for his achievements.[29]

As well as Eric Ambler, *The Magic Box* included other eminent British film personnel among its production team. The cinematography was the work of Technicolor's star cameraman Jack Cardiff, the music was composed by William Alwyn and conducted by Muir Matheson and the set designs were by John Bryan. Ronald Neame produced the film and John Boulting directed it. As is to be expected of such a prestige production, the critical press was generally positive. Many of them made the point that the film was not making a case for Friese-Greene as the sole inventor of cinematography, but merely suggesting that he should be recognised for his work alongside Edison, Le Prince, the Lumière Brothers and others. In *Sight and Sound* Ernest Lindgren suggested several reasons why everyone should see the film, including 'its restraint, its fidelity, its acting, its colourful period reconstructions, its humour'. However, most importantly he thought it a 'human picture of a type of individual to whom we all unknowingly owe much: the obscure, unrecognized, patient, ever-hopeful, dabbler in inventions who is prepared to sacrifice everything to his ruling passion'. The *Monthly Film Bulletin* noted that it was a 'leisurely, slow-paced, sober view of events with occasional ventures into near burlesque', and that it was 'excellently photographed and handsomely mounted'. The trade paper *Today's Cinema* thought it an 'appealing story' with 'stand-out box-office attraction ... assuring stimulating entertainment for all but the heedless'. Even the usually acerbic Richard Winnington writing in the *News Chronicle* thought the film-makers had 'made a thoroughly worthy job of a difficult subject'. The American trade paper *Variety* summed up the film as an 'okay prestige pic [*sic*] for the U.S. market', adding that it was a film of 'great sincerity and integrity, superbly acted and intelligently directed'. However, despite these predictions of wide audience appeal, *The Magic Box* failed at the box office.[30]

It is interesting to compare the way film was used in the 1951 festival to the way in which the moving image was used to mark the millennium nearly fifty years later. No feature films were commissioned for showing either at the Millennium Dome in Greenwich or at cinemas around Britain. The opportunity to showcase the newly revitalised British film industry of the 1990s was not taken and only two productions were made for screening at the Dome. These were a specially commissioned episode of the television series *Blackadder* and a four-and-a-half minute musical piece about British life called *The Good Ship Citizen* starring the television comedian Vic Reeves. The thirty-five-minute *Blackadder: Back and Forth* was shot on 35mm and projected in 70mm on to two 20 by 20 metre screens at the Dome's Skyscape accompanied by *The Good Ship Citizen*. Two major productions were incorporated into exhibitions. In the 'Timekeepers' Zone' a live action, computer-animated episode of the television series *Timekeepers* called *Timekeepers of the Millennium* was shown, and a BBC production, *Navy in Action*, was screened at an interactive exhibition on the Royal Navy at the University of Portsmouth. The BBC also featured all-day live coverage of the millennium celebrations as well as broadcasting a ten-part series surveying the last thousand years of history. New media technology was used in the production of a CD-ROM about the history of Stirling, and BBC Wales created a 'virtual art gallery' for a seven-part series on five hundred years of Welsh art. It is interesting to note that it was the television sector rather than the film industry which was called upon to produce films to reflect the cultural life of Britain for the millennium celebrations.

Film, as a whole, played a successful part in the Festival of Britain. The box office receipts of the Telekinema testify to the popularity of the stereoscopic films and also to the attraction of television, which was on the way to becoming a serious threat to cinema. It is not within the scope of this essay to discuss the place of television in the Festival, but it should be said that the film industry trade press was aware of its increasing presence. *Kinematograph Weekly* reported in May 1951 that the newsreel companies 'succeeded admirably in showing to a far wider public than [was] available to the Television News Service, a concise and permanent record of the event'. Although reaching a smaller share of the audience, the BBC provided five months of Festival-themed programming. As well as outside broadcasts of Festival events including the opening ceremony, they scheduled a season of Festival Theatre in their television drama slot, the light entertainment department broadcast a series on the history of British entertainment in the twentieth century and a cookery series featured regional British cooking.[31]

However, it would take another two years, with the coronation of Queen Elizabeth II, for television to make any real impact on British society. At the time of the Festival, film was more popular and affordable. Consequently, the opportunity to celebrate the medium was embraced by both publicly funded and privately owned sectors of the film industry. The publicly funded sector suffered a setback when almost all their funding was withdrawn, but managed to complete a good number of projects with the assistance of sponsorship. After reports in the press that the feature industry was bubbling over with ideas for Festival films, only one was completed – a cooperative venture between Rank and ABPC, amongst others, with a cast of over sixty British actors. Despite the initial problems and the limited time scale, over twenty films were made including one feature, at least fourteen documentaries, four experimental films and four stereophonic films, as well as the countless short films made for the exhibits themselves. Travelling exhibitions and local festivals of British features and documentaries ensured that the celebration of film was nationwide. Only the 3-D films were confined to screenings in London and at the Edinburgh Film Festival. Film appreciation sessions sprang up in arts clubs around the country to discuss the history of British film. Even so, the trade press complained that the industry should have taken greater advantage of the opportunities the Festival offered for 'the exploitation of its own wares'.[32] Certainly more films could have been made, but this was not just an occasion to highlight the present, it was also a time to celebrate the past. Although the films made for the Festival of Britain did not have a lasting impact on British cinema history, a legacy of sorts does remain. The concept of the BFI establishing a production fund with government monies for experimental film-making evolved directly from the Festival and is still in operation, albeit in a different guise. The Telekinema, under the auspices of the BFI, remained on the South Bank site until the institute built a new cinema close by, the National Film Theatre, which is still in use today.

Notes

1 'The Festival', *Manchester Guardian* (15 October 1948).
2 There appears to be some confusion over what the South Bank cinema was actually called. Although festival literature and BFI press releases refer to it as the 'Telecinema', the name on the outside of the building was 'Telekinema'.
3 Festival Film Productions consisted of the J. Arthur Rank Organisation, Associated British Picture Corporation (ABPC), National Film Finance Corporation (NFCC), London Films/British Lion group, Sidney Bernstein, Technicolor, Kodak and Berman's (the costume rental business). From a Jack Worrow press release: BFI National Library FG/1 29 June 1950, *The Magic Box* microjacket.
4 The BFI Panel Sub-Committee was composed variously of Cecil King (chair), Lady Allen of Hurtwood, Anthony Asquith, Michael Balcon, Arthur Elton, John Grierson, Harry Watt, one representative each from the Kinematograph Renters' Society and the Cinematograph Exhibitors' Association, two representatives from the Association of Specialised Film Producers, Dilys Powell (*Sunday Times* film critic), F.A. Hoare, F. Hill, Paul Wright of the Festival Office and Oliver Bell of the British Film Institute.
5 Many other sponsored documentary films were made for the festival, such as *Bristol – British City* (Bristol City Corporation), *City of London* (City of London Corporation), *Home of Your Own* (Hemel Hempstead Corporation), *In Black and White* (Bowater Paper Corporation), *Model Flight* (Shell), *Proud Preston* (Corporation of Preston), *Voices Under the Sea* (Cable and Wireless) and *We've Come a Long Way* (Anglo-Iranian Oil Company). A film about the problems in Pakistan, *Kashmir Conflict* made by Peter Lennox and Lawrence Mitchell, was deemed too controversial for screening. Its exhibition was banned by the LCC unless it was shown alongside a film showing the Indian point of view.
6 *British Film Institute: Report on Film Activities, Festival of Britain 1951*, Subject file: Festival of Britain 1951: BFI National Library.
7 Minutes of the Third Meeting of the British Film Institute Festival of Britain 1951 Panel (16 March 1949), No. 16, Subject file: Festival of Britain 1951: BFI National Library.
8 Douglas Railton, 'They Didn't Have This in 1851', *Today's Cinema*, 76, 6242 (1951), p. 31.
9 *The Story of the Festival of Britain*, HMSO (March 1952), p. 12.
10 Minutes of the Second Meeting of the British Film Institute Festival of Britain 1951 Panel, 18 February 1949, No. 9 (d), H/33, Aileen and Michael Balcon Special Collection, BFI Collections.
11 Several films were made for the Land of Britain Pavilion, including *Fossils Which Come to*

Life and *Land Fauna and Reptiles* (Signal Films), *Earth in Labour* (Halas and Batchelor) and *Landscape Scenes* (Greenpark Productions).

12 'Festival of Britain: Five Busy Months for Projectors in Villages, Towns and Cities', *Film User* 5, 55 (1951), pp. 246–8.

13 *Festival of Britain 1951: The Catalogue of Activities throughout the Country*, Festival of Britain Office (1951).

14 'Arts Club Ends Instructive Film Session', *Barrow News* (14 July 1951).

15 'Varied CMA Plans for the Festival Programme', *Today's Cinema* 76, 6242 (1951), p. 25.

16 'Festival Cinema Week', *Evesham Standard and West Midlands Observer* (7 September 1951), p. 6.

17 *Recommended 16mm Films for Distribution during the Festival of Britain 1951: List 2* (December 1950), BFI. Subject file: Festival of Britain 1951: BFI National Library.

18 Neil Baran, 'Films in Depth', *The Mini-Cinema* 5, 9 (1951), p. 33.

19 See Baran, 'Films in Depth', p. 32.

20 *Times Educational Supplement* (14 September 1951), Edinburgh International Festival 1951 file, BFI National Library.

21 'The Kine Takes an Exhibitor as Guest to the Festival's Telekinema', *Kinematograph Weekly* 2, 288 (1951), p. 6.

22 *Monthly Film Bulletin* 18, 209 (1951), p. 284.

23 *Film User* 5, 58 (1951), p. 405.

24 *The Mini-Cinema* 5, 11 (1951), p. 35.

25 *Weekly Scotsman* (6 September 1951), Edinburgh International Film Festival 1951 file, BFI National Library.

26 Lindsay Anderson, 'Postscript: October 1981', in Mary Lou Jennings (ed.), *Humphrey Jennings: Film-maker, Painter, Poet* (British Film Institute in association with Riverside Studios, 1982), p. 59.

27 In the documentary movement there had often been a blurring of the boundary between drama and documentary. For example: *North Sea* (1938), *The Silent Village* (1943), *Highland Doctor* (1943), *Western Approaches* (1944) and *Blue Scar* (1949). The last film was also shot in a Welsh mining village.

28 Research continues into the validity of Friese-Greene's place among the pioneers of moving image technology. See Alan Burton's article 'Seeing is Believing: *The Magic Box*' in Alan Burton *et al.* (eds), *The Family Way: The Boulting Brothers and British Film Culture* (Flicks Books, 2000), pp. 164–8.

29 See Michael Chanan, *The Dream That Kicks* (Routledge, 1996), pp. 92–3.

30 On 29 April 1952 *The Times* reported that the NFFC had sustained a loss of £45,851. 'The loss', it stated, 'arises almost wholly from the failure at the box-office of *The Magic Box*, the Festival of Britain film, for the production of which the corporation made a large loan. In fact, the corporation lost nearly all the money put into it.' *The Magic Box* microjacket, BFI National Library.

31 Cecil McGivern, 'Television and the Festival of Britain', *Radio Times* 111, 1433 (1951), p. 43.

32 'The Festival', *Kinematograph Weekly* 2259 (1951), p. 4.

The national health: Pat Jackson's *White Corridors*

CHARLES BARR

WHITE CORRIDORS, a hospital drama first shown in June 1951, belongs to the small class of fictional films that deny themselves a musical score. Even the brief passages that top and tail the film, heard over the initial credits and the final image, were added against the wish of its director, Pat Jackson. Jackson had spent the first ten years of his career in documentary, joining the GPO Unit in the mid-1930s and staying on throughout the war after its rebranding as Crown, and the denial of music is clearly part of a strategy for giving a sense of documentary-like reality to the fictional material of *White Corridors*.

There is a certain paradox here, in that actual documentaries, like newsreels, normally slap on music liberally. To take two submarine-centred features, released almost simultaneously in 1943, Gainsborough's fictional *We Dive at Dawn*, in which Anthony Asquith directs a cast of familiar professionals headed by John Mills and Eric Portman, has virtually no music, while Crown's 'story-documentary', *Close Quarters*, whose cast are all acting out their real-life naval roles, has a full-scale score by Gordon Jacob. Other films in this celebrated wartime genre have even more prominent and powerful scores, by Vaughan Williams for *Coastal Command* (1942), by William Alwyn for *Fires were Started* (1943) and by Clifton Parker for Jackson's own *Western Approaches* (1945). One can rationalise this by saying that documentary has enough markers of authenticity already at the level of dramatic and visual construction, and a corresponding need for the bonus of

---

I had the not untypical experience of being taken to a lot of worthy British films by parents and teachers in the 1950s, and then reacting against them when the riches of non-British cinema were opened up, notably by *Movie* magazine, in the 1960s. Since then I have progressively overcome the *Movie* conditioning in the course of writing books on *Ealing Studios* (1977, new edition, Cameron & Hollis, 1999), *English Hitchcock* (Cameron & Hollis, 1999) and *Vertigo* (BFI, 2002). I co-scripted, with Stephen Frears, the British programme in the BFI/Channel 4 series on the centenary of cinema, *Typically British* (1996). Current projects include a study of Pat Jackson in the Manchester University Press series about British directors. *Charles Barr*

music to give it extra shape and impact; and that the fiction film, conversely, can create enough momentum through its own dramatic and visual structures to 'afford' the lack of a score, and to turn this lack into a positive and compensatory marker of realism.

The absence of a score does not of course *make* the film in any way more real, but it is evidence of the kind of project that *White Corridors* represents: that of sustaining, in the changing post-war world, something of the impetus of the realist British cinema of wartime. The critical consensus of the 1940s may have given excessive weight to this realist trend, at the expense of the less austere cinema of, for instance, Powell and Pressburger and Gainsborough melodrama, but there was, indubitably, a significant coming together of feature and documentary at various levels, leading on the one hand to 'story-documentaries' of increased ambition and accessibility, and on the other to a cycle of fiction films, such as *Millions Like Us* (1943), that were rooted in contemporary realities and acknowledged a specific documentary influence.[1] The pairing of *We Dive at Dawn* and *Close Quarters* is a good instance of this crossover, or, as it was often termed, 'marriage', between the two modes.

At the end of the war, the story-documentary lost the support of sponsors and exhibitors with startling rapidity. *Western Approaches* was the last of the feature-length Crown products to get wide distribution. It earned Pat Jackson a Hollywood contract, but he postponed taking it up in order to fight for the survival of this mode of film-making. In a paper written in 1945 and submitted to the Rank Organisation in early 1946, he lists the key films, and argues that

> A country with such a record of achievement in any field of activity cannot now afford, through lack of foresight, to allow that activity to disappear. Yet just as the documentary method of story telling is reaching full maturity, just as it has broken down so much prejudice from both the public and the commercial industry, just as it has found its most persuasive method of putting Britain and her people on the screen – this type of film is in danger of disappearing from the cinemas altogether.[2]

There was no response, and Jackson soon went to MGM, where he was to direct just one film (*Shadow on the Wall*, 1949 – the first time he worked with actors) before returning to England in 1950. Meanwhile, his associates from Crown had gone in various directions. Some stayed on with the Unit, struggling with little success in the bleaker post-war climate; of the others, Harry Watt (director of *Target for Tonight*, 1941) had already gone to Ealing, and Jack Lee (*Close Quarters*) would likewise soon go into feature films, but only Watt's *The Overlanders* in 1946 has any real continuity with the big idea of wartime. The anticlimax of the post-war career of Humphrey Jennings is well-known, and symptomatic. What might he have done as a genuine follow-up to *Fires were Started*? Even if he had not died in an accident in Greece in 1950, we might never have had an answer.

This context makes the achievement of *White Corridors* all the more striking. The absence of a musical score does not render it austere; it was a popular success at the time, and was thought worth re-releasing in 1963, when I recall watching it in an Irish suburban cinema among a packed and attentive afternoon audience. There are three main ways, in addition to the soundtrack strategy, in which it recalls the wartime marriage or crossover between fiction and documentary:

1   *The use of non-professionals, alongside experienced actors.* A talismanic role is played by H.F. Hills, a ship's officer whom Jackson had used in a small but important part at the end of *Western Approaches*. Unlike Fred Griffiths, whose casting in *Fires were Started* launched a long career as a character actor, Hills had nothing more to do with films until Jackson summoned him again to play the hospital porter; the film opens with his walk through the dawn streets to begin his stint at the reception desk. Like another non-professional cast as a Scottish ward sister, Grace Gavin, he blends in seamlessly. A third in this category is the boy whose illness constitutes a central thread in the story; compared with most of the stage-schooly child actors of the time, Brand Inglis is notably fresh and affecting.

2   *The instructional mode.* Basil Radford plays a confused gentleman who is just back from abroad and doesn't understand the workings of the new National Health Service. The porter patiently talks him – and us, if we need to know – through the procedures for getting onto a doctor's list and obtaining an NHS card. His cluster of comic-relief scenes add up to something very reminiscent of the short films of wartime in which the instructional pill is sugared by humour, for instance those of Richard Massingham – right down to the payoff where he breaks an ankle and is admitted as a casualty, thus bypassing the bureaucracy. On the inside of the hospital, we go through a comparable learning process via the experience of a nursing recruit (Petula Clark) who is finding her way around on her first day (compare the structural roles of the new fireman, Barratt, in *Fires were Started*, and the new recruit to the Fleet Air Arm in Ealing's *For Those in Peril*, 1944). Overall, the film works to familiarise us with the workings of an NHS hospital – and this shades into a third kind of echo of the big wartime films.

3   *Celebration of a public service and of the team that delivers it.* This had
been a main impulse behind the highest-profile documentaries, from
Night Mail and its postal workers to the dramatisations of the work of
the various wartime service units. With the end of the war, the demand
for such films had, as we have seen, tailed off, to the dismay of the left-
leaning documentary loyalists who hoped that a Labour government
would make imaginative use of them to promote its social agenda.
Instead, Labour acquiesced in the contraction of official film sponsorship and in the marginalisation of the Crown Unit, which led to its abolition by the incoming Conservative government in 1952. The achievement
of *White Corridors* is to find both an appropriate topical subject in the
NHS and an absorbing way of dramatising it as a commercial project.
In this, it can be compared with the police drama *The Blue Lamp* (1950),
made by the most public-spirited and documentary-influenced of the
commercial companies, Ealing, at the end of a few years of uncertainty
as it cast around for a post-war identity. The two films even share a
screenwriter in Jan Read, credited along with three others for *The
Blue Lamp*, and with Pat Jackson for *White Corridors*. Important as
The Blue Lamp is, *White Corridors* is bolder, less cosy, more adult.

Jackson's first wartime assignment was a short film released in November
1940, *Health in War*, an early example of the type of documentary that takes
the enforced changes of the time as the foundation for a better future. In the
words of the commentary, it shows how 'the voluntary and municipal
hospitals were linked together into one national health service'. The lower-
case initials are correct here, but the film is recording, and in a small way
contributing to, the momentum that will lead to the creation of an upper-
case National Health Service. After *Western Approaches*, Jackson spent six
months preparing a film about the Beveridge Report – the weighty blueprint
for a new system, NHS included, that would create security 'from the cradle
to the grave', published in 1942 and widely discussed – but the project never
got beyond script stage.[3] *White Corridors* can be seen as an unofficial sequel
both to *Health in War* and to the unrealised Beveridge film. It is based,
appropriately enough, on a novel of wartime: *Yeoman's Hospital* by Helen
Ashton, published in 1944 and set in December 1943.[4] That hospital struggles along, financed by a combination of public money, private subscription
and 'provident scheme' contributions, but state control is already in the air.
The film updates the book unobtrusively into the world of the NHS, where
finance is still tight but provision is free. The novel covers a period of
twenty-four hours, which the film expands into a few days.

Health in War, while acknowledging 'the evils of the past', was typical of official documentary in its upbeat rhetoric about present and future, backed by sunny imagery. 'Whatever it is, no hospital, even in the danger area, will fail to give you attention if your case is urgent.' 'Here come the finest surgeons in the country, to give their skills to all the people.' We see white coats, gleaming instruments, wise and caring faces, and country settings. *White Corridors* honours the ideals while being honest about the obstacles, both material and human.[5] This is urban austerity England: white coats grow shabby, new equipment has to be fought for. Surgeons are fallible.

'No hospital … will fail to give you attention if your case is urgent.' The narrative weaves together a number of ongoing cases with two new admissions who get a contrasting quality of care. A woman arrives in casualty at an inconvenient time, with head pains; the young doctor on duty, Dick Groom (Jack Watling), is impatient to get away, examines her cursorily, and sends her away with some pills. Later she is found unconscious, and others diagnose a cerebral abscess. This episode is taken from the book; the other casualty admission is – like the Basil Radford character – new. A boy with a poisoned hand, Tommy Briggs, is brought in by his anxious mother, and both are received by doctors and nurses alike with warm care and concern. Ironically, it is the woman with a cerebral abscess who lives, saved by an emergency operation, and the boy who dies, since he turns out to be resistant to penicillin.

These two stories, absorbing in themselves, allow the main plot issues to be carried forward and resolved. The film combines its strong documentary elements with the kind of tight construction that is characteristic of 'classical Hollywood', leaving no loose ends, and interweaving the public life of the hospital with the personal life of its doctor protagonists. Gavin Lambert, the new young editor of *Sight and Sound*, was an outspoken critic of the mainstream British cinema of the time, and had recently caused great offence by his scathing attack on *The Blue Lamp*, but he praised *White Corridors* for its 'rare professionalism', suggesting that this might owe something to Jackson's experience in Hollywood.[6] Lambert was referring to directorial style and handling of actors, but the economy of the scripting deserves equally to be called professional, and it may be significant that Jan Read had likewise spent time after the war in Hollywood, working with Fritz Lang.[7]

Sophie Dean (Googie Withers) is a surgeon attracted by the offer of a glamorous job in London. Two things make her hesitate to leave, her attachment to a colleague, Neil Marriner (James Donald), and the prospect of a secure staff appointment at Yeoman's; but her rival for the appointment, Dick Groom, has strong support on the relevant committee, led by his surgeon father (Godfrey Tearle). When Dick mishandles the abscess case, it is Sophie who finds the woman unconscious, makes a correct diagnosis, and saves her life, which leads Dick's father to transfer his support to her. Meanwhile, Neil has been absorbed in his research on penicillin-resistant cases, developing the kind of serum that might have saved Tommy Briggs, had it been fully tested and approved for use. In taking a blood sample from Tommy, he has, by a careless – and plausibly 'Freudian' – slip of the needle, infected himself; and when, predictably, he in turn fails to respond to orthodox treatment, he urges Sophie to inject him with the unauthorised experimental serum, even though both realise that his death would then result in criminal charges against her. His decline, and the devastating death of Tommy, decide her; she injects the serum, he lives, and she will stay on at Yeoman's Hospital, presumably to be given promotion and to marry Neil.

Summarised thus, the drama may sound neat to the point of glibness (Lambert qualified his praise by referring to 'material that is basically synthetic'), but it is realised with subtlety and conviction, and a historical perspective leads one to respect and value it all the more strongly, centred as it is on two types that were soon virtually to disappear from British films: the visionary researcher, and the strong female professional.

The film seems to foreshadow the drastic 1950s narrowing down of the role of women in an earlier dialogue scene, in which Sophie insists to Neil that 'I'm not a careerist, honestly I'm not. I'd like to do some good in the world if I can, but I'd much rather you were the big success'. Her final decision to stay in the provinces could be read, like so many last-minute British film decisions of the *Billy Liar* kind, as abject, subordinating herself to him; but she is not exactly embracing domesticity, and can continue, like him, to 'do some good in the world', even if she is no longer going for 'big success' in London. It is a delicate balance, and the long-held final shot of her walk down the corridor, away from the camera into long shot, has complex connotations, like the identically constructed and equally portentous one of Midge (Barbara Bel Geddes) walking down the hospital corridor and out of *Vertigo*. It represents Sophie's absorption into the provincial hospital, Googie Withers ending her last decent British film role, after playing a series of impressively forceful 1940s women, notably for post-war Ealing, and the figure of the strong professional woman walking out of British cinema.

'I'd much rather you were the big success.' In the event, her male opposite number does not have much of a future either in British films, and this applies, likewise, both to the type and to the actor. The frustration of the inventor, played by Alec Guinness, of the miracle new fabric in Ealing's *The Man in the White Suit* (Mackendrick, 1951) acts as a prescient comic diagnosis of the imminent loss of this spirit of inventiveness, a loss which goes strikingly in parallel with the attenuation of female ambition.[8] The passionately committed aircraft designer of Anthony Asquith's *The Net*, released at the start of 1953, is the last of a line. Like Neil Marriner, he is played by James Donald, an actor with a remarkable ability to combine sardonically detached humour with idealistic commitment to the goals of scientific enquiry.[9] Googie Withers and James Donald are the most expressive possible casting for *White Corridors*, and their playing brings to mind the comment made by Lindsay Anderson on a film with which it has certain affinities, *The Small Back Room* (Powell and Pressburger, 1949), that the relationship there between David Farrar and Kathleen Byron is, in contrast to so much screen artificiality, 'recognizably one between a man and a woman'.[10]

One of the consistent pleasures of *White Corridors* is, indeed, its shrewd casting. Around this admirable central pair there circulates an evocative range of familiar and unfamiliar faces. The pre-war, pre-welfare state mind-set is neatly represented not only in the cameo of confusion by Basil Radford, an actor identified forever with his role as half of the reactionary Charters–Caldicott team in *The Lady Vanishes* (Hitchcock, 1938), but also in two senior committee members whom Sophie and Neil have to contend with, played by men whose career goes right back into the dark ages of British cinema: Godfrey Tearle as the older Dr Groom, and Henry Edwards as Brewster, the local magnate whose daughter is set to make a dynastic marriage to Groom's son. Edwards was a leading star and director of silent films from 1914 onwards, while Tearle's Romeo was filmed as early as 1908.[11] This professional back story helps to give the two men a formidable 'weight', and to give corresponding weight to their gradual reorientation – Groom's especially, as he comes to recognise both his own failing powers and his son's unworthiness, and acknowledges Sophie's superior claim to the vacant post. The son, and the nurse whose affections he trifles with, are Jack Watling and Moira Lister, both giving a hint of depth to their familiar personae, callow and flighty respectively. The new nurse is Petula Clark, poised between her child and adult careers, and coping well with some rigorously extended vulnerable close-ups as she listens to important advice, or watches the off-screen unbandaging of a mutilated face. Further down the cast list, reliable character players like Jean Anderson (as a nurse) and Megs Jenkins (Tommy's mother) mix with the various non-professionals already referred to, and with faces that we see briefly here but that will later be familiar: the Brewster daughter is Dagmar Wynter, soon to be Dana in Hollywood, and waiting-room patients include Dandy Nichols and Patrick Troughton, stars of the future TV series *Till Death Us Do Part* and *Doctor Who*.

Many films of the time inevitably have some kind of comparable mix, but *White Corridors*, through a combination of luck and judgment, has an especially charismatic and precisely chosen range, and is distinctive both in its integration of non-professionals and in the artful way it deploys them all in the service of a story about gradual, unspectacular, but significant change. To return to Godfrey Tearle: not only will he play a comparable role soon afterwards in a film of comparable stature, *Mandy* (Mackendrick, 1952, for Ealing), but it was his role as the elderly aircraft gunner in *One of Our Aircraft is Missing* (1942), and his relations with the younger crew members, that inspired its makers, Powell and Pressburger, to go on to explore further the theme of continuity and change between generations in *The Life and Death of Colonel Blimp* (1943); and Tearle's Dr Groom, like his grandfather in *Mandy*, has affinities with Blimp, both in his obstinacy and in his final graceful concessions.[12] *White Corridors* can, then, be linked with equal plausibility both to wartime documentary and to the war films of a team who positioned themselves in explicit opposition to documentary; two important streams come together that revive the wartime story/documentary 'marriage' in a particularly fresh and apparently promising way.

But the promise was scarcely fulfilled. Powell and Pressburger, whose great achievements were made possible by finance from Rank, had left the company when it began to adopt a policy of greater caution and closer control; ironically, the trigger for this was the management's hostile reception of *The Red Shoes* (1948), which became their greatest commercial success.[13] Something comparable now happened to Pat Jackson. Despite the commercial and critical success of *White Corridors*, the film made the Rank Organisation uneasy, with its lack of a score and its reluctance to compromise:

> When Arthur Rank saw the film he was flattering about it and said, 'I congratulate you, Mr. Jackson, it's a nice film, but I don't think the little boy ought to die. I think you should retake that.' I replied, 'Mr. Rank, if the boy doesn't die, you haven't got a film.' He didn't know what I was talking about. I realized he hadn't a clue about drama, how it is conceived and constructed. This applied to his right-hand and left-hand men. The death knell of British cinema was starting to be rung.[14]

Pat Jackson resisted the offer of a Rank contract, anxious to maintain control over his own projects, but in the rigid duopoly conditions of the 1950s it was not easy to negotiate an independent career. As *Film Dope* magazine put it, 'The battleship-grey decade of the 1950s ... was the era of the company man, and Pat Jackson had the misfortune to turn up at the wrong time and with the wrong kind of temperament.' Like Powell, he came to see himself as the victim of a Rank 'vendetta' and his work for the rest of the decade and beyond was, on the whole, similarly unfulfilling.[15] Though Gavin Lambert wrote that '*White Corridors* should set a new standard for popular entertainment in films of this country', there was no real successor to it, from Jackson or anyone else, except, to some extent, in television. But that is a story of the 1960s.

Notes

1   For an insider's account of this process, from one who was active during the war both as a critic and as a film producer, see Basil Wright, *The Long View: An International History of Cinema* (Secker & Warburg, 1974), pp. 199–200. Among the terms he uses are 'rapprochement' and 'shot-gun wedding'.

2   'Crisis in Documentary', unpub. six-page typescript, originally dated 16 April 1945; I am grateful to Pat Jackson for supplying me with a copy.

3   Jackson refers to the Beveridge script, 'Now or Never', in an interview for *Film Dope* 27 (July 1983), p. 4.

4   Helen Ashton, *Yeoman's Hospital* (Collins, 1944). A prefatory note (p. 10) indicates that 'the whole action takes place during twenty-four hours in December, 1943', and the completion of the text (p. 248) is dated with equal precision as 'Feb. 1944'.

5   For a sourly hostile presentation of the National Health Service reforms, in a comparable popular narrative format, see Nevil Shute's novel *The Far Country* (Heinemann, 1952). Though this forms a minor strand of the novel, and deals more with general practice than with hospitals, it has considerable weight in motivating the heroine's, and the novel's, preference for post-war Australia over England. A classic account of the establishment of the NHS, by means of legislation passed in July 1948, is given in an essay by Peter Jenkins, 'Bevan's Fight with the BMA [British Medical Association]', in Michael Sissons and Philip French (eds), *Age of Austerity: 1945–1951* (Hodder and Stoughton, 1963).

6   Gavin Lambert, review of *White Corridors* in *Sight and Sound* 21, 1 (August–September 1951), p. 20.

7   Read's work as an 'assistant' to Lang, immediately after the war, is referred to in Patrick McGilligan, *Fritz Lang: The Nature of the Beast* (St. Martin's Press, 1997), pp. 347–8.

8   It could be argued that, just as repressed sexuality is released in the Dracula films at the end of the decade, so the repressed spirit of scientific enquiry finds its way into the figure of Dr Frankenstein.

9   For a fuller discussion of this actor and of the values he represents, see my essay 'Madness, Madness: The Brief Stardom of James Donald', in Bruce Babington (ed.), *British Stars and Stardom: From Alma Taylor to Sean Connery* (Manchester University Press, 2001), pp. 236–54.

10 Lindsay Anderson, 'British Cinema: The Descending Spiral' in *Sequence* 7 (Spring 1949), p. 9. Farrar's bomb expert is a similar flawed and sardonic visionary, ready to put himself in danger in the cause of advancing knowledge and saving life; Kathleen Byron overcomes frustrations to commit herself to him at the end. In both films, the experts have to choke back their irritation with ignorant but influential visitors to their workplace, and the obstacles to rational progress are conveyed in lucidly staged committee meetings. *The Small Back Room* is, like *White Corridors*, based on a wartime novel, though the subject matter meant that updating it was not an option. In visual texture, the films are at opposite extremes, of white and of noir.

11 On Tearle, see Rachael Low, *The History of the British Film: 1906–1914* (Allen & Unwin, 1948), p. 117, and on Edwards, Rachael Low, *The History of the British Film: 1914–18* (Allen & Unwin, 1950), p. 79 and many other references.

12 On the genesis of *The Life and Death of Colonel Blimp*, see Michael Powell, *A Life in Movies* (Heinemann, 1986), p. 399. On the generational conflict in *Mandy*, and, indeed, on the other Ealing material referred to earlier, see the third edition of my *Ealing Studios* (Cameron & Hollis/University of California Press, 1999).

13 Powell, *A Life in the Movies*, pp. 653–4 and 670.

14 *Film Dope* (July 1983), p. 8.

15 *Film Dope* (July 1983), editorial introduction to interview with Pat Jackson, p. 1.

The long shadow:
Robert Hamer after Ealing

PHILIP KEMP

Louis Mazzini, serial killer and tenth Duke of Chalfont, emerges from jail, cleared of the murder for which he was about to hang. Waiting for him, along with two attractive rival widows, is a bowler-hatted little man from a popular magazine bidding for his memoirs. 'My memoirs?' murmurs Louis, the faintest spasm of panic ruffling his urbanity, and we cut to a pile of pages lying forgotten in the condemned cell: the incriminating manuscript that occupied his supposed last hours on earth.

So ends Robert Hamer's best-known film, *Kind Hearts and Coronets* (1949). It's an elegant, teasing sign-off from a movie that has teased us elegantly all through – luring us into complicity with its cool, confidential voice-over, holding us at arm's length with its deadpan irony. The final gag, with an amused shrug, invites us to pick our own ending: Louis triumphant, retrieving his manuscript, poised for glory and prosperity; or Louis disgraced, doomed by his own hand. (For the US version, the Breen Office priggishly demanded an added shot of the memoirs in the hands of the authorities.)

Films have an eerie habit of mirroring the conditions of their own making – and of their makers. Or is it that we can't resist reading such reflections into them, indulging ourselves in the enjoyable shudder of the unwitting premonition? Either way, *Kind Hearts*' ambiguous close seems to foreshadow the options facing Hamer himself on its completion. His finest film to date, it could have led to a dazzling career. Instead, it marked the high-point before an abrupt and irreversible decline. Apart from Preston Sturges, it's hard to think of another director who has fallen so far so fast.

I am a freelance writer and film historian based in London, and a regular contributor to *Sight and Sound* and *International Film Guide*. I have written various articles on British cinema, and am the author of *Lethal Innocence: The Cinema of Alexander Mackendrick* (Methuen, 1991). For longer than I like to remember, I have been working on a biography of Michael Balcon. A version of this essay, in a slightly different form, appeared in *Film Comment* 31, 3 (May–June 1995). *Philip Kemp*

Kind Hearts confirmed Hamer as one of the most individual of British directors, only four years after his directorial debut. Like many of his contemporaries, he got his break at Michael Balcon's Ealing Studios. He started out as a clapper-boy at Gaumont-British, graduated to the cutting-room at London Films (where 'I had the inestimable good fortune to be put to work for Erich Pommer') and joined Ealing as an editor in 1940. Balcon liked to advance promising young men, and editors in particular: Hamer was promoted to producer on *San Demetrio London* (1943) and got his chance to direct when the credited director, Charles Frend, fell ill. He did the same on *Fiddlers Three* (1944), taking over from Harry Watt, and having proved himself was assigned an episode of the omnibus ghost film, *Dead of Night* (1945).[1]

Hamer's episode, 'The Haunted Mirror', locates him on the shadow side of Ealing, in the maverick strain that included Alberto Cavalcanti and Alexander Mackendrick. The episode not only conjures up a dark, dangerous world of violence and sexuality, but finds it perversely attractive. (It also introduces Hamer's key motif of the malign, enticing alter ego.) To the disquiet of the morally strait-laced Balcon, these subversive elements resurfaced in Hamer's first two features, the Victorian melodrama *Pink String and Sealing Wax* (1945) and *It Always Rains on Sunday* (1947), a fair shot at transplanting Prévert/Carné poetic realism into an English context. In both films, respectable family values come under threat from anti-social forces: in *Pink String* the glitzy, ruthless demi-monde of a Brighton pub; in *Rains* a convict ex-lover on the run. In the end the lowlifes are defeated, but with them all vitality drains out of the films. What's left is the family structure, smug and suffocating. As if settling the score, Hamer proceeded to make a film that 'paid no regard whatever to established, although not practised, moral convention, in which a whole family is picked off by a mass murderer'.[2]

Balcon hated the idea of *Kind Hearts and Coronets* ('I'm not going to make a comedy about eight murders'), but capitulated to a united front of Ealing's top creative personnel. What alarmed him about the finished film, though, wasn't the violence but the sexual charge of the scenes involving Joan Greenwood's deliciously manipulative Sibella.[3] He demanded they be toned down; Hamer indignantly refused. The disagreement flared into a public row – a rare event at Ealing, where quiet conciliation and compromise were the norm. (None of which deterred Balcon, when *Kind Hearts* was released, from publicly hailing it as being 'an entirely new level of comedy', and 'the best film we have made'.)[4]

For his next film, Hamer embarked on an adaptation of *The Shadow and the Peak*, a novel by Richard Mason (author of *The World of Suzie Wong*). Set in Jamaica, the story has (for its period) a high erotic content, which

Hamer intended to retain. He planned a location shoot in the West Indies, with Vivien Leigh for the female lead. Unhappy about the subject matter – and the budget – Balcon reluctantly secured the rights and gave Hamer the go-ahead. With pre-production well advanced, he suddenly changed his mind. Furious, Hamer quit Ealing on the spot.

The break would have come anyway, sooner or later. Ealing, with its upbeat, wholesome ethos, was no place for a man who wanted 'to make films about people in dark rooms doing beastly things to each other'.[5] A more devious film-maker like Mackendrick would contrive ways of sneaking his 'perverted and malicious sense of humour' into seemingly anodyne subjects, insidiously subverting Ealing from within. But Hamer, contrary and quick-tempered, courted confrontation.[6] He wanted to win publicly as well as privately, to have his right to make his kind of film officially conceded. It was a hopelessly unrealistic demand even at Ealing, let alone any other post-war British studio.

Between quitting Ealing in 1949 and his death in 1963 Hamer completed – or at any rate is credited with – seven more films. They're commonly written off as bleak and emotionally atrophied, blighted by his losing battle with alcohol. 'His later films are all disappointing,' wrote David Thomson, voicing the consensus.[7] And so they are, if we come to them expecting the malicious energy and suave black comedy of his masterpiece. But a masterpiece casts a long shadow, and at least four of Hamer's post-Ealing films – *The Spider and the Fly*, *The Long Memory*, *Father Brown* and *The Scapegoat* – deserve to be brought out from under. None of them wholly works and the last of them was reduced to a mutilated torso. But they share a haunted, teeth-gritted quality that marks them out as particular to Hamer. They could have been made by no other director.

Since Ealing held the rights to *The Shadow and the Peak*, Hamer couldn't take his unrealised project with him. Instead, he made a film about as far as he could get from the tropical sensuality of Mason's story. *The Spider and the Fly* (1949) is set in Paris, but not the fluffy, ooh-la-la city beloved of British movies. This is a grey, grim Paris poised on the abyss of World War I, where even the nightlife has a hard professional gleam in its eye. Hamer's protagonists, Maubert (Eric Portman) and Ledocq (Guy Rolfe), are also professionals – one a policeman, the other a criminal, united in their contempt for the fools and incompetents around them on both sides of the law.

Throughout Hamer's later films he explores the Jekyll-and-Hyde theme of a man pitted against his *doppelgänger*, a person whom he opposes but feels tempted to resemble. Often there's a strong undertow of homo-eroticism to the relationship. Ledocq, handsome and dashing, uses women but keeps them at emotional arm's length. The repressed Maubert, who lives alone, nagged by an elderly housekeeper, speaks of Ledocq in the petulant tones of a discarded lover. Told that the criminal has accused him of 'having no heart', he retorts bitterly, 'He should know. He and his kind have pulled it from me piece by piece.'

Hamer was himself a suppressed homosexual. Sent down from Cambridge after an affair with a man, to the horror of his middle-class family, he tried to go straight by marrying Joan Holt, would-be actress and sister of another Ealing director, Seth Holt. Joan, strikingly beautiful but low on acting talent, matched her husband for boozing and outdid him at drunken bitchery; Diana Morgan, Ealing's only woman screenwriter and a close friend of Hamer, felt the couple were 'modelling themselves on Scott and Zelda'.[8] After the marriage broke up in the early 1950s Hamer drifted through affairs with several women, none of them lasting long.

In *The Spider and the Fly* the attraction between Maubert and Ledocq is re-routed through Madeleine, the woman both love but neither can commit to until, by a cruel irony of the kind Hamer relished, they unwittingly join to destroy her. This unconventional triangle is twisted into unexpected shapes by moral ambiguity. Intelligent, dispassionate, sharing a sense of honour but not of loyalty, each of the three avidly exploits the others for personal ambition – rather than for love, a warm, risky emotion to be quizzically noted, then filed safely away. 'I admire you, and you say you love me,' Ledocq tells Madeleine. 'That's the best time to part.'

The ending is the bleakest in all Hamer's work. The trio – like that of *Jules et Jim* (1962) but in a darker register – self-destructs: Madeleine is led off to execution, Ledocq in effect commits suicide. The coda plays out in a nocturnal railway station where Maubert moodily watches troops embarking for Verdun and near-certain death. Among them he spots Ledocq who, exempt from conscription, has perversely volunteered. The two men exchange a wry gesture – a stripped-down précis of all those tearful railroad farewells in standard-issue war movies – before Ledocq vanishes into the train, whose closed, cattle-truck-style carriages recall other death trains in a later war.

The scene is typical of *The Spider and the Fly* in its emotional asphyxia and its night-time setting. Hamer was a practitioner of that relatively sparse genre, British noir, and all the film's prime scenes are set in noir's universal City of Dreadful Night. Daytime episodes are consigned to gloomy offices dulled by the sulky grey light of an overcast sky. *La ville lumière* this isn't, and only once does the film evoke sunlight: an insipid boating expedition on the Seine, filmed with the insolent offhandedness Hamer reserved for scenes he despised. Unevenness, as Charles Drazin notes, 'is almost the hallmark of a Hamer film'.[9] Strewn through all his movies (barring only *Kind Hearts*) are scenes where you sense the director sneering or yawning behind the camera; bland, conventional stuff he shot because he had to, but was damned if he'd put any effort into. A more visual director like Mackendrick could have taken refuge in technical resource. Hamer responded to banality with boredom, which he never bothered to conceal. It fits his jaundiced view of humanity that these dead stretches mostly afflict scenes of happiness. Happiness wasn't something Hamer believed in; what spoke to him were dark, destructive emotions like guilt or vengeance.

One or two Hamer films are sheer dead-stretch from start to finish. One such followed *The Spider and the Fly*, during a brief return to Ealing. This was unusual in itself; Balcon placed a high value on loyalty, and those who quit the studio were rarely allowed back. But Balcon's conscience was troubled by Hamer, whom he felt he had handled badly. He was even willing to reconsider *The Shadow and the Peak*, scheduling it among Ealing's forthcoming projects, and meantime Hamer was assigned to a filmed play, *His Excellency* (1952). The original, a West End hit about industrial unrest in a British colony, held nothing for him; he took it on as a *quid pro quo* for the film he wanted to make, and his indifference glares through every frame. In any case it was wasted effort. Once again Balcon fought shy of the Jamaican project, and Hamer left Ealing for a second time.

There was more to attract him in *The Long Memory* (1952), whose set-up is archetypal noir: a man framed for murder comes out of jail years later, bent on getting the people who put him away. Hamer's bid to create an English *Quai des brumes* is a touch too blatant, and it needed a crueller actor than John Mills (James Mason, perhaps?) for the lead. Mills does a staunch professional job, giving us the tenacity but missing the malevolence; the role calls for a cold, harsh venom that isn't within the actor's compass. What makes *The Long Memory* worth seeing is spirit of place: its exceptional use of landscape. On previous form, this was the last thing to expect from Hamer. His films had been largely studio-bound, not always to their detriment: studio artifice suits the stylised elegance of *Kind Hearts* and the shadowy claustrophobia of *The Spider and the Fly*. *The Long Memory*, though, not only uses locations but chooses a region of England few other films have exploited – the desolate mudflats of the Thames estuary beyond London where the Kent coast slumps despondently into the sea. Windswept and salt-scoured, the flats express the seared mental landscape of Davidson, the ex-con plotting revenge. Early in the film Davidson appears on the flats for the first time. Shooting in long shot from a low angle, Hamer picks up the small, stocky figure far off on the barren expanse. Instead of cutting to a close-up, he simply holds and waits while Davidson trudges up to camera. Even before we know who he is or what he wants, we sense the distance he has to go and his bitter loneliness.

The Long Memory is a film of acutely captured detail – tacky, sleazy detail for the most part. A decade before the trumpeted naturalism of the British New Wave, Hamer was exploring townscapes far from the official picture-postcard locations. This is a scruffy, back-alley Britain of cracked pavements and corrugated-iron lean-to sheds. A petty crook's deserted wife sits in a parlour stuffed with sad, tawdry knick-knacks – china cats, samplers, cheap reproductions, a portrait of Queen Victoria. The villain's warehouse is located in Shad Thames (a richly Dickensian name) in the shadow of Tower Bridge, hemmed in by cranes and bombed-out buildings. As Davidson climbs its bare wooden stairs you hear the grime crunching underfoot. These lowlife milieux contrast with the pristine suburban home of Fay, Davidson's ex-girlfriend, whose false evidence put him away. She has married the police inspector involved in the case. (It's that kind of plot, too dovetailed for its own good.) When Davidson confronts her amid the sterile gentility of her sitting room she flings herself desperately about it like a trapped bird, terrified less at what he might do to her than at the idea of her husband or schoolboy son finding out. As so often for Hamer, domesticity is a snare.

In the event, Davidson refrains from taking physical vengeance on Fay. 'I can't be bothered … You're not worth it.' When he catches up with the chief villain, Boyd, the idea gets a further twist. 'When it comes to the point revenge isn't worth it. You plan it and plan it, and then when it starts it makes you feel as filthy as the other person.' Again a Hamer protagonist fears turning into his opponent – with the added barb that, this time round, the gay element is displaced on to the baddies. Boyd, a suave, menacing figure, sports a fancy waistcoat, a flower in his button hole and a cockney-genteel accent. His boyfriend doubles as chauffeur and receptionist, a punk-ish youth slouched in a booth leafing through male-physique magazines.

The negative attraction between Davidson and Boyd skews the film, being far more intense than the nominal love interest. The heroine, a waifish East European refugee, hangs around imploring Davidson to let her stay, but Hamer's impatience with this pallid and underwritten figure is palpable. The action's also saddled with a *deus ex machina*, a creakingly symbolic tramp borrowed from *Les Portes de la nuit* (Carné and Prévert's last and weakest film together), who saves Davidson when Boyd finally hunts him down on the mudflats.

But even this scene is redeemed by its sheer physical immediacy. The landscape, a brooding presence throughout, now sides with the villain, threatening literally to engulf the hero. Fleeing the armed Boyd, Davidson falls off a derelict barge into the mud – which holds him fast as he squirms like a beached fish. The soundtrack pitilessly captures the glutinous, squelchy noises of his struggle, and his rescue comes as reprieve from a nightmare. The plot of *The Long Memory* fades fast from the mind, but its texture stays vividly with you.

Hamer's next three films all starred Alec Guinness, a friend since *Kind Hearts*. 'We spoke the same language and laughed at the same things,' Guinness recalled; 'He was finely tuned, full of wicked glee and marvellous to actors – appreciative and encouraging.'[10] The actor's remote, withdrawn persona suited the emotional obliquity of Hamer's work, and with his gallery of quirky, oddball characters Guinness was a natural for the title role in *Father Brown* (1954) as G.K. Chesterton's mild-mannered priest-detective.

The plot derives from Chesterton's story 'The Blue Cross' – a brief, straightforward tale in which the priest foils a master criminal, Flambeau, who is trying to rob him of a jewelled crucifix. Brown and Flambeau themselves hardly figure until the last page or two; the story focuses on a Sûreté detective who is trailing them. Hamer and his co-writer, Thelma Schnee, dumped the detective, reduced the cross to a McGuffin and turned the film into an extended intellectual and moral duel between priest and criminal – the central *Spider and the Fly* relationship replayed as comedy. But it is comedy of the most sombre kind. There aren't many laughs in *Father Brown*, and such as there are feel thin and uneasy, chilled by a freezing whisper of melancholia. What the film latches on to – what may well have attracted Hamer to the project in the first place – is the dark side of Chesterton, the horror squirming around under the compulsive jokiness. 'Something in the make-up of his personality,' wrote Borges, Chesterton's great admirer, 'leaned toward the nightmarish, something secret, and blind, and central.'[11] That would go for Hamer too, though he lacked the balances that kept Chesterton sane – his bonhomie, and the consolation he found in Catholicism.

Though not religious, Hamer felt a grudging envy for the certainties of faith – as does his surrogate in the film, played by Peter Finch with saturnine charm. A renegade aristocrat (like Ledocq in *The Spider and the Fly*), Flambeau steals not out of greed or viciousness, but to requite a world that has no place for him. 'I was trained as a good swordsman,' he tells Brown, 'but in a world of guns and bombs it is no longer ... an accomplishment to know how to die gracefully at dawn.' Instead he courts death with his criminal audacities, much as Hamer courted it with his reckless drinking.

Flambeau is Brown's quarry, body and soul – to be redeemed from crime and atheism and restored to the fold. But there's a desperation in the priest's quest that reaches beyond piety into aching personal need. Both men, Brown in particular, seem wretchedly lonely, clutching at each other to escape a sense of futility. This Hound of Heaven pursuit reflected reality; Guinness, himself poised to convert, was urging the solace of Catholicism on Hamer. He failed – which may be why the ending, with Flambeau restoring the cross and himself to the bosom of the church, doesn't seem complacent, just miserably lacking in conviction.

Once more an attraction between mirror-image opposites dominates the film. (Flambeau likes to disguise himself as a priest; Brown has some skill as a pickpocket.) The only significant female character – Joan Greenwood, sadly wasted – is even sketchier than her counterpart in *The Long Memory*. Now and again, suddenly recalling that he's making a comedy, Hamer tosses in a spot of slapstick, but his heart isn't in it. When Brown consults a librarian (Ernest Thesiger as yet another lonely obsessive), the two men are made to teeter on high ladders and lose their spectacles. The effect is irritating and embarrassing, as though two pensive, dignified birds – a pair of storks, say – had been press-ganged into a circus and induced to juggle.

Physical comedy was never Hamer's forte, as was all too plain from his next film. Dispiritingly jocular, *To Paris with Love* (1955) blunders into every frou-frou cliché about the French capital that *The Spider and the Fly* so dourly rejected. A father (Guinness) and son visit Paris, where each meets a Frenchwoman his own age but falls for the other one. The Brits are inhibited but susceptible; the French gesticulate and address each other in comic-accented English. The whole affair would deserve utter oblivion had it not foreshadowed Hamer's next project, the great unrealised film that haunted the remaining years of his life.

Although *For Each the Other* was never made, Hamer's shooting script survives. It makes poignant reading. Into it he poured everything of himself – his melancholia, his wit, his wistful francophilia and his conviction that life had dealt him a rotten hand. It may be that the script is better than any film of it could have been at the time. Today Hamer's doom-laden romanticism might come through unscathed, but in 1950s Britain some crass happy ending would surely have been imposed.

The script is adapted from a French play, *L'Âme en peine* by Jean-Jacques Bernard. At its heart is the passage in Plato's *Symposium* where Aristophanes explains sexual attraction: that human beings were originally perfect spheres until the malicious gods sliced them all in half. Since then each half yearns to reunite with its fellow, and roams the earth embracing countless others in the hope of finding the one true match.

The three main characters are Marceline, a beautiful and intelligent

Frenchwoman, obscurely discontented; her husband Philip, an English country gentleman, kindly and comfortable though not stupid; and Anthony, handsome and raffish, who offhandedly runs a London bookshop and drifts from one half-hearted liaison to another. Marceline and Anthony are destined soulmates. Their paths, in England and France, repeatedly cross but never quite meet until, at a hunt, they instinctively recognise each other. Marceline's horse, scared by a low-flying plane, bolts and Anthony gallops after her. Both are killed.

Charming, cultured and dissipated, Anthony is an unmistakable self-portrait, revealing a chilling degree of self-awareness. Hamer, it's clear, knew exactly what he was doing to himself. Such merciless lucidity recalls a line of Zola's (about the writing of *Thérèse Raquin*) Hamer once quoted to explain the kind of films he wanted to make: 'J'ai simplement essayé ce que fait un chirurgien sur deux cadavres'.[12]

The script's chief weakness is its mannered tone. Anthony is given to musings on malign Fate, the 'croupier in the sky ... who's in charge of dis-appointments, thwartings, frustrations ... He waits until it will hurt most. He'll let the stars grow even more beautiful before he decides to turn them into rats' eyes'. (It isn't only Anthony who talks like this. Referring to Mar-celine, the supposedly prosaic Philip speaks of 'some deep, central, reason-less insufficiency which is private to her'.) But the overwritten dialogue – which Hamer would no doubt have toned down before shooting – never detracts from the agonised intensity behind the words. Hamer was too sophisticated to believe in the ideal Other, but his script throbs with a desperate wish that he could.

Guessing that Rank, producers of the inane *To Paris with Love*, would hardly appreciate his latest offering, Hamer turned once again to Michael Balcon. Balcon was impressed by the script's qualities but doubted its commercial appeal. Hamer, though, was still on his conscience, so *For Each the Other* was announced as a forthcoming production, with Peter Finch pencilled in for Anthony, and Hamer was given an interest-free loan of £2,700 to secure the rights to Bernard's play. But by the late 1950s Balcon's power base was shrinking. Ealing Studios were sold in 1955, and he was now running Ealing Films from a corner of the MGM lot at Borehamwood. In theory the unit was autonomous; in practice any project had to be sold to the Metro hierarchy. When Ealing finally folded in 1959, *For Each the Other* was still in limbo.

In 1958, to compound Hamer's frustration, there appeared a film version of *The Shadow and the Peak*. Produced for Rank, who had picked up the rights when their deal with Ealing lapsed, *The Passionate Summer* was scripted (flatly) by Joan Henry, directed (turgidly) by Rudolph Cartier and acted (stolidly) by Bill Travers and Virginia McKenna. If Hamer hadn't long since been driven to drink, this film would have been enough to do it.

To keep himself occupied, and to pay off his loan, Hamer took on another film for Balcon, *The Scapegoat* (1959), adapted from a novel by Daphne du Maurier. The troubled project had already run through multiple scripts and several possible directors, including Laslo Benedek, David Lean and George Cukor. (So improbable a trio hints eloquently at desperation. Kenneth Tynan, Ealing's script editor, even suggested Ingmar Bergman.) Though Balcon was producing, Ealing had no financial interest in the film. Production control was split between MGM and an ad hoc partnership of Alec Guinness and du Maurier herself – the only terms on which the novelist would make the rights available. It was an arrangement calculated to enthuse no one: not MGM, who resented having Guinness imposed as the lead, nor Balcon, who noted worriedly that 'neither du Maurier nor Guinness ... have the slightest conception how to organise and start a picture'.[13] Du Maurier disliked every version of the script submitted to her, taking particular exception to the final version by Gore Vidal. Her comments incensed Hamer, who described them as 'a compound of stupidity, egomania and gross bad manners', and demanded to be taken off the picture.[14] It took all Balcon's diplomacy to smooth everyone's ruffled feathers.

On the face of it, *The Scapegoat* looks like an ideal Hamer subject. Once again a disaffected loner tangles with his alter ego – literally his double this time, since the film pushes Hamer's *doppelgänger* theme to its extreme. John Barrett, a college professor of French on holiday in 'the France I love so well', ponders the lukewarm void of his existence: 'Only a few personal belongings and a blank life ... Nothing in the past to be particularly ashamed of – nothing, in the future. Perhaps a man has to be empty before he can be used'. And used he is, by his evil twin Count Jacques de Gué (also played by Guinness), who sees in the Englishman a chance to get shot of his debts, discontented wife and importunate family.

The film sets out in Hamer's most authentically downbeat vein, with Barrett musing as he clears French customs, 'You can't declare an emptiness of the heart' – neatly defining the malady afflicting so many Hamer protagonists. (A brief glimpse of his passport shows his birthplace as Porlock, home of the visitor said to have interrupted Coleridge in the midflow of 'Kubla Khan'. Barrett is Superfluous Man par excellence.) Early scenes capture the nightmare mood: a man tracked by his double through the darkened streets of an old town, like a scene from *The Student of Prague*. Even when the two are seated together in a cafe the other-worldly dread

lingers. 'You couldn't perhaps be the Devil?' asks de Gué ironically. 'No –
could you perhaps?' responds Barrett, only half joking. He could, almost.
Getting Barrett drunk, de Gué hijacks his clothes and his identity, leaving
his own in unfair exchange. Hung over and dismayed, Barrett is driven off
to de Gué's chateau where his protests are brushed aside as another of
Jacques' sadistic jokes. So far, the nightmare holds – the horror of finding
yourself trapped in another man's bad dream, guilty of his past, ignorant of
everything you ought to know. But from here on the fabric of the film wears
steadily thinner: mood and tension drain away, vital plot elements are
fudged and the film crumbles down to a botched and perfunctory ending.

The failure of *The Scapegoat* is usually put down to Hamer's declining
powers, but on all the evidence he can't be blamed for the mess. The
brooding atmosphere of the opening, and random flashes of dramatic power
thereafter, suggest he succeeded in weaving a taut moral spider's web out of
du Maurier's melodramatic original. With its theme of the principled
commoner taking on and finally supplanting the decadent aristocrat, *The
Scapegoat* could even have stood as a serious counterpart to *Kind Hearts and
Coronets*. All we have, though, is what was left after MGM had taken a blunt
axe to it. Hamer's original cut ran just on two hours. Metro chopped out
some forty minutes, spliced in 'clarifying' material directed by the film's
editor, Jack Harris, and dubbed on a new score by in-house composer
Bronislau Kaper. Balcon, aging and weary, fought the cuts for a time but at
last gave in. Viewing the final result, Hamer vainly tried to have his name
taken off the credits.

The débâcle of *The Scapegoat* finished him. He had promised Balcon to
stay off the booze throughout the shoot, and he kept his promise. The
cinematographer, Paul Beeson, remembers him on location in France
recommending a local wine. 'We'd all be drinking around him, and he
wouldn't touch it. He was on some white tablets, God knows what they
were. You could see him suffering. He'd come out in a greasy cold sweat and
take another of these bloody tablets.'[15] The moment the final shot, on the
quayside at Boulogne, was in the can Hamer took off on an almighty bender.
He had to be poured back on to the ferry, and tried to pick a fight with the
Customs at Dover.

The ruin of his film convinced him the effort just wasn't worth it. There
was one more movie bearing his name as director: *School for Scoundrels*
(1960), a comedy based on Stephen Potter's cynical 'Lifemanship' books.
Much of it was directed by Cyril Frankel, asked to take over after Hamer
showed up drunk on set one morning.

It was terribly sad. One couldn't help him … I said, 'I won't take it over, Robert, what I will do is hold the reins for you provided you promise you'll go into hospital for a week and get over this.' We shook hands on that, but he didn't go into hospital and didn't get better. So I finished the film, did the basic editing, then Robert came in to do the final edit.[16]

Frankel insisted Hamer take sole directorial credit.

Hamer's last few years were a fast downhill slide; not even the hope of making his pet project could keep him level for long. In May 1960 his agent, Dennis van Thal, wrote to Balcon, 'The "problem" really seems a thing of the past. Robert still has the rights of *For Each the Other* and … seemed very appreciative of your continued interest in the subject'.[17] But two weeks later he reported, 'I feel in all honesty I must tell you that Robert did a "flip" yesterday … I wrote to him yesterday to say I could not do anything for him unless and until he was completely cured'.[18] By mid-1961 Balcon, now heading the Bryanston group, had given up on Hamer as a director. 'At one time,' he told an associate, 'Robert Hamer insisted that [*For Each the Other*] should be directed by him, but I now believe that the rights can be acquired without any trouble.'[19]

Scriptwriting was the only job left open. Hamer worked for a while on an adaptation of C.E. Vulliamy's 1920s black comedy *Don among the Dead Men*, about an Oxford don who bumps off rival colleagues. The film was offered to Charles Crichton, who turned it down, finding the main character too unpleasant. It was eventually directed by Don Chaffey as *A Jolly Bad Fellow* – a feeble echo of *Kind Hearts and Coronets*. Hamer's final credit was 'additional dialogue', on Nicholas Ray's sprawling *55 Days at Peking* (1963). Before it was released he was dead, aged 52.

In *For Each the Other*, the work into which he put more of himself than any other, Hamer wrote:

> People think they have some right to be happy, and are doubly unhappy because they are not. It is only when they come to accept that the natural human salary is one of unhappiness, and that interims of happiness come as a bonus and must be hungrily seized and savoured, that they have a chance of coming out anywhere near even in the unequal contest with fate.

With a little adjustment – 'Directors think they have some right to make the films they want to', perhaps? – he could have applied the same message to his own career, but such wise detachment was never in his character. He remained doubly unhappy, and came out a lot worse than even.

Hamer was in the wrong country at the wrong time. It wasn't only Ealing: at that period there wasn't a studio in Britain – or in Hollywood, most likely – that could have accommodated his savage, sombre vision. (He might have done better across the Channel; an industry with room for Carné, Clouzot and Bresson could easily have accepted Hamer. But for all his passion for France he seems never to have tried working there.) His later films, dismissed as the sad products of alcoholic decline, can equally be seen as his response to the frustrations he was undergoing, desperate attempts at self-expression by a thwarted talent. Balcon's verdict on Hamer is often quoted, that 'he was engaged on a process of self-destruction'.[20] True, but the process was hastened by an industry that could find no place for such an exceptional and idiosyncratic film-maker.

Notes

1 Freda Bruce Lockhart, 'Conversation with Robert Hamer', *Sight and Sound* 21, 2 (October–December 1951), p. 74.
2 Hamer, quoted in John Russell Taylor (ed.), *Kind Hearts and Coronets: Masterworks of the British Cinema* (Lorrimer, 1974), p. 9.
3 Author's conversation with Charles Crichton (26 March 1991).
4 'Sir Michael Balcon on ... Martyrs to Fun', *Picturegoer* (6 August 1949), p. 6.
5 Author's conversation with Monja Danischewsky (26 May 1991).
6 Interview with Alexander Mackendrick for *Omnibus*: 'Ealing', BBC-TV (2 May 1986).
7 David Thomson, *A Biographical Dictionary of the Cinema* (Secker & Warburg, 1980), p. 245.
8 Author's conversation with Diana Morgan (27 February 1991).
9 Charles Drazin, 'Robert Hamer', *London Magazine* (February–March 1994), p. 125.
10 Alec Guinness, *Blessings in Disguise* (Hamish Hamilton, 1985), p. 199.
11 Quoted by Marie Smith in her foreword to *Daylight and Nightmare: Uncollected Stories and Fables by G.K. Chesterton* (Xanadu Publications, 1986), p. 7.
12 Freda Bruce Lockhart, 'Conversation with Robert Hamer', in *Sight and Sound* (October–December 1951).
13 Letter from Michael Balcon to George Muchnic of Loew's Inc. (25 February 1957), Michael Balcon Collection, British Film Institute.
14 Memorandum from Robert Hamer to Michael Balcon (21 February 1958), Michael Balcon Collection, BFI.
15 Author's conversation with Paul Beeson (13 January 1993).
16 Author's conversation with Cyril Frankel (9 March 1991).
17 Letter from Dennis van Thal to Michael Balcon (25 May 1960), Michael Balcon Collection, BFI.
18 Letter from Dennis van Thal to Michael Balcon (10 June 1960), Michael Balcon Collection, BFI.
19 Letter from Michael Balcon to Maxwell Setton (18 May 1961), Michael Balcon Collection, BFI.
20 Michael Balcon, *Michael Balcon Presents ... A Lifetime of Films* (Hutchinson, 1969), p. 163.

Quotations from the screenplay of *For Each the Other* are taken from a copy of Hamer's unpublished script loaned to the author by the late Diana Morgan.

'If they want culture, they pay': consumerism and alienation in 1950s comedies

DAVE ROLINSON

FOR EVERY 1950S British comedy assimilated into the academic canon, there are many which have fallen into obscurity, reinforcing the alleged disposability of the form. One of the highest-profile casualties is *The Horse's Mouth* (Ronald Neame, 1958), which was justly celebrated at the time for Alec Guinness's performance as aggressively anti-social artist Gulley Jimson, but has since suffered from the critical neglect regarding Neame's work. It is true that the film dilutes the complex themes of Joyce Cary's novel with broad comedy, and its removal of darker plot points – not least Jimson's death – reinforces complaints grounded in fidelity criticism that 'beside the novel it looks very small'.[1] However, acknowledging the dispersal of authorship inherent in adaptation and judging the film in its own right, *The Horse's Mouth* is an intriguing oddity which proves that there is more to British comedy films of the 1950s than meets the eye. Neame's assured direction exploits Arthur Ibbetson's gorgeous colour photography, Guinness's performance and the art of John Bratby to succeed where the novel partly failed to show how the artist 'expresses himself in colour rather than words'.[2]

In particular, *The Horse's Mouth* is a fascinating starting point for a discussion of 1950s comedy, because of its treatment of the genre's defining themes: consensus and its breakdown through the alienating individualism of consumerism. It shares key characteristics with such 'canonical' Ealing comedies as *The Lavender Hill Mob* (Charles Crichton, 1951) and *The Man in the White Suit* (Alexander Mackendrick, 1951). As in those films, Guinness plays an obsessive (Jimson) whose pursuit of a financially configured personal vision (attaining the means to paint) leads him to clash with the

I am a research student at the University of Hull, writing a Ph.D. on the television and film director Alan Clarke. I have written articles on documentary and the 1950s *Quatermass* television serials and films. Although I'm 27 years old, I can easily relate to the puritanical austerity and yearning for escape in my favourite 1950s films because I've spent all of those years in Hull. *Dave Rolinson*

community (violence, vandalism, verbal assault). This is particularly striking given that Guinness himself wrote the screenplay, adapting Joyce Cary's 1944 novel (for which he was nominated for an Academy Award). Meanwhile, its acidic one-liners give it a similar edge to late-1950s satires like *I'm All Right Jack* (John Boulting, 1959), while sharing that film's limitations through 'its socially determined need to adopt a 'broader' style'.[3] Like *I'm All Right Jack*, *The Horse's Mouth* questions the efficacy of Ealing's representations of consensus, but does so by assimilating its tropes. The attempt of a group to save a church wall from demolition echoes the recurring Ealing plot in which 'ordinary people enacting the value of co-operation and community' rally around symbolic objects, but the group's failure and degeneration into violence problematises national solidarity.[4] Of course, some Ealing films were themselves aware of the limitations of their consensual representations. *The Lavender Hill Mob* satirises Ealing's 'projection of Britain' by way of its ironic representations of America – through the lurid gangster tales read to Mrs Chalk – and France, where traders sell tourists Eiffel Tower paperweights made in England by Pendlebury, who admits 'I perpetuate British cultural depravity'.

For many critics, this comment could be extended to 1950s comedy, an attitude which finds symbolic expression in the Bijou Kinema in *The Smallest Show on Earth* (Basil Dearden, 1957), an outdated purveyor of lowest-common-denominator entertainment. In *The Horse's Mouth*, Jimson, possibly referencing critical responses to Neame's occasional flourishes, warns against artistic cleverness as 'the kiss of death'. Responding to the threat of television, British cinema found a winning formula in the *Doctor*, Norman Wisdom and *Carry On* series, which were rooted in a rhetoric of consensus: 'Uneven, loose or non-existent at the level of narrative, these films depended on the mise-en-scène of particular, isolated sequences which were paced specifically to create and deliver a sense of audience communality.'[5] However, there is a constant tension between a form built on consensus and content built on alienation. Rather than harking back to wartime collectivism, the decade's comedies are shaped by the general election of 1951, particularly its anti-collectivist sub-texts. The communities of *The Titfield Thunderbolt* (Charles Crichton, 1953) and *The Mouse That Roared* (Jack Arnold, 1959) reflect the triumph of the British spirit over Nazi Germany's unsportingly ruthless professionalism, but their villains, rather than being improbably moustached failed Austrian artists, are profiteering businesses. Throughout the decade's comedies, consumerism is the enemy of consensus, an alienating presence impinging on the value of work and, through the individualising agency of television, the domestic space.

The Horse's Mouth opens with Gulley Jimson emerging from a short prison sentence, growling at the desire of his would-be protégé Nosy to see him made 'a citizen, recognized by society'. Jimson seeks not the recognition of the community, but payment for the products he has made. Therefore, he recommences the threatening phone calls to his former sponsor Hickson for which he was originally imprisoned. He also nearly kills former wife Sarah in his attempt to recover one of his rare early pieces, and on a private commission demolishes the flat of Lady and Sir William Beeder. The unlawful, and anti-social, pursuit of finance is a key theme of Ealing's 1950s output, stemming from the construction of a 'new' nation in *Passport to Pimlico* (Henry Cornelius, 1949), as Charles Barr wrote: 'Insofar as the anti-controls, anti-rationing feeling means outright acquisitiveness, every man for himself, Ealing plainly means to present it as frightening ... the question is whether it can reconcile the desire to maintain the wartime spirit with the desire to be freer and more affluent.'[6] In *The Lavender Hill Mob*, the attempt of entrepreneurs to attain affluence is presented as a criminal act, recognising the ability of institutions (in this case the Bank of England) to resist the claims of private individuals and the working class. Alienated from a sense of inclusion in the invisible product of his employers, the Bank of England, Holland seeks to reward his 'worth' in their terms. In order to achieve the theft of their invisible product, he has to conspire with Pendlebury, a maker of visible products. Morality asserts itself as the robbers are caught by the collective action of the police, but this is possible because of the intervention of anti-consumerist consensus. The robbers are first obstructed by a stall keeper who mistakenly thinks that Pendlebury has stolen a painting. The arrival of the police warns of the dangers inherent in the gang's inability to grasp that consumerism is dependent upon exchange value – all they can exchange for the bullion is their freedom. The gang's nemesis is an Eiffel-Tower-clutching schoolgirl who will not be bought off. This innocence reflects back the selfishness of the gang's acquisitive motives and asserts the moral authority of consensus against the gang's oppositional thinking. Because the consensual rhetoric of ideology has led to an internalisation of capitalist modes as natural, the public view the Bank of England as part of their society, so that stealing from them means stealing from innocent children.

The internalisation of economic consensus is further explored in *The Ladykillers* (Alexander Mackendrick, 1955), in which a lone moral voice championing the status quo destroys a bank-bothering gang from within. Professor Marcus's attempt to articulate an oppositional economic reading (because of insurance, 'nobody *wants* the money back') is thwarted because

Mrs Wilberforce has become the mother figure, acting as a conduit for the family-unit model of ideological indoctrination. Reading her as a mother figure requires a psychoanalytical interpretation of the film, in part inspired by its source material in a dream by writer William Rose. Called 'Mum' by most characters at some point, Mrs Wilberforce emasculates the gang, for example interrupting an argument between Marcus and Louis with a pot of tea: 'Shall I be mother?' Just as in *Psycho* (Alfred Hitchcock, 1960), another film set around an expressionistically designed lodging house, a domineering mother figure provokes transferred murderous impulses ('mother hate', or, on the licence plate of one of the gang's cars during the robbery, 'MUV 8'). In the best British tradition, *The Ladykillers* represses and makes respectable the impulses that *Psycho* more clearly exposes, but the characters are driven on by a wish to hide guilty secrets, particularly those involving bodies and trains plunging through tunnels. The final round of carnage is caused by One Round's uncompromising statement 'I'm staying with Mum', as the others react with Oedipal jealousy to this closer relationship. Mirroring a Gramscian reading of consensus as the '"spontaneous" consent given by the great masses of the population to the general direction imposed on social life by the dominant fundamental group',[7] Mrs Wilberforce indoctrinates the gang with the dominant ideology to such an extent that they murder each other. Reflecting this insidious process, Alexander Mackendrick problematises the notion that 'good' consensus has prevailed over antisocial impulses by undermining Mrs Wilberforce as a representative of society. She is introduced with twinklingly harmless music, but when she stands over a pram the baby screams; later, her effect on a crowded street is to provoke a decidedly non-consensual punch-up.

Several 1950s comedy series achieved success with narratives showing the upward mobility of the individual. The series that began with *Doctor in the House* (Ralph Thomas, 1954) follows aspiring professionals along their career path. Doctors prove their worth to society, and implicate the public in their accession to power, a trope subverted in *The Horse's Mouth* by Jimson's disdain for public respect. This affirmation of the meritocracy is a key feature of both the Norman Wisdom and *Carry On* series, in which bumbling individuals endure disasters but ultimately prove their worth. In *Trouble in Store* (John Paddy Carstairs, 1953), Norman is seen apparently in the boss's car, only for it to pull away, revealing him to be on a pushbike. The film follows Norman's struggles to become a window dresser advertising consumer goods, and its climax takes place in a sale, a consumerist feeding frenzy ripe for criminal exploitation. Identical sequences in *Trouble in Store* and *The Square Peg* (John Paddy Carstairs, 1958) show Norman assuming the voice of authority, using the boss's phone to baffle sales staff, and imitating a drill sergeant to confuse obedient soldiers with silly orders. In both sequences, Norman breaks into hysterics at the incongruity of attaining power, but, like Will Mossop in *Hobson's Choice* (David Lean, 1953), deserves his eventual success all the more for not pursuing it aggressively.

Carry On Sergeant (Gerald Thomas, 1958) establishes the early *Carry On* formula, following the progress of staggeringly incompetent groups within institutions. In often surprisingly sustained parodies of dramatic forms, the result is not so much a professionalisation of amateurs as an amateurisation of the professions. *Carry On Nurse* (Gerald Thomas, 1959) opens with the stock dramatic scenario of an ambulance hurtling back to hospital, where the crew's dash is revealed to be motivated not by a public-service imperative but by a desire to get the racing results.

Consumerism is acceptable when it is used to beat the profiteer at his own game; Matt and Jean in *The Smallest Show on Earth* act not through 'an intrinsic love for the old flea-pit, but rather to increase the asking price'.[8] Audiences abandoning the Bijou for the comfort of the Grand are lured back through consumerist roles; the wheeze of turning up the heating during desert films to sell more refreshments predicts the evolution of the industry to a point where films have become trailers for their merchandising.

This internalisation of dominant ideology, a shaping of 'the imaginary relationship of individuals in their real conditions of existence', expresses itself in *I'm All Right, Jack* and *The Man in the White Suit*.[9] Alienated, individualistic publics appropriate the languages of consensus to protect their own interests. The speech by Stanley Windrush that gives *I'm All Right, Jack* its title illustrates the idea that 'underneath the apparent divisions there is, at root, consensus: that is to say, the common self-interest and greed uniting all in the modern consumer society'.[10] Therefore, 'the phoney patriotic claptrap of the employers' is linked with 'the bilge I've heard talked about workers' rights'. Although Windrush goes to court for his crime against consensus, he receives leniency as, like the limited satire, he has exposed general trends rather than the real ('businessmen') villains. *The Man in the White Suit* reveals the limitations of consensus by opening with a voice-over which places subsequent events in the past tense, giving a foreknowledge of all returning to 'normal' which makes the audience complicit with repression. This enables the film, and Mackendrick's other Ealing work, to subvert the circularity of the studio's comedies with 'an intimation of stasis and stagnancy, of a system seizing up under the dead weight of tradition'.[11] This tradition has assimilated the new consumerism; Sidney is punished for his crimes against capitalism, producing the suit for its 'use' value and not for its exchange value. He craves not the ownership of consumer goods but the free use of private space and equipment, and works obsessively but announces 'I don't want to be paid'. Kierlaw is prepared to pay him handsomely not to produce his work. Daphne negotiates herself a wage ('Aren't you rating my value a little low?') to reward a seduction she does not intend to go through with. Mackendrick reflects Sidney's interruption of the progressive rhetoric of capitalism in smooth camera movements that Sidney brings to a halt by crashing into scenes. Sidney realises the extent to which human relationships are determined by economic relationships when an old woman asks, 'What about my bit of washing when there's no washing to do?' The workers ignore the white suit's socialist symbolism; they want to be defined by the products they make. This reflects a process of alienation described by André Gorz: 'The height of alienation is reached when it becomes impossible to conceive that an activity should have a goal other than its wage.'[12] The use of economic rhetoric by employers in *I'm All Right, Jack* – 'If we cannot sell the things we produce, we cannot buy the things we need' – results not in consensus but in indolence, as it alienates the workforce from the true 'value' of their work.

This alienation is central to the film version of *The Horse's Mouth*. Gulley Jimson loses his motivation after assisting in the commodification of his work, arguing that 'If they want culture, they pay'. Rather than basking in the social admiration of having his work displayed in the Tate Gallery, he attempts to cash in on the display by selling an earlier piece. He seems unaware of the contradictions in his description of one of his pictures because of his inability to distinguish value: 'It's a work of genius, Cokey. It's worth fifty thousand pounds. It's worth anything you like, because it's unique.' Exploiting the commodity value of his work, he pursues Lady and Sir William Beeder for a private commission, sardonically linking ownership with understanding in his statement that the rich are 'the most enlightened people in the world'. Jimson bypasses commissions to attempt a huge artwork on a church wall, which due to time constraints is made as a composite work. This involvement of the community implies that Jimson has grasped the importance of spectatorship in the construction of art, the 'reception by the primary imagination of the disparate images that will be broken up and reunited by the secondary imagination'.[13] Neame captures this aesthetically with a fluid reverse tracking shot over the rubble of the church, which reveals the bigger picture available to the spectator. However, subsequent events reveal the gaps in the consensual rhetoric of the act of viewing.

The transition of Jimson's art from the private domestic space to public display enacts a tension at the heart of the decade's comedies, the interaction between televisual and cinematic forms. Throughout, his artistic experiments are related not to content but to form, a search for the correct wall. As Jimson states in the novel: 'Walls have been my salvation ... In form, in surface, in elasticity, in lighting, and in that indefinable something which is, as we all know, the final beauty of a wall, the very essence of its being.'[14] In his early work on an interior wall at the Beeders' home, this represents itself as an attempt to overcome the reproducibility of television. The presence of a unique artwork counteracts the theory that 'that which withers in the age of mechanical reproduction is the aura of a work of art'.[15] But individualised spectatorship within the home is an alienating experience, so Jimson attempts to find a public canvas, tracing the shift from cult value to exchange value. His use of the church wall symbolises the cinema screen, an artwork validated by the presence of a crowd, and particularly by their diegetic involvement in the picture's construction. This juxtaposition of individualised viewing and the communal viewing of cinema is a recurring concern in 1950s comedies.

The communality of genre is reinforced by many comedies' attempts to assimilate oppositional discourses. Youth rebellion is assimilated into the mainstream by the redirection of leather-clad hooligans in *Barnacle Bill* (Charles Crichton, 1957) and the hidden conservatism of destructive pupils in *Carry On Teacher* (Gerald Thomas, 1959) who 'cheer uproariously at the maintenance of the *status quo*'.[16] However, it is overly simplistic to see the rhetoric of consensus in 1950s comedies as a unifying force; for example, 'working-class British people were depicted in terms of patronizing ignorance'.[17] *The Smallest Show on Earth* is aware of this, demonstrating the form's inability to represent non-hegemonic discourse. The opening sequence utilises a crane shot to show Jean coming down from her home 'above', prefiguring a plot in which she and Matt are drawn to Sloughborough. As tuxedo-clad Matt later barks to an unruly audience: 'You down there! I shall come among you!' In a semiotic struggle with the signification of names, Matt and Jean interpret Sloughborough in their bourgeois terms as 'Slahw-brahw' and imagine the delights of Samarkand ('Doesn't the very name ...?'), which seems less exotic to them than the industrial North. Matt is amused to find that a Marilyn Monroe lookalike is called 'Miss Hogg'. The representational value of words is a constant problem; the plot turns on a misunderstanding between Old Tom and Matt for which the latter refuses to take responsibility, arguing that 'he was always saying things that didn't mean anything'. Jean disagrees with a local's description of his area's glue factory – 'pungent's hardly the word' – then ironically assimilates the discourse to call the Bijou's foyer 'pungent'. The film acknowledges cinema's weaknesses but states its consensual elements. Although satirising British cinema and Ealing whimsy, the film seeks to achieve 'the redefinition of cinema as an institution, and plays upon the nostalgia for a sentimental notion of cinema as a social practice'.[18] If the enemy here is the Hollywood symbol of the Grand, elsewhere the enemy – both of cinema and of society – is television.

The impact of television on British film comedy was more insidious than the use of vehicles for its stars – like Benny Hill in *Who Done It?* (Basil Dearden, 1956) – or such spin-offs as Hammer's *I Only Arsked* (Montgomery Tully, 1959), derived from *The Army Game* (Granada 1957–61). Low-cost, quickly made film series borrowed the aesthetic and performative modes of television situation comedy, particularly the *Doctor* series, with its recurring characters involved in episodic farce plots in a fixed idiom. Although the settings of each *Carry On* film are different, the cast are recurring characters, and the style itself enables a self-reflective continuity. An incident in *Carry On Nurse* involving a daffodil and a Wilfred Hyde-White orifice is referenced when Frankie Howerd bristles at a daffodil in *Carry On Doctor* (Gerald Thomas, 1967): 'Oh no you don't! I saw that film!' Although cinema's swipes at television, in *Simon and Laura* (Muriel Box, 1955), or the set in *The Titfield Thunderbolt* which breaks down after attempting to contain a (filmic) Western, are so playful as to become mutually supportive, some 1950s comedies view the medium in darker terms.

I'm All Right, Jack links television with the consumerist impulse. Commercial television is a vehicle for the consumerist propaganda of advertising that sells products and encourages people to work harder to attain the lifestyle they portray. Windrush experiences the faceless factory behind the Num-Yum adverts, which marry a lively jingle with images of leisure. The contrast between life and lifestyle is made clear when a Num-Yum hoarding is glimpsed on a rubbish dump near Sidney's more prosaic seduction. The effect is to portray consumerism as the 'false consciousness' that distances people from an understanding of their place in society. An Althusserian reading of 'false needs' is foregrounded when a voice-over about the post-war ability 'to supply those vital needs for which the people had hungered for so long' is followed by a jingle advertising Detto detergent. The construction of consumer needs through advertising is so pronounced that, in the Arthur Askey vehicle *Make Mine a Million* (Lance Comfort, 1959), characters cannot sell their detergent because of an inability to advertise on television. This limited satire on the elitism of the monopolistic BBC reclaims popular entertainment as a consumer product from the imposed consensus of hegemonic public-service discourses. The film satirises the content of commercial television, but shows a link between commercial television and the public through advertisements paid for by consumer spending. Although alienated from the lifestyles presented to them, the fragmented television audience derives a sense of freedom, as *Make Mine A Million* 'puts forward the perspective of the British working class for whom advertising was seen as a symbol of the end of postwar austerity'.[19]

Such duality between the consumer-based consensual rhetoric of television content and the social fragmentation necessitated by its form is further addressed in the climax of *I'm All Right, Jack*. After the establishment-supporting soundbites of BBC and ATV news reports, a television debate offers the people a chance to speak for themselves. 'Argument', claiming to put 'YOU' In The Picture, has an adversarial format to appeal to television's fragmented viewers. The alienated consumerist audience storms the stage to grab the money Windrush tosses away: 'This is what they all want! Something for nothing!' The scene's location within a film legitimises the communal experience of being an audience in a cinema. The contrast between the communality of the cinema experience and the individualising experience of television (an 'instrument of the Devil') is similarly explored in *Meet Mr Lucifer* (Anthony Pelissier, 1953). Television erodes communality to the extent that families ignore each other to gaze at it, fooled by the convention of direct address into reading 'communion between the viewer and the screen'. Through a misunderstanding of broadcasting codes, the viewer fails to grasp their alienation from the social space of cinema viewing. Entertainment which takes place in a public space can be encoded as an extension of the work process, an act of conditioning as individuals take their cue from the responses of others (hence television's enduring use of canned laughter). Responses without this validation are dangerous, as shown by a man's unrequited affection for a TV image. The film's ending prioritises mass viewing as 'a fictional diegesis which is clearly recognised to be fiction' configured in the pantomime subject-relationship desired by the lead character.[20]

In the film version of *The Horse's Mouth*, Jimson shocks the community gathered before the public screen by personally bulldozing his own creation. This act reclaims the film from the lazy category of consensual comedy, illustrating the theory that artistic insight 'is an act of the imagination asserting the noncommunality of the mind'.[21] While the novel ends with Jimson being killed by the falling wall, in the film Jimson is inspired and liberated by it, setting sail in the boat which has long been marooned on dry land. Seated alone on deck as if in a living-room armchair, Jimson is passed by a liner which Neame allows to dominate the frame as another cinematic 'wall'. In the film's most expansive shot, the camera moves to track Jimson's attempt to compose his/the director's vision, again viewing the community – the passenger ship – from the outside. This non-communality enacts the threat of television's individualism to social cohesion, and its capacity to undermine a Lacanian impression of the screen as an extension of the 'mirror stage', an Imaginary conception of unity before the mediating screen. The self-reflexivity of media-based plots undermines the psychological processes of suture; if television is constructed, then so is film. In *The Smallest Show on Earth*, the Bijou's problems with projection draw attention to the beam of light above as a hitherto unseen creator. This culminates in the collision of diegetic and non-diegetic sound as a train arrives outside the cinema simultaneously with a train's arrival in the Western being viewed. The intrusion of the outside world ('The train now standing at Number Three Platform') breaks the 'spell' of suture, uniting both diegetic and non-diegetic audiences in an understanding of their constructed status as audiences, made amusing by the spectator's ironic understanding of the film illusion. Comedy narratives have their own levels of 'realism', acting generically to incite expectation, an interiorised knowledge of cause and effect which enables an audience to 'know' the modes of film-making. Therefore, the Bijou's audience leaves as soon as the hero and heroine kiss, because this connotes 'The End' seconds before the end titles come up.

It is this familiarity which problematises the attempt by 1950s comedies to construct an 'aura' around the cinematic experience. Jimson's destruction of the wall becomes a deconstruction of form, reconstituting its viewers' responses to it. However, critics may be tempted to read the wall as a symbol for British film comedies of the 1950s – a gaudy, enjoyable construction that is ultimately transitory and disposable. Perhaps they were the appropriate entertainment for a period negotiating the effects of consumerism. As Cary wrote in a new preface in the film's year of release, Jimson 'has to create not only his work but his public ... the public consists of creative artists. Every living soul creates his own world, and must do so'.[22] Regardless of whether 'forgotten' 1950s comedies are simply consumer products with as short a shelf-life as Num-Yum blocks, *The Horse's Mouth* found its public. In the 1950s 'British audiences' taste for American comedy declined sharply, and they soon preferred the home-grown product'.[23] In an age when sporadic (and American-financed) comedy hits like *A Fish Called Wanda* (Charles Crichton, 1988), *Four Weddings and a Funeral* (Mike Newell, 1993) and *The Full Monty* (Peter Cattaneo, 1997) are heralded as triumphs for British cinema, 1950s comedies remain one of Britain's most successful forms of indigenous popular cinema.

Notes

1 Penelope Houston, '*The Horse's Mouth*', *Monthly Film Bulletin* (March 1958), p. 28.
2 Enid Starkie, 'Joyce Cary: A Personal Portrait', *The Virginia Quarterly Review* 37 (1961), p. 130.
3 Alan Burton, Tim O'Sullivan and Paul Wells, Introduction to *The Family Way: The Boulting Brothers and British Film Culture* (Flicks Books, 1997), p. 11.
4 Stuart Laing, *Representations of Working-Class Life: 1957–1964* (Macmillan, 1986), p. 113.
5 John Ellis, 'Cinema as performance art', in Justine Ashby and Andrew Higson (eds), *British Cinema: Past and Present* (Routledge, 2000), p. 102.
6 Charles Barr, *Ealing Studios* (University of California Press, 1998; 3rd edn), pp. 102–3.
7 Antonio Gramsci, *Selection from Prison Notebooks* (Lawrence & Wishart, 1971), p. 12.
8 James Chapman, 'Films and Flea-Pits: The Smallest Show on Earth', in Alan Burton, Tim O' Sullivan and Paul Wells (eds), *Liberal Directions: Basil Dearden and Postwar British Film Culture* (Flicks Books, 1997), p. 197.
9 Louis Althusser, *Essays on Ideology* (Verso, 1984), p. 36.
10 John Hill, *Sex, Class and Realism: British Cinema 1956–1963* (British Film Institute, 1986), p. 147.
11 Philip Kemp, *Lethal Innocence: The Cinema of Alexander Mackendrick* (Methuen, 1991), p. 58.
12 André Gorz, trans. Michael Sonenscher, *Farewell to the Working Class: An Essay on Post-Industrial Socialism* (Pluto Press, 1982), p. 36.
13 Giles Mitchell, *The Art Theme in Joyce Cary's First Trilogy* (Mouton, 1971), p. 102.
14 Joyce Cary, *The Horse's Mouth* ([1944] Michael Joseph, 1958), p. 297.
15 Walter Benjamin, 'The Work of Art in the Age of Mechanical Reproduction', in Hannah Arendt (ed.), *Illuminations* (Jonathan Cape, 1970), p. 223.
16 Christine Geraghty, *British Cinema in the 1950s: Gender, Genre and the 'New Look'* (Routledge, 2000), p. 68.
17 Kenneth O. Morgan, *Labour in Power 1945–1951* (Oxford University Press, 1984), p. 323.
18 Paul Wells, 'Sociability, Sentimentality and Sensibility: Basil Dearden and the English Comic Tradition', in Burton, O' Sullivan and Wells (eds), *Liberal Directions*, p. 50.
19 Jane Stokes, 'Arthur Askey and the Construction of Popular Entertainment' in Justine Ashby and Andrew Higson (eds), *British Cinema Past and Present* (Routledge, 2000), p. 130.
20 Charles Barr, 'Broadcasting and the Cinema: Screens Within Screens', in Barr (ed.), *All Our Yesterdays: 90 Years of British Film* (British Film Institute, 1986), p. 211.
21 Mitchell, *The Art Theme*, p. 89.
22 Joyce Cary 1958, prefatory essay to *The Horse's Mouth* (Michael Joseph, 1958), p. 8.
23 Sue Harder and Vincent Porter, 'Cinema Audience Tastes in 1950s Britain', *Journal of Popular British Cinema* 2 (Flicks Books, 1999), p. 76.

Boys, ballet and begonias: *The Spanish Gardener* and its analogues

ALISON PLATT

T HE SIXTH SENSE, an American film of 1999 from an Indian director, M. Night Shyamalan, with an all-American star (Bruce Willis), seems a very long way from British cinema of the 1950s.[1] But the boy in this film (Haley Joel Osment) seems almost a revenant from the British post-war era, with his lack of teenage quality, his innocence of youth culture and, more importantly, his anguished concern for and with the adult (Willis) whom he befriends. Here there is something of Carol Reed's *The Fallen Idol* (1948), Anthony Pélissier's *The Rocking Horse Winner* (1949), Philip Leacock's *The Spanish Gardener* (1956) and other films of the period that centre upon the child/adult relationship or incorporate it as a theme: Anthony Asquith's *The Winslow Boy* (1948) and *The Browning Version* (1951), and Philip Leacock's *The Kidnappers* (1953). Perhaps the template for this type of isolated child is Pip in David Lean's *Great Expectations* (1946). Anthony Wager as young Pip seems an irrevocably old-fashioned child victim, the Little Father Time of Hardy's *Jude the Obscure*, as does John Howard Davies asking for more in Lean's *Oliver Twist* (1948). This sensitive-looking child returns in *The Sixth Sense* and indeed in another film of 1999, Paul Thomas Anderson's *Magnolia*.

Neither of the children who feature in these films exemplifies today's idea of 'normal' children in cinema, which is based on a concept of young, tough 'kids' that does not show children as people. Stuart Jeffries recently bemoaned the similarities of late 1990s/early 2000 British films, including 'the spate of sentimental films about the travails of small boys in the provinces.'[2] He attributes this to British cinema's desire to play it safe, to

---

I lecture in English Literature at the Centre for Continuing Education at the University of Liverpool where I did my doctorate on the fiction and philosophy of George Eliot. I became interested in the films of the 1950s through the Sunday afternoon television of the 1970s, such films now irrevocably associated with childhood and the digestion of roast dinners. Particularly interested in literary adaptations, both past and recent, I have published on Hardy and Eliot, including an essay on the BBC *Middlemarch* with Ian Mackillop in *The classic novel* (Manchester University Press, 1999). I must confess there are no begonias in *The Spanish Gardener*. *Alison Platt*

take a successful formula and 'continue mining the same seam' (p. 4), a view particularly applicable to Stephen Daldry's *Billy Elliot* (2000), which surely looks back to Ken Loach's *Kes*, recycling a motif that worked in 1969 but is stale in the year 2000. It is a manipulative pretence of realism that mars *Billy Elliot* (streetwise kids of the 1980s never attempted to erase spray-painted graffiti off gravestones by licking their sleeves and rubbing) and in the general scheme of things it feels like a greater achievement to watch Billy Caspar rear and train a wild kestrel in a mining district than to see Billy Elliot gain a place at the Royal Ballet School, even if, as Billy's father points out, 'lads do football or boxing or wrestling not frigging ballet'.[3] Perhaps it's not simplistic to propose that *Billy Elliot*, so to speak, *trusts* ballet less than *Kes* trusts falconry or, more importantly, Leacock's *The Spanish Gardener* trusts gardening. The ancient sport of falconry and the primal experience of gardening feel like lessons in growth in that they contribute to a changing character, but in *Billy Elliot* ballet functions simply as entertainment for a toe-tapping audience. It feels replaceable, it is an obviously 'feminine' alternative to that masculine sport of boxing (Billy's mother and grand-mother are both associated with dancing and Billy uses his father's boxing gloves) and a complicated means of escaping from the pit, the profession of the male line. If falconry in *Kes* functions as inspiration, enriching Billy's constricted existence with new meaning rather than replacing it altogether, it does so unsentimentally and believably. His harsh family life (absent father, ineffectual mother and brutal half-brother) is not suddenly trans-formed into 'The Waltons' part way through out of recognition of his talent, as occurs in *Billy Elliot*. In effect the family Billy Elliot has at the end of the film is not the family he has at the beginning: they change; he doesn't.[4] In *Kes* the opposite is true – the child grows, the family remains static, which is at least a more truthful response to childhood.

So what of the British post-war era? In *The Sixth Sense* there is an unashamed example of the sensitive relationship between males, adult and child, that figures as so strong a motif in British post-war cinema. It is therefore tempting to say that Britain in this period left a legacy that America inherited. Although films such as Alexander Mackendrick's *Mandy* (1952), Roy Baker's *Jacqueline* (1956), Leslie Norman's *The Shiralee* (1957) and J. Lee Thompson's *Tiger Bay* (1959) all deal in varying degrees with a young girl's relationship with her father, or father-substitute, it is also the male child's 'search for a satisfactory father-figure' which most interests this era in its portrayals of child-as-hero.[5]

In Michael Anderson's *Waterfront* (1950) a 12-year-old boy whose father has absconded to sea gets into a fight at school with a boy who has told him 'there's some who have fathers alive and some who have fathers what's dead but some don't have any fathers at all'. Implied illegitimacy, a traditional male taunt, was a particular concern for a post-war generation. (In Melvyn Bragg's 1999 novel of post-war familial readjustment, *The Soldier's Return*, Wigton's prosperous bookmaker says 'there are women in this town with little kiddies whose fathers have nothing to do with Wigton and have moved on to faraway places! Say nothing'.) The boy, George Alexander, has at his older sister's request not been named after his father, Peter McCabe (a wonderfully villainous Robert Newton), but after a well-known actor, Sir George Alexander. His name therefore incorporates another man's surname. George Alexander, like Dickens's Pip, gains a good education, a passport to a life far removed from that of the male parental figure.

At the beginning of Lean's *Great Expectations* there is a similar concern with names. We learn that Pip is so called because he is unable to pronounce his father's family name, Pirrip, or his Christian name, Phillip. 'So I called myself Pip and came to be called Pip,' he says, in an act of self-naming. The film then shows young Pip running across the marshes against a darkening sky between a pair of gallows like a miniature saviour. He enters a churchyard and places flowers upon a grave on which the name 'Phillip Pirrip' is deeply engraved. As he looks fearfully round, already sensing Magwitch (Finlay Currie), just the name 'Phillip', without the surname, is highlighted on the far right of the screen. In effect Pip's real father is erased by the time Magwitch appears. Joe Gargery (Bernard Miles) is no substitute due to his wife's resentment at being 'a second mother' to her young brother; and the space is filled instead by Magwitch, who is able to offer Pip an inheritance, a true father's legacy. 'Why I'm your second father Pip and you're my son,' he informs him proudly. The film, unlike the novel, ends with a very definite promise of union between Magwitch's actual child Estella (Valerie Hobson) and his substitute one, Pip (John Mills). In one sense Magwitch has unwittingly brought Pip up to be fit to marry his daughter, who has lost her rich suitor now that her true parentage has been revealed, a shadow which also partly covers Pip but which can now be kept in the family.

Parentage, the place from which one is made and named, is a concern in Anthony Asquith's *The Winslow Boy* (1948), adapted from the play by Terence Rattigan. Young Ronnie Winslow (Neil North), having won a scholarship to naval college, shows off his new uniform to his father, Arthur Ronald Winslow (Cedric Hardwicke), who says, 'he's no longer our master Ronnie. He's Cadet Ronald Winslow, Royal Navy'. 'R. Winslow' is highlighted several times on screen as Ronnie's trunk is forwarded and we see it again on his locker at college. Accused of stealing a five-shilling postal order, Ronnie is discharged ('sacked') in disgrace, and sent home without his trunk. 'They're sending it on later', he informs his father. 'R. Winslow' is separated from the name that makes him his father's son. The letter addressed to his father detailing his discharge refers to the theft of the letter 'by your son, Cadet Ronald Arthur Winslow'. The signature of the letter is indecipherable; there must be no distractions from this issue of the Winslow name. The father's unremitting fight to clear his son of all charges is, above all else, a fight to clear his name, a name that is contained within his own ('Ronald Winslow'). It is, in a sense, then, a question of providing the most basic of birthrights: a father's name. This is emphasised in the House of Commons when the representative of the Admiralty refers to the 'Onslow' case (perhaps a Freudian slip, given the substitution for 'win'). On a train two businessmen argue over the case. 'Winslow's only doing what any father would do,' says one. 'Nonsense,' replies the other, 'if he hadn't made such a fuss no one would ever have heard the name Winslow.' This is what the case is reduced to: 'the name Winslow', that of a father and that of a son. 'I'm going to publish my son's innocence before the world,' Arthur informs his wife, a gesture of very public ownership. This is how a father lets 'right be done', that phrase which has, to quote the Winslows' debonair barrister, Sir Robert Morton (Robert Donat), 'always stirred an Englishman'.[6] In spite of being set in pre-World War I England the film has a post-World War II concern with names, with legitimacy, with ownership. The opening scene refers to Arthur's retirement and the film asks, 'What legacy can be passed on from father to son?' Virtually bankrupting himself, Arthur is forced to withdraw his daughter Catherine's marriage settlement and take his eldest son from Oxford; but at the end of the film the Winslow name is intact and Catherine turns down two suitors. holding on to the patronymic for the foreseeable future.

The child/adult bond resonates again in Asquith's *The Browning Version* (1951), where the desiccated classics teacher Mr Crocker-Harris (Michael Redgrave) finds himself, at the very end of a long and undistinguished career, unable to say, like Mr Chips, that he had many children 'and all of them boys'. In fact it is this recognition of his inability to 'father' that causes him such regret. His pupils refer to him as being already dead, his unfulfilled wife (Jean Kent) has emasculated him and he has also, he says in his improvised farewell speech, 'degraded the noblest calling that a man can follow – the care and moulding of the young'. A running motif in the film concerns Taplow (Brian Smith), the only pupil who is able to understand Crocker-Harris enough to actually like him and for whom the film functions as a kind of quest narrative (he seeks promotion from classics Lower V to science Upper V with the groovy Mr Hunter). Taplow's desire to find out if he has been promoted is given so much space in the film that it represents more than a simple graduation from one class to another (the sign that Crocker-Harris's private tutoring has paid off), but comes to signal a kind of fatherly bequest. Taplow is the sole pupil who wants what Crocker-Harris has to give, a reciprocation which has been painfully absent from the Crocker-Harris marriage. 'A single success can atone and more than atone for all the failures in the world,' Crocker-Harris tells his unimpressed successor Mr Gilbert as he 'bequeaths' (his word) him the Classics Room. More important than Crocker-Harris's 'I am sorry' speech is the film's final moment when he not only finally informs Taplow of his promotion, but tells him by means of a joke: 'If you have any regard for me you will refrain from blowing yourself up next term in the science Upper Fifth.' For once it is a joke that Taplow finds funny, rather than one of Crocker-Harris's Latin apophthegms that he laughs at out of politeness. What Taplow has given to his teacher, the grammatically correct epigram he writes in 'the Browning version', Crocker-Harris returns here in language Taplow appreciates. The dead cannot make jokes and this humour at the end is the sign of returning life.

Michael Redgrave's wonderfully understated performance in *The Browning Version*, a compelling study of mannerism and temperament, is owed much by that of Michael Hordern in Leacock's *The Spanish Gardener* (1956).[7] Hordern's portrayal of the British diplomat Harrington Brande who becomes jealous of his young son Nicholas's relationship with his gardener may be captured in wonderfully bright Technicolor VistaVision, but like Crocker-Harris his character is coloured only in shades of grey. In *Fatherhood Reclaimed: The Making of the Modern Father* (1997) Adrienne Burgess discusses the way in which our culture has severed the ancient association of males with nurturing, with birth and rebirth, in favour of the image of father as ruler, the nexus of patriarchy and domestic fathering.[8] In *The Spanish Gardener* this battle between 'earth father' and 'patriarch' takes place over the parenting of young Nicholas Brande (Jon Whiteley) and takes for its field the garden of Harrington Brande's newly acquired house, a garden that has been previously attended to by his predecessor's wife. Brande's wife has left him at a very bad time, a time when the nuclear family model was being heavily promoted. Not only does he not have a wife as homemaker but his role of breadwinner is also in doubt as he fails to gain the promotion he believes he deserves. Brande's separation from his wife, the other contender for his son's affections is, then, the reason why he needs to hire a gardener in the first place (and he believes it is the reason why he has been passed over for the consulship in Madrid; 'my wife left me of her own volition, without cause or motive,' he protests too much to his son's physician, Dr Harvey). Dr Harvey's 'the boy is perfectly well' is set against Brande's 'my son is delicate', a belief dictated by his own Crocker-Harris sickness of the soul. However, Crocker-Harris is in part a victim of his unhappy marriage; Brande, one senses, is more purely the victim of his own inhibited and bitter nature. 'It's as a man that you've failed,' the consul general informs him. Yet how one fails 'as a man' is in this film inseparable from how one falls short as a father. Raymond Durgnat in *A Mirror for England* is right to point out the absence of female characters which, he says,

> suggests the primacy of male allegiance in the public school spirit. The feeling of growing up as something that goes on between boys and men, not involving, or only very elliptically, a feminine presence, has sufficient anthropological precedent to be defensible as absolutely normal and not, as it's latterly fashionable to allege, homosexual. (Durgnat, p. 178)[9]

The exclusion of women in the film may seem to be taken quietly for granted but it is certainly not allowed to pass uncriticised. Not only is Nicholas's most intense relationship formed with a nurturing male but he is 'restored' to the companionship of his mother at the end of the film (albeit in the school holidays). Brande's involuntary flinching every time his wife is mentioned (Hordern's deep facial lines visibly straining for recomposure) clearly highlights the exclusion as a problem; it is undoubtedly one reason why his love for his son is so tenacious.

Although Brande's love for Nicholas includes ensuring that he is fed a balanced diet, administering tonic and watching over his prayers, there is an unnecessary fussiness that makes it feel like supervision rather than care. It is the gardener José (Dirk Bogarde) who makes Nicholas a swing after his father tells him he is too busy and it is José who takes him on that recreational male pursuit, fishing. He plays with him on the beach, shelters him from the corrupt and insinuating butler Garcia, in fact provides him with the opportunity to be a child, something which his father's regimen inhibits. There is a telling scene near the beginning of the film when Brande's 'personal treasures' arrive in a box marked fragile. 'Look Nicholas,' he says, 'they've arrived at last, all our friends. Isn't it nice to see them again?' Nicholas is unimpressed, his mind on his real friend José and his newfound gardening duty, watering the seedlings. With his father's desire to contain him within the house (as well as in his shirt, jacket and hat which Nicholas removes at every opportunity) set against Nicholas's desire to garden, the symbolism is clear: he is not a piece of porcelain to be hidden away and he is in danger of etiolating if he is not given the right kind of care. ('I did it to make him strong,' José explains, in defence of Nicholas's outdoor pursuits.) At the local pelota competition where Nicholas has taken his father as a surprise to see José play, Brande sees himself for the first time as a fallen idol in his son's eyes. In one of the most chilling speeches of emotional blackmail ever made to a child on screen he says, 'you and I are alone now since your mother left us. There are times when it isn't easy but I've never wavered in my devotion to your care. I ask little in return Nicholas but the knowledge of your love', sounding latterly like a jealous god. Brande's constant resort when his own shivering ego is threatened is to insist upon his son's fragility: he is too 'delicate' to attend the local boys' club and the fish José brings as a peace offering are 'too rich' for him. When Brande forbids his son to speak to José, José and Nicholas decide between them that such a command is 'childish' ('we'll be like men and not like children,' José says). It is an important word to describe Brande's behaviour for childishness is easily recognisable to a child and it is this that fuels Nicholas's newfound ability to judge his father's actions. It is not, as Brande assumes, José's 'poisonous' influence that has filled his son with 'new boldness' and 'disobedience' (turning him into a teenager).

In 1950 Martha Wolfenstein and Nathan Leites in *Movies: A Psychological Study* used three stills to differentiate between the father/child relationship in American film (*All My Sons*: 'son judges father'), British film (*The Rake's Progress*: 'father judges son') and French film (*Marius*: 'son will resemble father whom he now fights').[10] In *The Spanish Gardener* there is an over-riding sense of Brande judging his son (and getting hot and bothered about the night Nicholas spends with José when Garcia threatens him), but what fuels Brande's increasingly unfair behaviour is the sense he has of being judged by his son, which is subtly conveyed through a series of scenes in which Nicholas glances from his father to José, a mental weighing up that occurs at his first sighting of the gardener when, momentarily arrested, he looks him up and down. This is *not*, I think, the initiatory moment in a gay love story, as Andy Medhurst has articulated (see note 9 below) but rather the signal that he recognises a quality quite unlike his starched, oppressive father and that he is going to like it.

Throughout the first half of the twentieth century the image of the father as playmate and confidant was actively encouraged, but Brande falls short on both counts. 'You don't like games,' Nicholas tells his father bluntly when he offers to take him to the boys' club. Brande only knows how to be that paternal archetype, the cold and distant father.[11] Between 1940 and 1970 the father's importance as sex-role model was heavily emphasised, as remarked by Adrienne Burgess, and during the 1950s in particular it was felt that fathers should not exhibit 'maternal' tendencies towards their children for fear of emasculating them. In this sense emotional distance had a specific function in terms of gender development. What is interesting about *The Spanish Gardener* is that the child chooses an alternative to this aloof kind of father, chooses instead the kind represented here by Dirk Bogarde, an actor who himself epitomised a new, sexy form of English manhood, most notably in Relph and Dearden's *The Blue Lamp* (1950).[12] In fact Bogarde's persona broadened the era's accepted definitions of masculinity, something which he was to explore more fully in the 1960s in his post-Rank years. It is easy to see why *The Spanish Gardener* could lend itself to a gay reading. The relationship of man and boy is easily the most analysed kind of homo-erotic relationship and its basic nature is initiatory, plus Bogarde's looks conform readily to a primary homosexual symbol of the Mediterranean lover.[13] Also there is a strong undercurrent of unresolved repression in the film, an overspill from A. J. Cronin's source novel of 1950 which depicts the relationship between adult and child in a much more ambiguous way (José is only nineteen and is not given a fiancée, and Nicholas shares a bed with him when he runs away rather than just staying in the family home). However, the novel's Dr Halevy, a rather caricatured French analyst, has more in common with the film's thieving butler Garcia (Cyril Cusack) than with the sensible Dr Harvey who speaks of this 'perfectly ordinary friendship' between man and boy. The butler, barometer of a master's moods, insinuates exactly what Brande wishes to hear, that Nicholas and José are inseparable, and when he gets drunk his pursuit of Nicholas has a surprisingly lascivious manner to it. To read this relationship between Nicholas and José as being anything other than 'ordinary' is to fall into the same trap Garcia sets for his employer. Medhurst asks why Brande reacts to the friendship with such alarm if it is not out of his own inexpressible feelings for the handsome gardener. But Brande has already lost his role of husband, has been passed over for the consulship in Madrid and now feels faced with the loss of his role of father ('after he's gone perhaps I'll regain my son's affection,' he remarks to an incredulous Dr Harvey). Returning from Madrid, where another man was appointed in his place, Brande finds at home an identical situation regarding his son. It is this redundancy that terrifies him, the loss of the final role open to him.

But what of Brande's painfully maintained repression? No other male figure in the film has anything in common with him; even the consul general, whom we might expect to share this particular 'brand' of upper-middle-class, public-school masculinity, tells him to try and 'behave like a human being'. What this film records, beyond the overt 'father judges son and is judged accordingly', is the passing of a type of Englishness, a stiff-upper-lipped, three-piece-suited paternalism that no longer works. In Cronin's novel Brande is American; in the film his Englishness is central to the theme. This is why it is significant that Bogarde maintains his particularly suave English accent throughout; he's not really Spanish, the film implies, even if he is the popular pelota champion of San Jorge (Saint George). Bogarde never removes his shirt in the film, but no doubt would have done had his physique more fully expressed his manual profession (Bogarde often wore a sweater underneath his shirt as padding to improve his build), but it is Brande who is, as his colleague points out, 'a stuffed shirt'. It is José who signifies the dawning of a new kind of fathering that differs from the patriarchal norm, that offers intimacy and involvement beyond that pattern strictly in place in the post-war years when demobilisation dictated the reinforcement of the gender roles so heavily disrupted by World War II.

Ultimately this is the story of an innocent child's first brush with human fallibility – sin, of a kind. Brande makes poor moral judgements but his son works by astute instinct: 'the little boy knows who is good and who is bad because he sees and feels. He understands already what kind of man you are,' José's fiancée tells Brande when he has had José imprisoned for a theft he did not commit (and inadvertently answers his own earlier question to his son 'who are you to say what's good or bad?'). If certain 1950s British films, Leacock's being one, detail an adult world in which restraint and solitude are givens, they also convey the cost to the child who must inevitably enter that world. What the post-war era seems to capture is a time when childhood, impinged upon by an uncomprehending adult world, is no longer tenable as a place for children. At the end of *The Spanish Gardener* José, having been framed for theft by Garcia, escapes from a moving train and seeks refuge in the mountains. Nicholas, unable to understand how his father could think José guilty, finds him and in the most climactic moment of the film tells him that he hates his father. Brande, realising how unjust he has been, travels through a heavy storm to find his son and begs José's forgiveness. There is a peculiar moment when José looks at Brande who looks at Nicholas, who is looking at his father before turning to look at José, who, in turn, looks back at Nicholas. As a set of stills this might combine all of Wolfenstein and Leites's categories but with a twist: 'father judged son who judged and fought with the father he will not resemble'. There is no convenient restoration of what has gone before – Brande will head to a posting in Stockholm, a climate better suited to his attire, and Nicholas will go to boarding school and to his mother in the holidays. Only José, the eternal gardener, returns to his old life (although it is not clear who is now paying his wages). The film leaves him in front of the house, facing the sea with his back to us, the same position he was in when Brande first met him. It seems fitting given that Brande and Nicholas are the ones whose lives have been irrevocably changed.

When José told Nicholas that he must find a way to forgive his father he said 'what has happened between your father and me is our affair', which rings falsely in a film in which a child has been caught between two adults and forced to acknowledge the nature of the trap. In spite of Nicholas's excitement at leaving for school the ending sounds an elegiac note and Brande is right to acknowledge that he and his son will never forget José. The same might be said of Phillipe (Bobby Henrey), the young boy in Carol Reed's *The Fallen Idol* (1948) who experiences an adult world of moral complexity through the agency of his father's butler. That the upper-middle-class father is either absent (*The Fallen Idol*) or ineffectual (*The Spanish Gardener*, *The Rocking Horse Winner*) partly explains the child's readiness to find a suitable paternal substitute, that of the domestic servant. In *The Fallen Idol*, based on Graham Greene's short story 'The Basement Room' (1936), Phillipe's father leaves him in the care of Baines (Ralph Richardson) whose malevolent wife affects his heart not by rendering it diseased in the manner of Mrs Crocker-Harris but by sending him into the arms of another woman.[14] The film is structured around a series of ascents and descents both literal (the main staircase is used to good effect) and metaphorical (Phillipe is caught up in a sort of adult game of snakes and ladders), and it is clear that Mrs Baines dies an accidental death, something which is far less clear in the story, where Baines moves the body to cover up his involvement. The story also makes it clear that Phillipe's involvement in marital intrigues and his desire to extricate himself from a world in which secrets lead somehow to death, ultimately destroy him, leaving him broken, an earlier version of L.P. Hartley's own tale of a young boy's traumatic initiation into the world of adult passion and deception, *The Go-Between*, published in 1953. The film shifts the child's desire to protect himself, to be free of all adult secrets, to a desire to protect Baines, his idol, at whatever cost. In the story Philip (not French as in the film) expresses a 'merciless egotism'; he refuses the burden of knowledge and reveals Baines's culpability, punishing him in a sense for involving him in a world that destroys his childhood.[15]

In the film Phillipe lies for Baines *because* he assumes he is guilty of murdering Mrs Baines and feels a responsibility towards him, even to the point of trying to take the blame himself. A child's conscience, the film implies, is governed by an instinctive care for the befriending adult, a theme explored more fully in J. Lee Thompson's *Tiger Bay* (1959). At the end Phillipe rejects only secrets and not life itself as he does in the story, but his oddly blank expression as he descends the staircase to greet his parents seems to register the change he has undergone: it is a look which has put aside childish things.

This brings me back to *The Sixth Sense* and *Magnolia*, to that child who started life in post-war British films. Raymond Durgnat has chronicled the era's obsession with the juvenile delinquent, a way of addressing an 'issue' (social unrest) that could be given an easy solution (a good hiding, better housing).[16] Delinquent teenagers, too old to seek alternative father figures, go up against the Establishment and invariably lose. Their younger selves were not the child heroes of early post-war cinema and their battles are portrayed as less complex.[17] This particular type of teenage delinquent no longer exists for contemporary cinema yet the child hero of this period undoubtedly does. Haley Joel Osment's Cole in *The Sixth Sense* begins as a case history (an acutely anxious child of divorced parents) for the adult, Dr Malcolm Crowe (Bruce Willis), but like *The Fallen Idol*'s Phillipe he is a figure burdened by secrets which he cannot comprehend. Cole wears his father's glasses without their lenses (which impede his vision) and his father's broken watch (abandoned in a drawer). Malcolm Crowe, the child psychologist who befriends him, is careful not to make the same mistake with Cole as he had made with a previous case, Vincent Grey. Crowe, honoured as Philadelphia's 'son', not knowing that Vincent, like Cole, can see and hear the dead, mistakenly puts Vincent's troubles down to his parents' divorce. Yet, complexly, this is Crowe's story too and like Harrington Brande, if he knew the truth about himself he would understand the child's needs too. If the 1950s were able to pinpoint one-parent families as being undesirable, 1999 seems too sophisticated to overtly blame child problems on marital separation; on the surface Crowe is simply wrong in this initial diagnosis.[18] Yet there are no happy families in this film any more than there are in Paul Thomas Anderson's tale of broken children and their cancer-ridden fathers, *Magnolia*. Crowe's wife speaks of the sacrifices he has made for his job; 'I haven't paid enough attention to my family,' Crowe tells Cole; Vincent Grey and Cole are both from broken homes; Tommy who bullies Cole remorselessly appears in a cough syrup commercial which harks back to a bygone age with its perfect mom and dad; the ghosts who visit Cole are primarily the ghosts of children past: a boy who shoots himself with his father's gun and a girl whose father fails to realise his new wife is poisoning his daughters. This, then, is a film in which fathers do not protect their children. Cole is visited by the ghost of his dead grandmother but no mention is made of his father's visiting rights; his religious icons and church visits are miserably ineffective – his metaphysical Father is as elusive as his literal one. Willis fills this particular role instead, finding a workable means for Cole to deal with his fears.[19]

The Sixth Sense, with its problem families, its isolated, serious boy and his complex relationship with an older paternal figure resonates with a previous (British) age. The righting of a wrong in order to protect a child is a theme this film shares with *The Fallen Idol*, *The Winslow Boy*, *The Spanish Gardener*, even *The Browning Version*. It takes a whole film to achieve it; there can be no miraculous adult shifts of heart (*Billy Elliot* take note) because the child's vision is a complex thing, as complex as that of the adult whom he befriends. More importantly, when the adult figure seems to be solving the child's problems he may also be solving his own if he knows where to look. It is this correlation between child and adult that permeates 1950s British cinema and is so evocatively recaptured in the contemporary Hollywood movie.

Notes

1 I take 'the 1950s' to refer not to a strict chronological timeline but to the post-war years, an historical era.
2 *Guardian* (13 July 2001), p. 4.
3 And indeed they do in two other British films of 2000, Mark Herman's *Purely Belter* and John Hay's *There's Only One Jimmy Grimble*.
4 Which is why 'adult' ballerina Billy makes so brief and hazy an appearance at the end, the film reverting back to the image it seems most comfortable with, the opening scene of Billy dancing on his bed to T-Rex.
5 Raymond Durgnat, *A Mirror for England: British Movies from Austerity to Affluence* (Faber, 1970), p. 143.
6 One thing which is notably absent from the film is the father's own grilling of his son. He simply asks him twice if he stole the postal order and is satisfied enough with the answer to carve the Sunday roast. It is Sir Robert Morton who has the role of browbeating Ronnie in the family sitting room. Arthur knows he has one son who is dishonest (his eldest son Dickie), which perhaps fuels his determination to accept his younger son's word.
7 Brian McFarlane calls this 'one of the finest films of the 1950s', *Sixty Voices: Celebrities Recall the Golden Age of British Cinema* (British Film Institute, 1992), p. 156.
8 Adrienne Burgess, *Fatherhood Reclaimed: The Making of the Modern Father* (Vermilion, 1997), pp. 5–6.
9 See Andy Medhurst, '"It's as a Man That You've Failed": Masculinity and Forbidden Desire in *The Spanish Gardener*', in Pat Kirkham and Janet Thumin (eds), *You Tarzan: Masculinity, Movies and Men* (Lawrence & Wishart, 1993), pp. 95–105.
10 Martha Wolfenstein and Nathan Leites, *Movies: A Psychological Study* (Free Press of Glencoe, 1950), quoted in Durgnat, *Mirror for England*, p. 141.
11 Both José and Dr Harvey abbreviate Nicholas's name, using Nico and Nicky respectively. Brande only calls him Nicholas and refers to José as 'the gardener'.
12 See Jeffrey Richards, *Films and British National Identity: From Dickens to Dad's Army* (Manchester University Press, 1997), p. 145.
13 Robert Aldrich examines this symbolism more fully in *The Seduction of the Mediterranean: Writing, Art and Homosexual Fantasy* (Routledge, 1993).

14 This was the first of three Reed/Greene collaborations, Greene calling it his favourite picture. It received a number of awards and Reed's direction of Henrey earned him a reputation as a great director of children.

15 Graham Greene, 'The Basement Room' (1936), in *Stories* (Heinemann, 1965).

16 Durgnat writes, 'the feeling for military-style paternalism, for the system and for the police, are special forms of a general acquiescence to father-figures of a quietly heavy kind' (*Mirror for England*, p. 140).

17 Unlike the American version, as complex a being as our child heroes.

18 In J. Lee Thompson's *Woman in a Dressing Gown* (1957) Jim Preston (Anthony Quayle)'s decision to leave his frowzy wife for his groomed mistress brings him to hit his son and drives his wife to drink. His reaction to his son's final farewell as he leaves arrests him much more strongly than the torrent of words his wife unleashes and he changes his mind. Harmony is restored as he bonds more closely with his son (Andrew Ray) and his wife (Yvonne Mitchell) abandons her dressing gown.

19 Above all else *The Sixth Sense* is a very good ghost story, the form that the critic Edmund Wilson predicted would die out with the dawning of electric light. It seems apt, therefore, that the opening shot depicts a bare light bulb glowing into life.

Intimate stranger: the early British films of Joseph Losey

NEIL SINYARD

In Hollywood you're still one of the bad boys. (*The Intimate Stranger*)

He doesn't like the world. It's a good beginning. (*The Damned*)

Ever an emotional soul, Dirk Bogarde confessed to being reduced to tears by the rave review in *The Times* when *The Servant* was premièred at the end of 1963. For Bogarde, this prestigious endorsement of his extraordinary performance as Barrett, the man-servant who brings the life of the aristocrat he serves crashing down about his ears, was a career turning-point, the fulfilment of his ambition to be recognised as a major screen actor and not simply a matinee idol. It marked a similar culmination for its director, Joseph Losey, who, after seeking work in England following his blacklisting in Hollywood during the McCarthy period, had struggled for a decade with, as he saw it, indifferent scripts, philistine producers and studio conformity. In an interview in *Films and Filming* in October 1963, he had declared: '*The Servant* is the only picture I have ever made in my life where there was no interference from beginning to end, either on script, casting, cutting, music or on anything else. The result, whether the film succeeds or not, whether one likes the film or not, at least it's something I can defend as being mine. It is all of one piece.'

As a film-struck teenager, I saw *The Servant* when it was first released and can recall being utterly bowled over by it. At that time, infected by a fashionable disdain towards British cinema in comparison with the panache

I have written over twenty books on film, including studies of Richard Lester, Nicolas Roeg and Jack Clayton. I am the co-editor of the ongoing series of monographs, 'British Film Makers', published by Manchester University Press. I grew up in the 1950s and my love of cinema dates from a childhood which left indelible filmgoing memories: of a cinema within walking distance of seemingly everyone's home, of copies of *Picturegoer* and the *ABC Film Review*, of usherettes, and choc ices before the main feature, of continuous programmes that permitted you to stay in the cinema all day and see the main feature more than once, of the undignified scramble at the end to get out before the striking up of the National Anthem. *Neil Sinyard*

of Hollywood and the passion of Europe, I was stunned by the film's make-over of Bogarde as a great screen character actor, and mesmerised by a Harold Pinter screenplay that seemed to set new standards for film writing in Britain. (Even a line like 'I'm afraid it's not very encouraging, Miss, the weather forecast,' as delivered by an insinuating Bogarde to a startled Wendy Craig, seemed to crackle with all kinds of underlying menace and cheek.) Above all, in a British cinema dominated by words and a ponderous visual imagination, here at last was a real film, full of sinuous and suggestive camera movement and visual symbolism, notably of décor, bars and mirrors, which I came to recognise as part of Losey's visual signature. It was that rare thing: a sexy British film. Indeed it was an even rarer thing in British cinema: a self-conscious art movie that combined prescient social criticism (it was *the* film that anatomised the Britain of the Profumo era) with a teasing density and ambiguity of theme and detail that one associated more with foreign directors such as Fellini or Resnais. Coming out of the auditorium, I became involved in an earnest conversation with an usherette who was puzzled by the moment towards the end of the film when Bogarde offers a befuddled James Fox a drink: what was in it? Whatever it was, its effect was devastating, reducing Fox to a state that seemed almost prophetic of the mental degeneration he would experience in Nic Roeg and Donald Cammell's similarly mind-blowing movie, *Performance* – perhaps the one other British film of this era to match up to Losey's art house audacity.

At the time, I knew something of Losey's reputation. I certainly remember seeing *Blind Date* (US: *Chance Meeting*) of 1959 because the predatory eroticism of Micheline Presle's socialite had burned deep in my youthful imagination, as had (for different reasons) Stanley Baker's brusque police inspector with a head cold, a characterisation some distance from the avuncular law officers of Jack Warner and Jack Hawkins one was accustomed to in British film and surely an anticipation of Stratford Johns's great Inspector Barlow in BBC-TV's classic *Z-Cars* series. I could also remember *The Gypsy and the Gentleman* (1957) for its unusual foreignness and the way this seemed to connote passion, particularly in Merlina Mercouri's devastation of the aristocrat's home ('I will smash everything you've got, everything you've got,' she shrieked in this strange accent), and I have no doubt that I later made the thematic connection with *The Servant*. However, I suspect Losey's name first really registered with me when listening to a feature on the making of *Eve* (1962) in the BBC radio magazine, *Movie-Go-Round*. I am sure people of my generation would remember this Sunday afternoon programme and its endearing routine of familiar ingredients: the theme tune from *Carousel*, the suave introductions of Peter Haigh, the star-struck news report of a breathy

Peter Noble, the excellent edited highlights of current releases, Stanley
Black often being contentious on film music, Gordon Gow invariably being
astute on the new films. In this particular programme featuring *Eve*, I was
startled to hear Jeanne Moreau describing Losey as one of the greatest of
contemporary film-makers. I was probably unaware then that what Moreau
was doing was contributing to a debate that was actually one of the most
heated critical issues about British cinema at this time: namely, the status of
Joseph Losey.

In an interview-article on Losey in 1961 in *Sight and Sound*, John Gillett
and Penelope Houston drew attention particularly to the contrasting
response to him in Britain and France, where he (surely alone amongst film-
makers in Britain at that time, albeit an American) was gathering a cult
reputation. Gillett and Houston tellingly illustrated this contrast by quoting
six critical opinions on Losey's *The Criminal* (US: *The Concrete Jungle*) of
1960, the first three hailing the lucidity and intelligence of the film's style,
the next three finding that same style hysterical and discordant in relation to
its material. As Gillett and Houston drily observed, the nationalities proclaimed themselves, so no prizes were offered for guessing that the first three
views were French and the next were British. The implication of this went
much further than a director's reputation, however: it seemed in some way
to go to the root of film aesthetics, of what a good film was, of 'what film was
for', of the relation between form and content. The debate was considerably
intensified by the appearance of the magazine *Movie* in June 1962 as an
aesthetic counterblast to what it saw as the insufferable and uncommitted
refinement of *Sight and Sound*. Bursting with *Cahiers du Cinéma*-type aesthetic
and auteurist polemic, *Movie* began with a sustained assault on what it
claimed was the irredeemable aesthetic poverty of British film, the only
significant exception, in its view, being Joseph Losey, left in splendid
isolation as the only director working in Britain deserving of *Movie*'s
accolade of 'brilliant'. If Losey is a fascinating case, then, it is not only
because of the particular quality of these early films: it is also because their
making and their reception have so much to say about what was going on at
the time in film criticism. As Losey was having his titanic struggles with
studios and actors and applying his outsider's perspective on English mores
(notably, sex and class), the films were also providing a focus and indeed a
battleground for conflicting critical ideas about the cinema in general and
British cinema in particular.

The Servant could be seen as the completion of the first phase of Losey's
English period, which had begun in 1954 with his first film in England, *The
Sleeping Tiger*. Here also we had Dirk Bogarde in the leading role as a

sinister guest (in this case a hardened criminal whom a psychiatrist is attempting to reform) let loose in an ostensibly respectable household of self-deceiving people, notably the psychiatrist (Alexander Knox) and his wife (Alexis Smith). The progression is similar to that in *The Servant*: the interloper causes havoc or, more precisely, brings to the surface weaknesses and dissatisfactions that were lurking in that household to begin with. Losey landed the assignment through the good auspices of fellow blacklisted American exile, Carl Foreman, who co-authored the screenplay under a pseudonym with another blacklisted screenwriter, Harold Buchman (brother of the more famous Sidney Buchman). Initially duped into thinking he was to be directed by Victor Hanbury, which was to be Losey's pseudonym on the credits, Bogarde at this stage knew nothing of Losey's previous work and rather crossly insisted on seeing a sample. Twenty minutes of *The Prowler* (1951) were enough to convince him that here was a director who, to say the least, knew what he was doing. The making of the film had its fraught moments, notably when Losey had to be spirited out of the hotel where he was staying when it was discovered that one of the other guests was the rabidly anti-communist Ginger Rogers, who was in England to make a thriller with David Miller called *The Beautiful Stranger* (one hostile word from her could have jeopardised the entire production). But from it came a close bond between actor and director that was to have a profound effect on both of their careers.

'We thought the script itself was frightful,' Bogarde told the editors of *Isis* in February 1964, 'and it embarrassed us incredibly to do it. Joe had to embellish this rubbish, as he always has had to do, and in consequence it was much more exciting to do: one found reasons for doing dreadful dialogue and making it sound all right.' Maybe this came out of Losey's theatrical experience, because in *The Empty Space* (1967) Peter Brook describes a similar experience: faced with a dreadful script, the cast had commissioned another, only to find that, by the time the improved and revised script was ready, they had found ways of making the original work. One could draw another lesson from this kind of experience, which was something that David Deutsch, the associate producer on *The Gypsy and the Gentleman*, had concluded: that the film was awful but the direction was extraordinary, the film's awfulness somehow showing up the director's exceptional qualities in the way that a good film might not have done (because there it is more difficult to separate one contribution from another). 'Joe showed an absolutely sure touch rarely seen in England in those days,' Deutsch told Edith de Rham. 'For the first time I came into contact with someone who truly recreated the Regency period visually. And he did this within the framework of a very conventional major studio. Joe was a lonely figure there [i.e. Rank], because they weren't used to people doing things that way.'

The characteristic that most distinguishes Losey's early films from other English films of their time is the energy of the visual style. With the exception of Michael Powell, British cinema of this time seemed mostly devoid of film stylists: form tended to be subordinated to content. Losey's films brought the form/content debate to the surface because the visual power and ornateness seemed, to many eyes, out of all proportion to the mundaneness of the subject matter. That, of course, begged the question of what the subject matter was. Ostensibly *The Sleeping Tiger* is a 'social problem' movie about a psychiatric experiment, which might seem to demand a clinical, objective approach. The sub-text, though, concerns a sterile marriage whose fissures are exposed by the arrival of a demonic, dynamic stranger and whose problems undercut both the motives and the validity of the psychiatrist's research. Like the philosophers in *Accident* (1967), he is a character who can pronounce loftily and smugly about the psychological problems of others without being fully in tune with his own emotions, the consequence being that his research is contaminated by his lack of self-knowledge. The noticeable self-consciousness of the style, then, operates in an almost Brechtian way to pull you out of narrative involvement into a more contemplative relation to the film. As with *Time Without Pity*, *Blind Date* and *Eve*, the plot is the weakest, or the least important, part of the film. In 1963, in *Films and Filming*, Losey remarked that the plot of *Blind Date* did not interest him at all, which is as well because, on the level of thriller, it is completely implausible. Similarly with *Eve*, he thought that the basic situation was so commonplace and classical that an audience could more or less take it as read, be trusted to tell that story for themselves, which in turn allowed Losey room to step back and use it as a frame to tell another story – a story within a story.

In *The Sleeping Tiger*, for example, the plot is merely a pretext for exploring different areas through means other than pure narrative – for example, expressive design, visual motifs, symbolism. Mirror shots predominate in a way that reflects the characters' narcissism, the brittleness of appearances, and the imminent reversals of power that will take place in the household. (For example, the psychiatrist is given six months for his experiment to work: towards the end, when his wife has started an affair with the criminal, she asks Bogarde for a trial period of six months for their relationship to work, a telling detail of how the power in the house has completely shifted.) Pictures are used to comment on character: the abstract in the psychiatrist's room says a lot about his dry, mechanical perception of personality, just as the total bafflement the picture induces from the policeman (Hugh Griffith) shows that man's down-to-earth, unimaginative pragmatism. The wife's tormented progress through the film can be mapped through her symbolic association with flowers (another Losey trademark), from, for example, the decorous way she arranges them early in the film to the way she crashes into a vase of flowers near the end when her life is spiralling out of control. The film's most portentous symbol is in its title. 'There is a sleeping tiger in the dark forest of every human personality,' the psychiatrist has told his patient, little realising the statement's applicability less to the patient than to his own wife, whose repressed and anguished passion will destroy her through no less an act than crashing her car through an advertising hoarding featuring Esso's famous leaping tiger ('Put a tiger in your tank'). Even the most flamboyant of directors might have hesitated at the blatant symbolism, but Losey goes straight for it. We are a long way there from British understatement and that may be a good thing. As Gavin Lambert said at the time: 'There is a splendour about this film, which has one of the most absurdly extravagant plots on record, and never flinches from it.'

As well as the energy of the visual style, what also marks out Losey's English films at this time is what one might call his American 'baggage' – his background and early experience in American cinema, which is signalled quite overtly in these movies. He is not the only director in England to be using American actors of below top rank (Lance Comfort is doing the same), nor is he the only American director of the time compelled to work in England (there is the interesting parallel case of the blacklisted Cy Endfield, who was to make the frenetic *Hell Drivers* in a style that also ruffled the feathers of the more staid of English critics). But the Americanism seems closer to the surface in Losey's case. For example, perhaps as a kind of safeguard or reassurance, he surrounds himself with American actors in leading roles: Alexis Smith in *The Sleeping Tiger*; Richard Basehart and Mary Murphy in *The Intimate Stranger* (US: *A Finger of Guilt*); Macdonald Carey, with whom he had worked in his 1949 American film, *The Dividing Line* (US: *The Lawless*), and Viveca Lindfors in *The Damned* (US: *These are the Damned*). The American background is also reflected in the writers he uses, frequently blacklisted comrades: Carl Foreman and Harold Buchman for *The Sleeping Tiger*, Howard Koch for *The Intimate Stranger*, Ben Barzman for *Blind Date*. The film in which Losey's background is most obvious is *The Intimate Stranger* in which the hero (Richard Basehart) is a former American film editor who, partly through an advantageous marriage, has become an important executive producer in England. The plot concerns an attempt by a jealous employee (Mervyn Johns) to discredit him by concocting evidence of an affair he is supposed to have had with a young actress (Mary Murphy).

The real concerns of the film seem to be quite different from this, however: more to do with the exploration of the difficulties of an American film man in an alien English environment where he is regarded as showy and extravagant; and also of a man trying to escape from, and live down, a so-called shady past that has compelled him to leave his country (in this film it is sex rather than politics that has landed him in trouble). It has its filmic in-jokes, such as the moment when Basehart seems about to commit suicide by jumping from a high building, an allusion to his most famous role at that time as the similarly suicidal hero of Henry Hathaway's *Fourteen Hours* (1951). More pointed, though, is the revelation of the identity of the villain – a peevish, small-minded individual – and the description of him, at a key moment, as a 'scheming, spying informer'. The equation of the villain with the tactics of McCarthyism is explicit there, as is the idea of the hero as someone who has been falsely 'victimised' (though it is also suggested that his behaviour has made him vulnerable to that form of attack). Made with modest means in twelve days, the film remains essentially a crisp B-picture thriller, but with a striking style and an unusually dense sub-text.

There is another way of reading the 'American baggage' in Losey's early films and it is less biographical than psychological. One of Losey's favourite actors, Alexander Knox, who appeared in three of his films (*The Sleeping Tiger*, *The Damned*, *Accident*), alluded to that when he opined to Losey's biographer Edith de Rham that 'Joe could have been one of the very great directors, but he was carrying around too much negative psychological baggage from his early days, and from the blacklist, and from having to adapt to the "old school tie" style of movie making in England, and in the society as well.' As it developed, the career was to become full of the tensions and contradictions that emanated from the man himself. He became eminent enough to work with the biggest stars and the greatest writers, and yet he always seemed to pull back from commercial success, his films teetering on the borderline between profundity and pretentiousness.

A man who was to work with Brecht, Pinter, Stoppard, Mercer and Tennessee Williams was also, through the quirks of the British distribution system, to have one of his films released as second feature to a Hammer horror film. He directed two of the biggest screen stars, Elizabeth Taylor and Richard Burton, in one of their hugest commercial flops, *Boom!* (1968), a film widely dismissed as incomprehensible rubbish but championed by its screenwriter Tennessee Williams and hailed as a major artistic achievement by one of Losey's staunchest allies in his first years in England, the secretary of the British Board of Film Censors, John Trevelyan. A man who always proclaimed the importance of a film having a personal signature also recognised that he was in an industry uniquely populated by people who 'cavalierly hire specialists at vast prices only to devote themselves to hampering the work of the specialist they have hired', as he said in *Films and Filming* in October 1963. The main creative contradiction in Losey is arguably something that was once asserted by Abe Polonsky about the Hollywood writer-director Robert Rossen (maker of such hard-hitting social dramas as *Body and Soul*, *All the King's Men*, and later *The Hustler* and *Lilith*), who roughly shared Losey's political orientation but who was to buckle under pressure from the House UnAmerican Activities Committee and name names: a tension between art house pretension and melodramatic propensity.

Was Losey 'melodramatic' or did he simply feel things deeply? Critics at the time certainly had to struggle with notions of 'excess' in relation to Losey's work, but the argument was really about what that 'excess' might portend. Contrasting his work with the more conventional naturalist style of British directors, Penelope Houston was to remark that Losey 'prefers something more high-powered: film-making in which, if one is not immediately aware of the horsepower under the bonnet, one is aware of nothing'. But this horsepower had several sources. It undoubtedly came from Losey's own temperament, as someone who felt deeply about his craft in an industry and country where, as he remarked to Houston and Gillett in their *Sight and Sound* interview, 'over here, I sometimes get the impression that they [the film executives] just don't like films'. Losey really cares. Trapped within archaic narrative stereotypes – or maybe the narrative obviousness opens up different possibilities – are films of raw anguish from a hypersensitive man who may have felt, having to rebuild his career from scratch in middle age and in poor health, that time was running out.

Time Without Pity is the early film of Losey's that particularly catches his peculiar qualities. Like its companion film of the same year, J. Lee Thompson's *Yield to the Night* (1956), it is a plea for the abolition of capital punishment, as an alcoholic writer (Michael Redgrave) is given less than twenty-four hours to save his son (Alec McCowen) from being hanged for murder. However, unlike *Yield to the Night*, in *Time Without Pity* capital punishment is the backdrop to the drama rather than the theme. The theme is time itself: time as enemy, as insistent presence that mocks man's attempt to get his life and relationships in order. The theme is sometimes conveyed through startlingly direct symbolism, such as the armory of alarm clocks owned by one character (Renée Houston) which at one stage all go off in unison, or the trial run of his new car by the actual murderer, the manufacturer (Leo McKern), where the race against time is an expression of his external power that is clearly compensating for inner insecurities. Leo

McKern's amazing performance is pitched somewhere between the extremes of Howard da Silva's crook in Nicholas Ray's 1948 film *They Live By Night* (like da Silva, McKern has an eye defect that carries symbolic overtones) and Rod Steiger's mogul in Robert Aldrich's *The Big Knife* (1954), whose gesture of hiding his head in his hands, as if warding off an invisible blow, is imitated by McKern, similarly a man of industrial power who feels emotionally impotent. The operatic turn is matched, in a different key, by Michael Redgrave, who comes lurching towards the camera in a paroxysm of self-torment as a disappointed character in desperate need of making up for lost time. For all their hostility and difference of circumstance, there is an eerie connection between the two men, both seeming driven by the Furies, both having contaminated blood (one by alcohol, the other by petrol), both being fundamentally isolated, insecure and self-destructive.

In his film dictionary Georges Sadoul remarks of *Time Without Pity* that 'this fevered film is a protest about the malaises of contemporary society'. It is true that Losey's films of this decade were sharply critical of British social institutions – one will see it also in the exposure of the 'old boy' network of the police in *Blind Date*, or the paralysing hierarchy of prison life in *The Criminal* that duplicates all that is wrong in the outside world. And certainly this film lays bare quite a number of contemporary malaises, which range from legalised execution, to irresponsible parenting, to a destructive combination of puritanism (Ann Todd) and philistinism (Leo McKern) that makes for a highly combustible marriage of elements in the English temperament. But what Sadoul calls the film's 'feverishness' is even more noticeable than the social criticism: it is as if Losey is making an Audenesque comment about a country in which nobody is well. A Goya bull looms in the background as McKern commits his murder of frustration; Tristram Cary's music comes in strident surges rather than unobtrusive accompaniment; and Redgrave's agitated gestures add up to a lexicon of his own guilt and failure, whether he be fiddling with a cat's cradle that reminds him of his son's imminent noose or thrusting away a drink with the jerky movement of a man who has just come into contact with vermin. If Losey has an edge on his English rivals of the time, it is precisely through this edginess, which gives the films their unusual visual attack and emotional energy.

Edgardo Cozarinski has a wonderful phrase for the core relationships in Losey's films: in his essay in Richard Roud's dictionary of cinema he calls them 'highly charged love–hate duets'. One can certainly feel this charge in the battle for masculine supremacy which takes place in the duets of Bogarde and Knox in *Sleeping Tiger*, Redgrave and McKern in *Time Without Pity*, Stanley Baker and Hardy Kruger in *Blind Date*, Bogarde and Fox in *The*

Servant: in all cases, the struggle for territorial advantage, physical and psychological, seems a working out of complex feelings of kinship as well as conflict. This is even true of Losey's short film *Man on the Beach* (1955), where the encounter between a transvestite criminal on the run (Michael Medwin) and a reclusive doctor (Donald Wolfit) who is only gradually revealed to be blind seems an odd anticipation of early Pinter in its depiction of tense male confrontations. The heterosexual relationships seem even more tortured. It is quite remarkable in these films how often the lovers resort to physical violence with each other, as if it is only through manifestations of anger that love can be recognised or released: an attempted blow is often abruptly followed by a passionate kiss. This is reversed in one of the most famous moments of *The Servant*, when, at the orgy near the end, Wendy Craig kisses the servant who has systematically humiliated her, but then, in a last act of defiance as he is showing her to the door, lashes him across the face. What is going on here? Is this commingling of love and hate some expression of fear – of loss of power, identity? Of being in thrall to another, in a shameful form of servility? Losey seems to have been working out here a very personal and private attitude to relationships, which he alluded to in a desolate comment to Tom Milne, in his book-length interview with him, when he identified a key theme in his work as 'the particular destruction and anguish and waste of most sexual relationships'. Whatever the cause of it, there was not another film-maker around in England at that time whose characters went through such emotional turmoil. It reaches its climax perhaps at the end of *The Gypsy and the Gentleman* (which, with its critique of the gentry and its inverted power relationships, seems more than ever like a fancy-dress rehearsal of *The Servant*), when the aristocrat, who has first rescued the gypsy from drowning, drags her down to the depths with him when he realises she wants to run off with her lover: the impulses of love and hate there murderously intertwined.

Blind Date offered something of a generic departure for Losey: the opportunity to make a British *film noir*. Classically, the story is told mostly in flashback, a journey into a past dominated by a deadly female, and the action hinges around a criminal investigation. In the tension it generates between the three main characters – the vulnerable artist-hero, the promiscuous and irresistible heroine and the stern incorruptible investigator – the structure is similar to the Billy Wilder classic *Double Indemnity* (1944). Losey gives it a British inflection through the emphasis on class. Whereas the American *film noir* often took the form of a covert, subversive attack on capitalism, the British variety – as in Robert Hamer's 1940s masterpieces *It Always Rains on Sundays* (1947) and *Kind Hearts and Coronets* (1949) – more often exposed the inequities of the class system and proposed a sinister connection between influence and corruption, wealth and depravity. Losey spoke to James Leahy of 'the degree to which the English class structure influences every Englishman's life, either in rebellion against it or acceptance of it, or simply through their being gotten at by it without realizing it, and sometimes whilst protesting that they're not'. In *Blind Date* the Inspector instinctively sympathises with the murder suspect because both seem at the mercy of the moneyed classes. Kruger is easily seduced by the elegant socialite and is framed, it seems, for her murder. Baker is hampered in his handling of the case by being instructed not to involve a highly respected and prosperous VIP who was dubiously associated with the murdered woman. 'I wanted to see what the soap smelt like,' explains Kruger when Baker asked why he washed his hands in the dead woman's flat. 'My father was a chauffeur,' says Baker when asked why he is so adept at distinguishing the givers from the takers. Both responses are very revealing about the social class and instincts of the two characters. The film's acute awareness of class tensions help disguise the occasional illogicality and awkwardness of the plot. Its expressiveness is on the level of style more than overt content: in its typical sensitivity to decor and to structural opposites; in the contrasting sets of the artist's studio and the woman's flat, which reveal so much about the personalities who occupy them; in the use of light and dark, as murky deceptions are brought out into the open. A cynical, social man (Baker) and an idealistic artistic one (Kruger) are brought into contact, as hunter and hunted, respectively, and discover a mysterious bond. Losey may have thought there was a message for him in that: a reconciliation between the cynic and the idealist, the realist and the artist.

His next two British films prior to *The Servant*, *The Criminal* (1960) and *The Damned* (1961), fall slightly outside the time-frame of this chapter; and as the films have been finely analysed by Robin Wood and by Paul Mayersberg, I will deal with them only briefly here. Suffice it to say, then, that *The Criminal* is arguably the finest prison drama made in Britain and that *The Damned* is one of the most distinguished examples of that offbeat and relatively neglected genre of the British cinema, the science fiction film. In the case of *The Damned*, a film that begins with curious anticipations of *A Clockwork Orange*, with its violent gangs and intimidatingly symbolic sculptures, surpasses even that film for future shock when it develops into an allegory of the nuclear age. The ending is particularly haunting as irradiated children, who for a scientific experiment are being schooled for assimilation into a post-atomic world, are heard crying for help in a heedless universe, and a hero and heroine, who have attempted to liberate them, are now dying from contamination at their touch. *The Criminal* is similarly remarkable for its uncovering of the vulnerability beneath Stanley Baker's tough-guy image; for an extraordinary ending as a dying Baker gasps for absolution whilst his criminal cohorts slither around the frozen ground in an undignified scramble for the buried money; and for an incisive vision of a penal system where authority seems either sadistic or ineffectually liberal, which only perpetuates the endless cycle of crime and retribution. This vision is clinched by a final aerial shot of the prisoners exercising in the prison yard by just jogging around in a circle. This motif, incidentally, has an intriguing similarity to one in *The Intimate Stranger* in which Losey at one stage lingers noticeably on a shot of an empty spinning chair, and the blackmailing actress says that 'you go around in circles and either you break the circle or the circle breaks you'. Breaking the circle: there is a sense in which Losey in his films seems to see society as an endless repetition of hypocrisy and deceit, of destructive circles (the noose in *Time Without Pity* being perhaps the most extreme example) that can only be broken by an act of will from the inside or by an outsider's clear and critical perception of the way these circles strangle development. It might even have been a perception Losey had of his own development in the 1950s, which seemed to be going nowhere until critical recognition (notably the French response to *The Criminal*) ignited his career and the artistry of *The Servant* clinched his status.

By 1963 I think Losey had established for himself an unusual position in British film culture of some symbolic importance and one that no other English director at the time could precisely match. In one way, his career was symptomatic of certain fundamental flaws in the industry. Because of his experience with Hammer studios and their tawdry, delayed release of *The Damned*, and because of his difficulties with Rank and their obstructiveness on *The Gypsy and the Gentleman*, Losey was that classic victim figure: an artist among philistines, whose misunderstood genius was being mangled by the money men. He seemed, if you like, the British cinema's Orson Welles; and, like Welles, a director unusually articulate in interviews in giving his version of the way his vision had been compromised by petty commercialism. At the same time, however, the critics of *Movie* magazine, examining what they called 'the case of Joseph Losey', were finding something different. If most British films of the time were dully written and directed, Losey, by contrast, was an example of someone who could transcend the mediocrities of a screenplay and studio limitations through sheer talent: the evidence was films like *Time Without Pity*, *Blind Date* and *The Criminal*, which could stand comparison with films being made anywhere. After all, ideal conditions were not necessarily guarantors of great art: John Huston had said that some of his worst films were made when he had most freedom. For *Movie*, what Losey had in abundance was something was almost entirely lacking elsewhere in British cinema of that time: namely, passion and style. The material was thus transformed through the intelligence and involvement he brought to it and through a style that was a vital dimension of that involvement, whether it manifested itself in visual bravura (like the kaleidoscope shot that introduces the Jill Bennett character in *The Criminal* and immediately suggests the woman's fractured personality) or even in Losey's stated dislike of dissolves, which seemed consistent with the edgy lucidity of his work. In the critical parlance of the time, Losey was the one auteur of the British cinema.

Of course, not everyone would have agreed with the *Movie* assessment of British film at this time, though it was undoubtedly influential. Nevertheless, in a period when cinema was entering what I would call its modernist phase and releasing an explosion of artistically challenging work from, for example, Antonioni, Resnais, Godard, Fellini, Buñuel and Visconti, it was clear that, for the critical intelligentsia in Britain, Losey seemed the only director who was capable of producing comparable work. Evidence of that attitude could be seen in the proliferation of critical monographs on directors that came out in the 1960s, as a result, no doubt, of the growth of film studies as an academic subject and the influence of the auteur theory. Two appeared in quick succession on Losey, by Tom Milne and by James Leahy; no other British director had that kind of representation. On the contrary, at this stage British cinema was struggling for critical and intellectual recognition. The perception was that Lean had gone Hollywood; Powell had gone bad, or mad; Reed and Hamer seemed in permanent decline, while Mackendrick had emigrated; and the New Wave lot were too literary. It was left to Losey to carry the artistic torch.

Today one would want to query that wholesale negative assessment of British film of the 1950s and 1960s, but, however one argues it, the figure of Losey will always loom large in the debate. The early English phase was a key stage in his career, just as the contribution he made to British film was invaluable. He was not easily assimilated, but he became one of the most fascinating film observers of the English scene. To be frivolous about it, there is not a better shot of someone pouring tea in the entire British cinema than in Losey's *Accident* (1967), nor can I think of any other film-maker who could have directed with such precision and sympathy Barry Foster's inflection of the line, 'He brewed a damn good cup of tea' in *King and Country* (1964), his character's poignant testimonial to a man about to be executed for an act of wartime cowardice.

As we began with him, perhaps Dirk Bogarde should be given the last word – or, more precisely, the last quotations. They give a flavour of what Losey meant to British film and the massive development he himself underwent while he was here. During the 1950s, after his exhilarating experience of working with him on *The Sleeping Tiger*, Bogarde had used his influence at Rank to land Losey a contract. It was not a happy association, because, as Bogarde put it, 'Joe was highly suspect because he was unknown and an intellectual, which absolutely terrifies them.' Nevertheless, through the association with actors like Bogarde and Baker, and writers like Pinter, and because of the foundation he had established with his 1950s films and the critical support they generated, Losey's intellect did find expression in British film. It is at its finest, I think, in *The Servant*, *King and Country*, *Accident* and *The Go-Between* (1970). These are at the core of Losey's achievement and, in my view, among the glories of British film. 'I'm passionately English, but sometimes I don't like the English,' Bogarde told Margaret Hinxman in the *Sunday Telegraph* (22 February 1970): 'They seem to resent success. I've never said this before, because it sounds so pompous. But I will say it now. When Joe Losey and I made those terribly difficult films which no British companies wanted to touch, we were doing it for Britain. We honestly wanted to make British cinema important, to lift it out of the domestic rut. And I think we did.'

Note

For this essay I have used: Dirk Bogarde, *Snakes and Ladders* (Chatto & Windus, 1975); David Caute, *Joseph Losey: A Revenge on Life* (Faber & Faber, 1994); Michel Ciment, *Conversations with Losey* (Methuen, 1985); Edith De Rhan, *Joseph Losey* (André Deutsch, 1991); Penelope Houston, *The Contemporary Cinema* (Penguin, 1963); James Leahy, *The Cinema of Joseph Losey* (Tantivy Press, 1967); Joseph Losey, 'The Monkey on My Back', *Films and Filming* (October 1963); Paul Mayersberg, *Movie* (May 1963): Tom Milne (ed.), *Losey on Losey* (Secker & Warburg, 1967); Richard Roud, *Cinema: A Critical Dictionary*, Volume 2 (Secker & Warburg, 1980); Robin Wood, 'Losey', *Motion* (February 1963).

Painfully squalid?

Women of Twilight

KERRY KIDD

WOMEN OF TWILIGHT (Daniel Angel, 1952) was adapted from the play of the same name by Sylvia Rayman. The play was first performed at the Embassy Theatre, London, in July 1951, going on to the Vaudeville Theatre. *Theatre World Annual* called the stage set 'painfully squalid' and many people would have applied the phrase to the piece as a whole. It might have been used, too, of J. Lee Thompson's *Yield to the Night* a few years later in 1956. It is a gritty and still shocking portrayal of the lives of those 'women of twilight' who, mostly as a consequence of unmarried pregnancy, find themselves shunned by respectable society, unable to find homes and prey to exploitation by 'baby-farmers' and unscrupulous land-lords. A melodramatic opening finds pregnant Viviane (*sic*) (Renée Ray) searching for accommodation after her boyfriend Jerry (a cocktail of macho aggression and petulant vulnerability created by Laurence Harvey) is arrested for murder. Repeatedly recognised and rejected by landladies, Viviane eventually sees and answers the advertisement 'Room To Let, No. 4 Albion Road, No References Required'. It turns out to be a boarding-house for unmarried mothers, run by unscrupulous and tyrannical landlady Helen Allistair (Freda Jackson). Squalid and overcrowded, it nonetheless functions for Viviane as an anonymous place of sanctuary, where she can temporarily conceal herself from the prying gaze of the outside world. Whilst she is there, Jerry is sentenced to death and executed. Initially, her despair at losing him means that she is lost in her own misery and able to ignore the blatant exploitation surrounding her. Less fortunate is Christine (Lois Maxwell), who arrives for what she hopes will be 'just one night' and is horror-struck at the conditions in which she is forced to live. As the incidents of brutality and neglect increase, Rosie's (Joan Dowling) baby is announced by the

I was a graduate student in the English Literature Department at Sheffield University in 2001 where I completed a doctoral thesis on the Royal Court Theatre and British culture in the late 1950s and early 1960s. I have been actively involved in theatre work, in Africa and in Britain. I am currently working on a research project at Nottingham University on the effects of TV on its audiences. *Kerry Kidd*

'clinic' to be suffering from malnutrition, and Mrs Allistair tries to make Viviane sell both her story and her child, revealing herself as an illegal baby-farmer. (She also confiscates her bracelet, a present from Jerry and symbol of her earlier happiness.) Next Mrs Allistair is instrumental in the death of Christine's child, whom Christine has left in Viviane's care: Mrs Allistair refuses to call a doctor, the baby slips into a coma and dies in Viviane's arms, just after Christine has returned. Gradually, these events awaken Viviane from her grief and she comes to protest repeatedly against this exploitative rule. Mrs Allistair blames Viviane for the baby's death, accusing her of neglect. Incensed, Viviane threatens to report Mrs Allistair to the authorities, but is prevented by Allistair's reminder that, as a criminal associate, she is unlikely to be believed. Shortly afterwards she hears a rumour that Allistair has not only farmed babies, but killed them: she confronts Allistair with the truth, and when Mrs Allistair sees she will not be bullied into silence any longer, she pushes Viviane down the stairs and leaves her for dead. However, Viviane is saved by one of the other girls, returning early from an evening outing; she survives, a nurse caring for her hears her story and in the last minutes of the film Mrs Allistair is arrested. Meanwhile, Christine's boyfriend has returned and married her. Unable to have children of her own, she adopts Viviane's child. The film ends with the baby in Christine's arms, reclaimed for respectability, while Viviane lies pallid but smiling on the bed.

The title of both play and film is doubly apt. *Women of Twilight* hovers uneasily in the twilight areas of post-war British society, but also in the grey area between two sets of competing and unresolved moralities. On the one hand, it has a liberal and progressive agenda, depicting criminality sympathetically, attempting to present a realistic and unsentimental view of contemporary Britain, and critical of the suffering imposed on young girls by society's attempt to preserve respectability at all costs. One of the more poignant touches is the moment where Sally (Dorothy Gordon) complains wistfully, 'I'm sure Daddy wouldn't let me stay here if he knew', the obvious point being that, having been cast out, Daddy neither knows nor cares how she lives. *Women of Twilight* thus accuses contemporary Britain of negligence, and lays the blame for these girls' suffering at the door of the contemporary social prejudice and hypocrisy which leaves them with nowhere else to go.

On the other hand, in both form and theme the film is consciously melodramatic, casting Helen Allistair as the villain of the piece whose abuse and exploitation are eventually appropriately punished. As a consequence the film clearly and honestly depicts contemporary abuses, but seems unsure whether to blame respectable social prejudice, more simplistic caricatures of villainy or even, implicitly, the sexual behaviour of the girls themselves.

This implication was deliberately strengthened by the censorship authorities. In its textual interventions on the play text, the Lord Chamberlain's office came firmly down on the side of respectability and a sternly moralistic interpretation, demanding that the bleak line 'There is nothing wrong in being raped' be removed. In preparing the film, the British Board of Film Classifications made similar requests. Of particular note is the insistence that the phrases 'I was raped' and 'I would never have let it go so far' be cut. (See Tony Aldgate's '*Women of Twilight, Cosh Boy* and the Advent of the X Certificate' in the *Journal of Popular British Cinema* for March 2000.) Such omissions suggest a strong desire on the part of both censorship bodies to simplify the women's plight, and render it more compatible with conceptions of unmarried motherhood as bad. For all her obvious sympathy with the plight of such vulnerable women, Rayman's original script also implies a degree of agreement with the moralistic view. This is best seen in the startlingly saccharine ending, where Viviane is unproblematically delighted to give up her child for the chance that it may grow up respectable and herself accuses her child of bearing potentially criminal genes, suggesting an attempt to reclaim the film for a respectable moral agenda and audience. This ending restores the morality of marriage and marks the final stages of Viviane's 'redemption' from social alienation and personal despair.

This despair is marked in the film by repeated visual reference to the iconography of imprisonment. We are never shown Jerry's prison cell, only his meetings with Viviane; but their moving final conversation through a glass window is echoed on the morning of his death, when Viviane looks out of the boarding-house window and the shadow of bars falls across her chest. Similarly, on Christine's first night in the house, when Viviane tells her she won't be able to get out and had better get used to the place, the light is switched out and shadows of prison bars fall across the bed. Most of the film is shot indoors, reinforcing the claustrophobic sensation of being caged in.

Nor is the final escape all that it seems. The inescapable plight of these 'twilight women', and the prison-like atmosphere in which they live, is reinforced in the final frame of the film as the camera cuts from Christine's verve and energy to the sickly Viviane's face on a white sheet. No longer confined by shadowy bars, Viviane nonetheless appears critically weakened. Unlike Christine, who can be rescued by marriage, she is only able to escape the 'twilight' of despair and alienation by renunciation. The central ambiguities of the film are emphasised in this final frame as she twists Jerry's bracelet, evocative of both happiness and grief. The giving away of her child has been presented as 'redeeming' her; but as she lies on the pillow, her stillness and pallor suggest that it is a kind of death, too.

Yield to the Night

MELANIE WILLIAMS

J EAN-LUC GODARD once remarked that all you need to make a film is 'a girl and a gun' and the opening sequence of *Yield to the Night* (J. Lee Thompson, 1956) looks like a textbook illustration of his axiom. The girl is Mary Hilton, played by Diana Dors, who whips out the gun from her handbag and promptly shoots the woman she holds responsible for her lover's suicide. As a result, she finds herself convicted for murder and sentenced to death. Most of the film's action takes place in Mary's condemned cell as she waits to hear if her appeal has been successful and relives her doomed love affair with Jim (Michael Craig) that led to her *crime passionel* and her arrest. The film, unusually, does not have a happy ending: there is no last-minute reprieve for Mary. The film concludes as she is led away to the gallows.

Yield to the Night is often mentioned in connection with the contemporary case of Ruth Ellis, the last woman to be hanged in Britain. Although the film's scenario has a number of similarities to the Ellis case (a glamorous blonde murderess, a shooting), it is not, as is sometimes stated, based on it. The screenplay had been written two years before, and the film's appearance in the wake of Ellis's execution was coincidental. Nonetheless, this was a film that sought to enter the contemporary public debate on hanging, and to argue the abolitionist case to as many people as possible, through the medium of popular commercial cinema. What is particularly interesting about *Yield to the Night* is that it does not deal with a miscarriage of justice, like the later American anti-hanging film *I Want to Live!* (Robert Wise, 1958). Mary Hilton is definitely guilty of her crime but the film still maintains that it is wrong for the state to hang her. To make a clear case against capital

I teach film studies at the University of Hull. I have written on British film for the *Quarterly Review of Film and Video*, the *Journal of Popular British Cinema* and the *Journal of Gender Studies* and I am currently completing a doctorate on the representation of women in the 1950s films of J. Lee Thompson. This interest sprang from spending countless afternoons watching the Channel 4 matinee when I should have been doing something more constructive with my time. I also harbour a secret crush on Stanley Baker, especially in *Hell Drivers*. *Melanie Williams*

punishment, director J. Lee Thompson argued that 'you must take somebody who deserves to die, and then feel sorry for them and say this is wrong'.

However, the film is far from being a straightforward statement of social protest on the part of its makers, which is partly due to the casting of Diana Dors, a notorious and flamboyant British film personality of the 1950s, in the role of Mary Hilton. Hailed as the only sex symbol Britain has produced since Lady Godiva, Diana Dors was a precocious teenager who had made her first film appearance at the age of 15 as a spiv's mistress in *The Shop at Sly Corner* (George King, 1946). By 1954, questions were asked in the House of Commons about her excessive consumerism (her most notable extravagance being a powder-blue Cadillac), and in 1955 she glided down the grand canal in Venice wearing only a made-to-measure mink bikini (Dors later admitted it was actually made from rabbit fur) as a film festival publicity stunt. And yet, the very next year, here was Britain's glitziest star discarding the persona of the glamorous starlet in favour of the serious actress, willing to swap mink for dowdy prison uniform and to let her immaculately dyed platinum hair grow out to show its dark roots for the role. This aspect of the film was one that fascinated the critics of the time, whose reviews of *Yield to the Night* are peppered with remarks about the change in her appearance, threatening to overshadow the ostensible point of the film, the plea for the abolition of hanging.

The style adopted by J. Lee Thompson to tell this story is also significant. Although he sought the greatest verisimilitude in the depiction of the condemned cell and what goes on in it, the film eschews the documentary-style realism that might be seen as the natural companion of this kind of attention to detail. Instead, Thompson opts for a melodramatic, expressionistic film style which makes use of oblique angles, strange compositions and unnerving extreme close-ups, all of which dislocate the film from any simple 'realist' aesthetic. The realism of the film is a subjective, psychological realism, suggesting the strange and fearful state of mind of the person who knows she will die in a matter of days.

In fact, what gives *Yield to the Night* its emotional force is how the monumental melodrama of Mary, having to face her imminent death, is played out against a backdrop of banal reality and bureaucratic ritual. The film gives a strong feeling of the absurdity of Mary's situation: the friendly inconsequential chit-chat with the prison wardens who teach her to play chess, change the dressing on her blister and make sure she is well fed when the same women will lead her to her death in less than a week. It is the cinematic equivalent of George Orwell's famous essay on witnessing a hanging where it is not until he sees the condemned man, on the way to the gallows, walk around a puddle to avoid getting his feet wet, a tiny inconsequential moment of futility, that Orwell realises the immensity of what is about to happen.

When there was a parliamentary bill to abolish the death penalty in the House of Lords, Gerald Gardiner QC and Arthur Koestler organised a special screening of *Yield to the Night*. Only six of the invited peers came along. The bill was defeated and capital punishment was not repealed until 1965. The film, despite its aim to be commercial, was a box-office flop. As an attempt to intervene in the debate on hanging, *Yield to the Night* might be judged a failure. But as the high point of both Dors's and Thompson's respective careers, by their own admission, and a brave attempt to tackle a pressing social issue, it remains one of the most interesting British films of the decade.

From script to screen: *Serious Charge* and film censorship

TONY ALDGATE

In May 1950 the Wheare Committee recommended that a new 'X' category be introduced and applied to films intended for exhibition to 'adults only'. By January 1951, the British Board of Film Censors (BBFC) agreed to the implementation of an 'X' certificate which limited the cinema-going audience to those over 16 years of age. 'It is our desire', said the BBFC secretary, Arthur Watkins, 'that "X" films should not be merely sordid films dealing with unpleasant subjects, but films which, while not being suitable for children, are good adult entertainment and films which appeal to an intelligent public.'

The difficulties in defining 'good adult entertainment' soon became apparent when, on 5 January 1955, director Ronald Neame informed the British Film Producers Association that he felt 'the "X" certificate was no longer serving the purpose for which it was intended'. 'The British Board of Film Censors had stated at the outset that it was intended to encourage the production of films for adult audiences,' he argued; 'in fact, however, the "X" certificate was being wrongly exploited and was assisting considerably wider distribution of Continental films in this country than might otherwise be possible whilst, at the same time, attempts by British producers to make films suitable for adult audiences had, more often than not, failed.'[1]

The problems encountered by the BBFC and the film-makers in this instance are indicative of the problems that obtained throughout the 1950s with the 'X' certificate and British cinema at large. But the story of British film censorship during the period is also inextricably linked with the system of censorship operated by the Lord Chamberlain over stage productions and

I am Reader in Film and History at The Open University. My numerous publications on British cinema history include *Cinema and History* (Scolar Press, 1979) and *Censorship and the Permissive Society: British Cinema and Theatre: 1955–1965* (Clarendon Press, 1995). I have also written, with Jeffrey Richards, *Best of British: Cinema and Society from 1930 to the Present* (I.B. Tauris, 2nd edn, 1999) and *Britain Can Take It: The British Cinema in the Second World War* (Edinburgh University Press, 2nd edn, 1995). *Tony Aldgate*

the theatre. Both the BBFC and the Lord Chamberlain's Office employed a process of censorship which depended as much on the application of pre-production scrutiny as it did on post-production review. Moreover, both regularly informed each other of their respective activities and followed a policy of 'keeping in step'. Nowhere is this more evident than in the case of Terence Young's 1959 film, *Serious Charge*.

The genesis of this film lay in Philip King's play of the same name which was first presented for consideration to the Lord Chamberlain's Office in March 1953 with an anticipated presentation date of November that year. In time-honoured fashion, one of the Lord Chamberlain's readers, Charles Heriot, began his report of 16 March with a synopsis of the play's essential plot and story line.[2]

Howard Phillips is a 30-year-old vicar in a village. He is unmarried, lives with his mother, has a flair for interior decoration and rather too obviously repulses the advances of a spinster, Hester Byfield, who is thereafter too liable to believe anything about the parson. A village girl, pregnant by the local bad lad, comes to the vicar for advice and on her way out sees his maid in the arms of her seducer. She flings herself under a car and is killed. The vicar has discovered that Larry Thompson is the man and sends for him to tell him he is morally guilty of the girl's death and to warn him to mend his ways. Larry is thoroughly rotten – the vicar has also discovered him to be a thief and has thrown him out of the choir for 'talking smut' – and, when he hears a ring at the front door, shouts for help and smashes ornaments and furniture. When the visitor enters – it is Hester – he accuses the vicar of trying to make a pass at him. Hester is horrified and disgusted; she is also a gossip. The mischief is done. The village hounds its vicar and matters are reaching a point at which he must leave when Larry visits Hester to brief her about what she may have to say. Unfortunately he cannot keep his fingers out of her cash box. She sees him and in the ensuing row realises that he has lied. He tries to silence her and she defends herself with a pair of scissors. She tries to summon the vicar by telephone but only manages to stammer out a broken phrase before Larry closes with her. The scissors pierce her breast and she staggers out of the room. Larry thinks he has murdered her and collapses. Then the vicar arrives and everything is duly disentangled. Hester is not dead and is able to testify against the unspeakable Larry and save the vicar's reputation.

Interestingly, given its subject matter, Heriot thought the play 'strong and sensible'. 'We are in no doubt at any time that the vicar is innocent of the "serious charge",' he commented, and 'therefore, though the forbidden topic of homosexuality shadows this play, it does so in an inoffensive manner.' 'In my opinion,' Heriot concluded, 'the play is recommended for licence.' To be sure of his ground, however, he marked the controversial passages in the play and sent it on to the Lord Chamberlain and his comptrollers for further scrutiny. By no means all the theatre examiners agreed with Heriot's judgment.

'How can you pass this if we are to be at all consistent?' asked Brigadier Sir Norman Gwatkin, the Lord Chamberlain's assistant comptroller. 'But I am being consistent,' Heriot responded. 'Here there is no suggestion of real homosexuality – it is all lies.' Gwatkin, adamant in his own conviction that the play transgressed the bounds of propriety, replied: 'This is where we want the Solomon touch.' And he duly passed all comments on to the Lord Chamberlain himself, Lord Scarbrough, for final consideration. Scarbrough sensibly played both ends towards the middle. 'I am not convinced by the retort that because the accusation was untrue no question of propriety can arise,' he argued, 'but neither am I convinced that the relevant part of the play should be cut out or altered.' 'Though it is conceivable that some embarrassment might be caused,' Scarbrough concluded, 'I think on the whole no great harm will be done and that the play should be licensed.'

Serious Charge was licensed, indeed, and proceeded into production. It opened at the Adelphi Theatre on 8 November 1953 where it was presented by the Repertory Players, with Nigel Stock in the role of Howard Phillips and Alec McCowan as Larry Thompson, and produced by Joan Kemp-Welch. This was a trial run, in effect, but in view of the favourable critical response the play received, not least from W.A. Darlington in the *Daily Telegraph* (9 November 1953), *Serious Charge* was given a full-scale professional production at the Garrick Theatre from 17 February 1955 where it was directed by Martin Landau and starred Patrick McGoohan.[3]

Even as the play was enjoying the first fruits of its 1955 London run, a film producer expressed interest in transposing it from stage to screen. Such interest was inevitable, of course. The West End theatre was a rich and regular source of supply for British films throughout the 1950s, as ever with British cinema. And, in this instance, it was John Woolf of Romulus Films who was most keen to adapt Philip King's *Serious Charge* for the screen. Within a month of the play's opening, Woolf sent a copy of the script to the secretary of the British Board of Film Censors, Arthur Watkins, with a view to ascertaining whether it would pass pre-production scrutiny or stand much chance of progressing easily into production as a film. 'It would be our intention to use the services of a distinguished director,' he assured Watkins on 17 March 1955, 'and not in any way to sensationalize it.' 'I naturally realize it would fall into the "X" category,' Woolf maintained, 'but think it such a powerful play that it would be worth taking the risk.'[4]

The BBFC moved into action immediately. No less than two film examiners were dispatched by Arthur Watkins to watch the Garrick Theatre production. Clearly, pre-production scrutiny by the British Board of Film Censors entailed extensive theatrical 'vetting', as well as the reading of play scripts, when it was deemed necessary. In this instance, however, it was to little avail. The BBFC examiners were not best pleased with the stage production of *Serious Charge* – nor, especially, the likelihood of a film arising from it. They had 'strong misgivings' about the whole project and were 'agreed in thinking the central incident (which is essential to the story) intolerable for "A" and very undesirable for "X"'. 'It will make it very nearly impossible to reject other films of a melodramatic kind which flirt with the topic of homosexuality,' they stated, 'and we think this unsavoury flirting is just as bad as depicting a real homosexual on the screen.' Though the examiners recognised the play had already been licensed for the stage, in short, they drew a line of divide between what might be tolerated for a small band of theatre-goers and what should be allowed for the mass of cinema-goers. 'We do not believe the Lord Chamberlain himself would think the story fit for the mixed and immature provincial cinema audience which would see even an "X" film,' was their considered if jaundiced and distinctly elitist reaction. It was a revealing remark.

Unsurprisingly, Arthur Watkins at the BBFC proceeded to tell producer John Woolf that 'under no circumstances could any film based on this play be placed in any other than the "X" category' and that 'we are not prepared to commit ourselves even to an "X" category without further consideration [of a screenplay]'. Given, however, that *Serious Charge* had plainly caused much controversy within his examiners' ranks, no less a person than the president of the British Board of Film Censors, Sir Sidney Harris, went along to see the play for himself. His judgments on reading the play script alone then watching the stage production make an illuminating contrast. On 21 March 1955, for instance, he stated:

> I am rather surprised that this squalid melodrama was thought worthy of presentation on the stage, and it might be worth while to find out from the Lord Chamberlain whether he received any complaints. It would make a very unpleasant film and one liable to sensational exploitation. For the reasons given by the examiners I think we should have nothing to do with it. The 'X' certificate would only exclude persons under sixteen and the greatest risk of damage would be to persons of sixteen and seventeen who form a large part of the average cinema audience. Incidentally, I dislike the picture of the country vicarage with the worldly mother and the ineffective vicar whose method of dealing with Larry is so unwise. We see many films in which Roman Catholic priests appear as dignified and spiritually-minded persons. Why should the British film depict

Anglican clergymen either as figures of fun or of incompetence? This is not entirely irrelevant to censorship.

But on 24 March 1955, by comparison, after viewing the stage presentation of *Serious Charge* Harris felt compelled to revise his initially hostile opinion:

> I saw this play yesterday afternoon and I must allow that I was pleasantly surprised. I found little to complain about. It is admittedly a rather squalid story, but this aspect of it is largely forgotten in the tautness of the play and the good acting. It remains, in my view, melodrama rather than a serious social problem play, though towards the end it does become rather more serious. It might have been a better play if the author had not overdrawn (in particular) the character of Hester Byfield. The whole moral of the play is good and if we are to have a film on such a subject, we might do very much worse. The main trouble is that once we allow this topic we may find it rather a slippery slope, but I do not see how we can possibly refuse this story for the 'X' category.

Having been prompted by Harris to find out what the Lord Chamberlain's Office had thought of the stage play, moreover, Watkins reported back the fruits of a discussion with Sir Norman Gwatkin on 28 March 1955:

> He told me that they had received one or two individual letters of complaint about the play since its opening at the Garrick Theatre. They were on the lines of the individual playgoer having been 'embarrassed' at the introduction of the subject of homosexuality into the theatre. Sir Norman added that, in his own personal view, his department had made a mistake in licensing the play and he was opposed to the decision. He remained of the view that it would be better to keep this subject out of plays altogether. He confirmed that the decision to pass the play was based on the fact that no character in the play was actually a pervert and no more than an unfounded charge was involved. At the end of our talk, he confirmed that although some letters had been received, there had been no serious volume of complaint.

None of this was communicated to John Woolf, needless to say, who returned on 28 March 1955 to tell Watkins that he was now set upon purchasing the rights of the play and would submit a film script in due course while reiterating, for good measure, that 'it is not our intention in any way to sensationalize the subject any more than it is in the play'. The screenplay that was tendered finally for BBFC consideration almost four months later, on 23 August 1955, did as much as the producer promised and more besides. It had dispensed entirely with the original 'serious charge' at the heart of Philip King's controversial play and even Woolf was inclined to describe it in correspondence with Watkins as an 'emasculated' version 'which I am sure will please you'. Plainly, despite Woolf's protestations throughout that he would be only too happy to see the film in the 'X' category, given its adult themes and nature, at the last he was making a desperate attempt with the changes to see whether it might not yet be allowed for an 'A'-certificate rating.

'The curse has been removed,' commented one BBFC reader of the screenplay: 'It is now a girl (Dora), not a boy, who accuses the vicar of trying to interfere with her.' 'I really think the story has lost nothing of value in losing the homosexual element,' the reader continued. 'The "emasculated version" in fact does "please me" (see Mr. Woolf's covering letter) and I really don't care how silly he thinks us to want the change as long as he sticks to the present version and makes the change.' Not that everything was acceptable in the new script as it stood. Profound misgivings were expressed about the fact that the girl was just 17 years of age and only two years out of school. And fears were evident about the proposed ending to the film which all readers felt should be changed yet again: 'We are told that Dora is to "get her deserts", so presumably the lorry driver episode will go (our point would not be satisfactorily met by Dora being raped and killed by the lorry driver, in case that should be what they have in mind).' 'But we are so well out of the homosexual element,' it was noted, 'that it would be a mistake to be too captious.'

Sir Sidney Harris, for his part, felt that something had been lost in the adaptation and was intent still upon further fostering the projected image of the vicar as a salutary and commendable figure, as he pointed out to Watkins on 7 September 1955:

> I agree generally but we seem to have got rid of our main preoccupation by exchanging it for a grubby story which can only be saved by good acting. In particular, it would be wise to stress the importance of presenting the vicar as fine character facing a squalid situation in a dignified and manly way. I agree as to the complete revision of the last ten pages. If we are to contemplate an 'A' certificate we should meet *all* the points made by the two examiners and yourself.

In the event, no more work was needed for John Woolf's purposes since he proceeded to withdraw from the project. The reasons why he did so are difficult to fathom with any degree of certainty. Perhaps he tired of the BBFC's continuing vacillations; perhaps he felt that the 'emasculated' version had gone too far down the path, anyway, of selling out on an otherwise laudable idea for a screenplay; or, maybe, he encountered problems in negotiating the rights on King's play.

Whatever the deciding factor as far as Woolf was concerned, the film censors had not heard the last of *Serious Charge*. It resurfaced again exactly three years later in the hands of Mickey Delamar of Alva Films. Much had changed during the intervening period in the fabric of British society, of course, not least with regard to its burgeoning youth culture. Delamar consciously sought to appeal to that quarter and, much to the film censors' consternation, reverted to Philip King's story line for the inspiration of the screenplay he tendered to the BBFC early in September 1958. 'The story point is the same as in the original stage play,' noted one script reader on 8 September, 'i.e., it depends on a charge of indecent assault by the vicar upon a youth.' But other matters were noted besides:

> The only important divergence from the stage play is that in the film script the vicar's mother persuades the frustrated Hester to trap Larry into damaging admissions by vamping him and then staging a struggle which is interrupted by the vicar, Larry's father and other witnesses arriving just as Larry is protesting that the scene is a parallel to the trumped up business at the vicarage. The picture of small-town life is filled out by rather unedifying sidelights on the life and loves of Larry and other potential Teddy-boys and girls; and the script has been, on the whole, somewhat vulgarized; but the vulgarization of motion pictures intended for older teenagers has proceeded so fast in the past three years that it does not seem anything out of the way now.

John Trevelyan, who had taken on the position of BBFC secretary in July 1958, did not like the script at all and made that very clear. 'I do not consider the play as a serious exploration of a serious problem,' he stated: 'It is pure melodrama and should be treated as such. I think a good many adolescents will snigger at it, and it may, I suppose, give some of them an idea of how easy it is for them to do a bit of easy blackmail.' But he felt wedded in principle, at least, to extend to Delamar the same commitment to consider the project for the 'X' certificate that had been forthcoming to Woolf previously. Ironically, any homosexual connotations to the assault were now deemed less troublesome in prospect, always provided the film-makers for their part were willing to contemplate an 'X' as well. 'We have not yet accepted the theme of homosexuality for anything other than the "X" category,' Trevelyan told Delamar, 'and I see no likelihood of our changing our policy.' His parting words were reserved for repeated admonition, however, that 'from the angle of censorship it would be helpful if the vicar were shown as a thoroughly admirable person, effective at his job but landed through no fault of his own in a position of great difficulty'.

The problem for Delamar was that from the outset he was set upon securing an 'A' rating for his film and an 'X' would not do. Given, especially, that his intention was to cast the young British pop star Cliff Richard in the newly written part of Larry Thompson's brother, Curley, Delamar felt certain an 'X' certificate could only serve to deny him the guarantee of the idol's many teenage fans among audiences for his film. At the face-to-face meeting with Trevelyan which followed on 22 September 1958, producer Mickey Delamar and director Terence Young clearly did as much as they could to convince the BBFC of their willingness to compromise where necessary in order to achieve the desired result. As Trevelyan reported:

> We discussed the present script in some detail and I was told that this was only a preliminary script which Mr. Young intends to revise personally. He has in mind modelling the parson on the David Sheppard type and wants either Anthony Quayle or Peter Finch for the part. He is quite prepared to tone down the Teddy-boy hooliganism and erotic behaviour with girls, and he wants also to alter the part of Hester considerably since he feels that at present it is overdrawn. Furthermore he proposes to have a completely different ending in which the parson realizes that he must stay in the place because he is able to intervene successfully when one of the boys from his club is threatened with Borstal; indeed he wants to use this film to show what a live and forceful young parson can do with a boys' club.
>
> Both Mr. Young and Mr. Delamar realize that the nature of the 'serious charge' is a major difficulty, but they will consider whether it would not be possible to make the nature of the charge intelligible to the thinking adult and unintelligible to the child who knows nothing of such things. For instance, there might be the implication that the parson has physically attacked the boy rather than assaulted him sexually. All unnecessary emphasis on the nature of the charge … will be removed and the whole thing will be treated carefully and discreetly. I said that, in view of their proposed alterations, the only thing that really stood in the way of an 'A' certificate was the nature of the charge and that if this could be treated in a way that made it acceptable for the 'A' category so much the better, but I could not give any guarantee about it at this stage.

In the ensuing correspondence with Trevelyan, Delamar repeated that he was determined about making 'an intelligent adult film of quality' and that he was 'hoping to get your "blessing" for the "A" (as against the "horror and sex" we want to steer clear of)'. Yet in the final analysis, neither party was able fully to deliver on their promises, as became instantly apparent when a rough-cut version was delivered to the BBFC for viewing, on completion of production, in January 1959. Delamar had secured the services of both Cliff Richard and Anthony Quayle, and Andrew Ray for the part of Larry, as well as Sarah Churchill for Hester. But he had failed to resolve the screen depiction of the 'serious charge' to satisfaction and, moreover, his finished film now posed profound new problems for the censors besides.

Both the BBFC president and secretary, along with two more examiners, watched the rough cut of *Serious Charge* on 13 January 1959. They were convinced the film could only be considered for the 'X' category, after all, and even then cuts should have to be made. Lines of dialogue like 'A bunch of creeps and fairies' and 'Who are you calling fairies?' would have to be excised for a start. The scene in which Larry tried to rape Hester when she was seeking to frame him would require to be shortened. So, too, would an opening scene where Larry and the village girl he seduced were shown dressing after making love. 'We are inclined to think that this scene is in fact unnecessary since their relationship is well enough established later, and that it starts the film off on the wrong note.' Shots of the vicar being threatened by youths armed with a flick-knife and bicycle chain would need to be reduced. 'We want to keep flick-knives and bicycle-chains (and all such weapons) out of films as far as possible,' Trevelyan told Delamar, 'since we do not wish to encourage any extended use of things of this kind.' In particular, the censors were now distinctly worried about the introduction into the proceedings of a nude bathing scene in which teenage girls, especially, were seen 'naked to the waist'. These, certainly, had to be removed.

Some things were easily dealt with. The word 'fairy' was replaced by 'cissy' (sissy) on the two occasions in question, though Delamar regretted this could only be achieved at the expense of lack of lip-synchronization, 'I am afraid it is noticeable but that's our bad luck.' He also managed to shorten or eliminate the 'bicycle chain' shots. Three cuts were made to the nude-bathing sequence and he promised to further darken the grading of the final-release print being processed in the laboratories in order to lessen its impact. Most of all, however, Delamar was distraught that his film might still end up with an 'X' rating, as he told Trevelyan on 9 March 1959:

> Finally, I would like to mention that so far people in the Trade who have viewed the picture privately have been kind enough to congratulate me on making a sincere and intelligent film of quality – and were most amazed when I told them you could only give it an 'X' certificate. In this day and age when we have to compete in Foreign markets to survive, and in view of the fact that *Serious Charge* is a meticulously 'clean' film with a moral lesson, it should most certainly not be classed with Sex and Horror pictures but receive an 'A' certificate. So I sincerely hope that you can reconsider your last decision in this respect and in view of your kind help and encouragement to date I am sure that your sense of fair play will help me in this matter, particularly in view of the fact that otherwise respectable families and teenagers under sixteen will not be able to see a film meant for them.

Ironically, it was judicious leaks to the press about the censorship done to the nude-bathing sequence that most captured attention when the film was given its première on 14 May 1959 before being put on general release in ABC cinemas from 29 June 1959 – not least when it was revealed that the version made for overseas distribution had, in fact, retained the scenes intact. But in Delamar's eyes the major damage had been done at the point when the BBFC determined upon an 'X' certificate.

Little was to change in Delamar's fortunes, moreover, when he returned in March 1962 seeking consciously to capitalise on what he saw as the principal setback. He now asked for complete restoration of the nude scenes in view of the fact his film was being considered for reissue and because it had, after all, already been given an 'X'. The case was made that 'the Board's attitude to screen nudity has changed considerably since this film was first passed and, under today's standards, scenes such as this are, of course, commonplace in many full length nudity features presently under distribution'. It made scant difference in the BBFC's opinion. 'I can tell you quite definitely that we would not accept the original "swimming pool" footage under an "X" certificate today,' was the Board's reply. 'Such changes as we have made in our policy on nudity do not relate to a scene of this kind in a feature film.'

Changes were afoot at the BBFC from the early 1960s, to be sure, as is evident from John Trevelyan's liberal-minded attitude to the advent of the British 'New Wave' cinema and his enlightened policy, thereafter, throughout the rest of the 1960s. But *Serious Charge* was arguably an unfortunate victim during a period of cautious transition in British film censorship between the 'doldrums era' of the 1950s and the height of the 'swinging sixties'.

Notes

1   Quoted in Anthony Aldgate, *Censorship and the Permissive Society: British Cinema and Theatre, 1955-1965* (Clarendon Press, 1995), p. 18, which discusses the question of the 'X' certificate and 'quality' cinema at length.
2   Lord Chamberlain's Plays Correspondence Files, Department of Manuscripts, British Library, *Serious Charge* 1951/5355, play reader's report (16 March 1953) and other memoranda or correspondence related to same. All references hereafter to the Lord Chamberlain's Office come from this file.
3   Newspaper reviews for the stage production of *Serious Charge* are held in the dossier for the play at the Theatre Museum, London.
4   British Board of Film Censors file, *Serious Charge*, letter from Woolf to Watkins (17 March 1955). The remaining BBFC references to *Serious Charge* cited subsequently are taken from this same source. My thanks go to the British Board of Film Classification for their kindness and helpful support in making the file available. The British Film Institute Library also holds Guy Elmes's screenplay for the 1959 production (12 October 1958: S 10429) and a breakdown for the film comprising set lists, dope sheets, location and studio shots, with inserts (S 10428), as well as a microfiche of all newspaper reviews.

Housewife's choice:
Woman in a Dressing Gown
MELANIE WILLIAMS

What was the first sexy British film Frears remembers? '*Woman in a Dressing Gown*,' he says without hesitation. 'Actually, I don't think I ever saw *Woman in a Dressing Gown*, but its title always gave me a powerful erotic thrill.'[1]

To anyone who *has* seen it, Stephen Frears's response to *Woman in a Dressing Gown* (1957) seems laughably inappropriate. The dressing gown of the title is not the flimsy négligé of a seductress but a decidedly unerotic shapeless old housecoat worn by middle-aged housewife Amy Preston (Yvonne Mitchell), whose inability to find time to dress in the morning illustrates her poor organisational abilities, rather than a *déshabillé* sexuality. Amy aspires to be the perfect housewife but, despite several frantic attempts to get her house in order, never quite manages it. The *mise-en-scène* acts as a constant reminder of Amy's failure, showing her home crowded with piles of unironed laundry, unwashed plates and unfinished mending, all of which prompted Raymond Durgnat to describe the film as 'a rhapsody of bad housekeeping'.[2]

Furthermore, Amy's husband Jim (Anthony Quayle) is having an affair with a young woman at work, Georgie (Sylvia Syms), who is neat, tidy and efficient; the absolute antithesis of Amy. On the surface, *Woman in a Dressing Gown* is a drama that counterpoints two different kinds of women: if Georgie is the ideal of 1950s femininity, serene, sexually attractive and 'mature', then Amy is its unacceptable face, scatty, scruffy and loud.[3] However, what prevents any simple reading of the film as purely an indictment of Amy as a bad housewife is, as Marcia Landy has argued, its insistent focus on 'the sights and sounds of Amy's life ... the visualization of her milieu'.[4]

I teach film studies at the University of Hull. I have written on British film for the *Quarterly Review of Film and Video*, the *Journal of Popular British Cinema* and the *Journal of Gender Studies* and I am currently completing a doctorate on the representation of women in the 1950s films of J. Lee Thompson. This interest sprang from spending countless afternoons watching the Channel 4 matinee when I should have been doing something more constructive with my time. I also harbour a secret crush on Stanley Baker, especially in *Hell Drivers*. *Melanie Williams*

Simply the fact that during most of the film we are with her rather than Jim or Georgie helps to skew our sympathies towards the character and prevent a one-dimensional portrayal of her as an object of contempt.

Yvonne Mitchell's bravura performance as Amy was the factor most frequently singled out for praise in contemporary reviews, but the distinctive landscape and atmosphere of Amy's world is primarily realised by J. Lee Thompson's direction. John Hill has noted how Thompson's baroque directorial style runs exactly counter to writer Ted Willis's more naturalistic bent.[5] Whereas Willis argued for a 'simple uncluttered approach' to drama, Thompson's direction of *Woman in a Dressing Gown* is a world away from the modesty and sobriety of Willis's preferences.[6] Indeed, it was this kind of conspicuous direction that incurred the wrath of no less a cinema luminary than Jean-Luc Godard: 'It is putting it mildly to say that his style is as maddening as his heroine's behaviour. From beginning to end the film is an incredible debauch of camera movements as complex as they are silly and meaningless, and of cuts and changes in rhythm on cupboards closing and doors opening.'[7] I think Godard is right to make the link between the style of direction and its heroine (both 'maddening') but entirely wrong to cite this as one of the film's weaknesses. To employ a smooth style in filming Amy's world would detract from the complete realisation of that world from within. The 'cuts and changes in rhythm' are entirely appropriate for giving an idea of the bitty, piecemeal, having-several-things-on-the-go-at-once nature of housework. The choppiness of Thompson's style goes some way towards communicating the idea of the housewife's fragmented day and also, in her attempt to stay on top of it all, 'the frenzy so often a regular part of an apparently mediocre existence'.[8] Similarly, the frequent foregrounding of intermediary objects and the use of 'impossible' camera positions (from inside a cupboard or behind the cooker) are not the ostentatious showing off Godard proposes. Rather, they powerfully indicate a sense of claustrophobia and domestic entrapment, when we see Amy obscured by the toast rack or an unmade bed and her movement intercepted by washing dangling from a line or piles of ironing. Interestingly, these blocked and barred shot compositions irresistibly recall Thompson's film of the previous year, *Yield to the Night*, about a woman's last days in the condemned cell. Its shot of the condemned woman Mary Hilton looking through the rails of her bedstead, a visual trope of her incarceration behind bars, is repeated in *Woman in a Dressing Gown* with Amy, suggesting a similarity between the two women's situations despite their ostensible differences, one a real prisoner in the bare condemned cell, and the other a metaphorical prisoner in her own home.

Examining Godard's review further, it seems that his poor opinion of the film has more to do with Anglophobia ('May the English lose the Middle East soon if the loss of their political power could restore their sense of beauty,' for example) and virulent misogyny. *Woman in a Dressing Gown* rejects Godard's suggestion that the basic situation 'should at least have been handled with humour. Alas! Alas! Alas! Cukor is not English'. Why is the possible abandonment and unhappiness of a middle-aged housewife an inherently funny subject, one might enquire. Instead *Woman in a Dressing Gown* both in style and the locus of its drama sympathetically attempts to enter the world of what Godard disparagingly calls a 'shrew' and a 'virago'. Looked at with this in mind, the film's frequent and striking use of extreme close-up and loud noises, singled out for opprobrium by Derek Hill in his review for *Tribune*, suggests another possible interpretation: 'Monstrous closeups of burnt toast and tea-cups fill the screen. Every speck of lather on Anthony Quayle's face is blown up to twenty times its size. China bangs, a radio blares, and a plate smashes with a crash that nearly bursts the loud speaker.'[9]

Hill, like Godard, fails to grasp the possible justification for Thompson's frequent focus on such mundane household items as squirting taps and button boxes. Thomas Elsasesser's essay on family melodrama, 'Tales of Sound and Fury', provides a clue to another way of looking at these shots. He notes how the peculiarly vivid visuals of melodrama can portray the characters' sublimated 'fetishist fixations', giving the example of Kyle Hadley in Douglas Sirk's *Written on the Wind* (1956), who is accompanied by shots emphasising oil derricks, fast cars and bottles of alcohol, all symbolic reminders of his sexual impotence and the ways he tries to compensate for it.[10] In exactly the same way, *Woman in a Dressing Gown* reveals the 'fetishist fixations' of Amy – toast and teacups. Amy's identity as housewife is dependent on the successful execution of her household duties and that is why burning the toast or dropping a plate is treated in the extreme manner that Derek Hill describes above; for Amy, these *are* important things. 'Life is more than burnt toast' is the title of Hill's review and indeed this is the truth; it is Amy's tragedy that her world has narrowed into the trivial and the domestic where burnt toast is her major concern. When John Gillett complains that the film's 'stylistic exaggerations too often stress trivial details at the expense of the significant', he unwittingly makes exactly that point, that the mind of the housewife, Amy's mind, is colonised and consumed by triviality; if significant events have been effaced from the plot, it is because they have been effaced from the life of the housewife.[11]

These are all interesting instances of *Woman in a Dressing Gown*'s *mise-en-scène* generating meanings that are concurrent with and often prophetic of feminist thinking. The idea of the housewife as a 'domestic prisoner' is a cliché today, but in the 1950s this was an idea that ran counter to popular discourses of femininity. In 1957, the year of *Woman in a Dressing Gown*'s release, these words were spoken by D.W. Winnicott, clinical psychiatrist and childcare expert, in one of his popular BBC broadcasts: 'Talk about women not wanting to be housewives seems to me to ignore one thing, that nowhere else but in her own home is a woman in such command. Only in her own home is she free, if she has courage, to spread herself, to find her whole self.'[12] In sharp contrast to Winnicott, *Woman in a Dressing Gown*'s suggestion that a woman might not always be free and in command of her own home, that in fact, it might actually be firmly in command of her, seems positively radical.

The most useful touchstone for approaching *Woman in a Dressing Gown* as a 'proto-feminist' film is Betty Friedan's groundbreaking study of the disparity between the happy housewife image and the malaise and misery that lies beneath it, *The Feminine Mystique*, first published in 1963. Although other feminist writers had mapped out the problems of women's confinement in the domestic realm before, Friedan's book reminded its readers that the 'woman question' had not gone away, merely mutated into a different form. Her work was instrumental in the international rebirth of feminism in the 1960s, especially her concept of 'the problem that has no name', that women's discourse lacks the means of public and collective articulation, because of shame and fear of ostracism, and consequently a widespread feeling of despair does not even possess that most primary means of identification, a name. Ironically, by calling it 'the problem that has no name', Friedan finally gives it a name and asserts that it does exist.

Of course, using Friedan's work as a critical tool for looking at a British 'social problem' film is not without its problems. Friedan is writing about Eisenhower-era American society; moreover, the majority of her work is concerned with the dissatisfactions of college-educated women living in the suburbs and not working-class wives in tower blocks. But despite these different national and class contexts, there is still a startling amount of common ground between Friedan's dissection of real-life female discontent and *Woman in a Dressing Gown*'s fictional hapless housewife of six years before. *The Feminine Mystique* often discusses and illuminates exactly the same problems that *Woman in a Dressing Gown* indirectly hints at or alludes to, through its presentation of the character of Amy.

In the preface of *The Feminine Mystique*, Friedan explains that she had first been put on the scent of 'the problem with no name' when she gradually came to notice 'a strange discrepancy between the reality of our lives as women and the image to which we were trying to conform, the image that I came to call the feminine mystique' – exactly the same discrepancy between image and reality that is dramatised in the opening scene of *Woman in a Dressing Gown* where Amy attempts to prepare a cooked breakfast for Jim.[13] She burns the toast and has to scrape off the charred bits, while the neglected bacon and eggs in the saucepan blacken. We see her arrange the food artfully on a plate and the camera lingers on its disgusting appearance. To complete the meal, she pours Jim a cup of tea but overfills the teacup. All the time that this scene continues, her struggle and ultimate failure to make a good meal are exaggerated by the contrast of the music on the radio, a smooth, lilting, string-laden piece of easy listening (suggesting the popular radio programme *Housewives' Choice*) that dominates the film's soundtrack. The calm serenity of the music provides an ironic counterpoint to Amy's frenzied activity and the quick cutting in this scene illuminates exactly this idea of a disparity between image and reality that Friedan sees as the cornerstone of women's discontent.

One of Friedan's most important notions, and one very pertinent to *Woman in a Dressing Gown*, is her idea that 'housewifery expands to fill the time available', that despite the invention of labour-saving devices the American housewife was spending the same amount of time, if not longer, on housework. In her research, Friedan noticed how the full-time housewives that she interviewed always seemed to be incredibly busy, rushed off their feet in comparison with the women who held full- or part-time professions. She also discovered that when these 'frantically busy housewives' started working or studying or developed some other serious interest outside the house, 'they could polish off in one hour the housework that used to take them six – and was still undone at dinnertime'. How to explain this phenomenon? Friedan asserts that this illogical sixfold expansion of worktime is due to the central role that the doing of housework plays in the feminine mystique. She unambiguously puts it thus:

1 The more a woman is deprived of function in society at the level of her own ability, the more her housework, mother-work, wife-work, will expand – and the more she will resist finishing her housework or mother-work, and being without any function at all. (Evidently human nature also abhors a vacuum, even in women.)
2 The time required to do the housework for any given woman varies inversely with the challenge of the other work to which she is committed. Without any outside interests, a woman is virtually forced to devote her every moment to the trivia of keeping house. (p. 239)

Viewed with this in mind, Amy's Sisyphean relationship to her housework takes on a whole new meaning. As Brian tells her in the initial breakfast scene, she does 'a bit of this, a bit of that ... but nothing's ever finished'. Amy's inability to finish anything is perhaps less an inability and, if we believe Friedan, more a strategy for covering up the emptiness at her life.

Amy's goal of finally tidying up the house once and for all, which she reiterates throughout the film, must never actually come to fruition and the home must remain in a state of flux because 'after all, with no other purpose in her life, if the housework were done in an hour, and the children off to school, the bright, energetic housewife would find the emptiness of her days unbearable'. And yet, the fact that her work could be done in half the time places the housewife in a guilty, defensive position. We certainly see evidence of this in Amy, who repeatedly says things like, 'Well, anybody would think I never did anything – I've been up since seven'. When her teenage son Brian says he doesn't know what she does all day, she tells him she'd like to see him try to do better. Amy tries to trump the working hours of the men by repeating how she gets up before them, and also attempts to make a claim for housekeeping as an area of personal expertise that Brian would not be able to do as well as she can. A similar reaction to Amy's was recorded by Friedan when a Minneapolis schoolteacher, a man, wrote a letter to newspaper saying that the housewife's long working week was unnecessary and that 'any woman who puts in that many hours is awfully slow, a poor budgeter of time or just plain inefficient' and the paper was inundated by letters from 'scores of irate housewives' who dared him to prove it.

This is where the concept of creativity in housework gains its significance. Creativity acts as a way of covering up the essential monotony of household chores by suggesting that the housewife has some kind of individual, specialist input into the work, and thus the menial worker is transformed into a 'professional'. As Friedan quotes from a study carried out by the advertising industry:

> Creativeness is the modern woman's dialectical answer to the problem of her changed position in the household. Thesis: I'm a housewife. Antithesis: I hate drudgery. Synthesis: I'm creative! ... The feeling of creativeness also serves another purpose ... It permits her to use at home *all the faculties that she would display in an outside career*. (p. 214)

Creative housekeeping tries to act as a recompense and a substitute for a paid career by taking on the appearance and the attributes of a profession so the housewife feels less like a drudge and more like 'an engineer, an expert'. One of the ways the housewife raises her stature is 'to "do things my way" – to establish an expert's role for herself by creating her own "tricks of the trade"'. All this comes together in one of the most interesting scenes in *Woman in a Dressing Gown*, interesting in terms of its portrayal of house-wifery because it hints at an edge of melancholy and dissatisfaction in Amy's character that is not as a result of Jim's possible desertion because at this point of the film she has no idea about Jim's affair – everything is normal. And yet, this scene suggests, already all is not well in Amy's world.

Amy has prepared a special meal for Jim including apple pie and cream and a bottle of beer, and when he comes home from work she sits him in the armchair in front of the fireplace and presents him with the meal on a tray. She then sits at his feet and watches expectantly as he eats the meal. The camera shoots the scene from a low angle with Amy in the foreground as she describes one of her 'tricks of the trade' exactly like one of Friedan's house-wives: 'I tried a new way with the chips. Cook 'em for a minute or so, then take 'em out. Leave 'em for another minute then put 'em back ... It makes 'em crisp. Don't you think it makes 'em crisp?' What is particularly interest-ing about this little monologue is the way it is performed and presented on film.

Throughout the speech, Amy does not look at Jim but gazes straight ahead of her into the fireplace and her face is shot in profile. The words are intoned very slowly with pauses between each of the sentences, and this combined with the vacant expression on her face gives the feeling of a recital by a somnambulant. When she gets to 'It makes 'em crisp', the intonation of the word 'crisp' is disconcertingly perky, like a bit of 'ad-speak' has inadver-tently slipped into her speech. Then she slips out of this reverie and asks Jim quickly and anxiously, 'Don't you think it makes 'em crisp?' – he is the audience for her 'creative' cookery, and only his approval can validate her efforts. No amount of congratulation can assuage the self-recrimination that must always follow from being totally dependent on another's approval for one's sense of achievement. The pronunciation of these last two sentences is brittle and (onomatopoeically) crisp, which suggests an edge of hysteria. All through this scene, the radio has been playing Tchaikovsky's *Pathétique* symphony – echoes of the use of Rachmaninov on the radio in the hearth-side scene in *Brief Encounter* – and at this point the music swells. The film switches from the medium shot of Amy in profile with Jim in the back-ground to an unobstructed close-up of Amy's face alone, as her thoughts shift from husband, hearth and home to herself and her feelings about the music; 'This Tchaikovsky, it makes me want to cry, it's so sad.' Music is used throughout in Amy's scenes but it is usually pop music, and it tends to be used as an ironic counterpoint to her action. This is one of the few times classical music is used at all and it seems to be used specifically to suggest deep and sincere feeling. Amy is able to name the composer, indicating, albeit briefly, an appreciation and knowledge of the world of high culture which is not in evidence anywhere else. Earlier Amy's intellectual capacities are satirised, but in this later scene the tone is different, and far from mocking. This consciously quiet moment in an otherwise hectic film, together with the bathetic juxtaposition of Tchaikovsky and chips, high art and household drudgery, suggests a strong feeling of human potential gone to waste, creative energy channelled entirely into the trivialities of housework, being frittered away on devising pointless complicated methods for cooking chips. The sadness of that waste is evoked by Amy's wistful comment on the music, and most of all, by the music itself, which suggests the depth of feeling that cannot be expressed by the emotionally inarticulate characters.

Throughout *Woman in a Dressing Gown* melodramatic tropes such as the use of lachrymose music described above are important. The melodramatic elements become even more pronounced after Jim announces to Amy that he wants to divorce her and go off with Georgie. Once again, Raymond Durgnat hits the nail on the head when he describes the film as '*embarrassingly moving*', even linking Yvonne Mitchell's performance to those of Judy Garland and Anna Magnani.[14] Certainly, *Woman in a Dressing Gown* is almost unbearably uncomfortable to watch at points, and there is no better example of this than when we see Amy prepare for an 'adult discussion' of the situation with Jim and Georgie back at the flat. Amy resolves to reincarnate herself as the ideal housewife and sets out on an ill-fated outing to get her hair done and to buy some whisky and soda. This is the only scene apart from a brief visit to the pub where she ventures outside the confines of the flat and on the evidence of this, it is easy to see why. The outside world is a hostile and inhospitable place where Amy's attempts to beautify herself are ruined first by a sudden downpour of rain and then by the everyday cruelty and indifference of ordinary people. When the bus she gets on is full up and she has to get off, she is told by a woman to get to the back of the queue. When she tries to take cover in a doorway, she is jostled back into the rain. She tries to hail a taxi but someone else jumps in front of her and as the taxi pulls away, she is splashed with water from the gutter. She attempts to explain her situation to a man with an umbrella ('my hair …') but he ignores her and refuses to let her share his shelter. Eventually she has to walk home as the rain continues to pour down.

The litany of disaster continues back at the flat when Amy rips her best dress trying to get into it, and ends up getting drunk on the whisky after her friend Hilda's encouragement to have a quick nip for Dutch courage. Another scene of frantic tidying up occurs but Amy's manic tipsy cheerfulness is deflated when a line from the song she is singing, 'O Antonio', reminds her what she is actually preparing for: 'I'd like to see him with his new sweetheart.' She sits down at the table and begins to sob but is denied even this meagre comfort when the table suddenly collapses beneath her. All this relentless pathos is difficult to justify in terms of a realist methodology, but as melodrama, it makes much more sense. Just as contemporary critics of Douglas Sirk saw him as a failed realist rather than an intense fabulist, a similar mistake is made with J. Lee Thompson's films. One might also link *Woman in a Dressing Gown* with a more recent film, Mike Leigh's *Secrets and Lies* (1995). Both films are, I think, primarily melodramas in the guise of 'social realism' – their power lies in the moments where the *melos* takes over. What is really striking though is the similarity between the performances of Yvonne Mitchell and Brenda Blethyn in the two films. Neither actor shies away from being over-the-top and pathetic, and the way Blethyn harps on the word 'sweetheart' is almost exactly the same as the way Mitchell uses 'Jimbo' (her pet name for Jim) repeatedly for the same effect of desperate neediness. Godard criticises Yvonne Mitchell's 'Look at me!' performance without understanding how well it fits the character. The more taciturn and neglectful Jim is, the more Amy must, in her own phrase, 'make a scene, or create', which suggests the performative nature of the character's life and her need for attention.

What does *Woman in a Dressing Gown* suggest would be the best thing for its heroine at this juncture? Again, we can discern an eerie prediction of Betty Friedan's ideas. For her, the only solution to 'the problem that has no name' is to go out to work. It provides the means of making contact with the larger world outside the home, and not having to live vicariously through husband or children. Towards the end of *Woman in a Dressing Gown*, when it looks as though Jim really will leave Amy, we see her face the prospect of paid employment with the following declaration of independence: 'I don't need you anymore, Jimbo. I can work ... Maybe this is the best thing that could happen to me. For years I haven't thought of myself, only you. Now it's changed. You go tonight.' It is true that in strictly realist terms this sudden burst of eloquence after years of inarticulacy is implausible, but like so much of the film, it obeys a different logic, one that works in melo-dramatic terms. It is interesting that Jim is firmly against Amy getting a job, and when he phrases this opposition as a statement in the imperative and not as a question ('You don't want to work, Amy'), he voices the terms on which he expects their relationship to continue. For a woman to work seems to be a blot on the character of the husband and his status as provider, despite the fact that not to work would reduce Amy to the status of domestic chattel to be maintained by Jim after his absence.[15] Amy protests against this: 'Yes, I do. I don't want to sit down and weep for the rest of my life.' Her face as she says these lines is shot in clear, unobstructed close-up and is brightly lit, which all suggest that this is a moment of clarity and self-realisation. At this point her character has a dignity and poise that is denied in the rest of the film, with its emphasis on her pitiable inadequacy. As John Gillett muses in his review, 'it is interesting to speculate what would have happened to Amy if Jim had in fact gone away with Georgie', and at this point the film seems to suggest that this might be the best thing for Amy.[16] However, the radical suggestion that her emotional dependence is fostered by her economic dependence and that Jim's departure would be as good for her as it would for him is curtailed by the ending. Although Jim packs his bags to leave with Georgie, his severance from the family home is short-lived, lasting only a few minutes. Halfway down the street he has a change of heart and returns to the flat.

Woman in a Dressing Gown concludes with a resumption of the nuclear family, but one that is far from untroubled. The deeply conservative final tableau is almost parodic in its inscription of traditional gender roles, father and son in the foreground discussing current affairs, Amy silent and in the background making a pot of tea. But of course, the fact that this scene occurs only minutes after we have seen the same family on the brink of collapse adds an air of unreality to proceedings and serves as an implicit criticism of the situation. If this version of the family is improvisatory at this point, how real is it the rest of the time? And as John Hill notes, the camera placement at the end of the film, outside the flat's window, means that the audience is 'critically distanced from the film's apparently "happy ending" by the deployment of a device … saturated with negative connotations'.[17] What we see in the closing moments of *Woman in a Dressing Gown* is certainly not the conventional closure of a drama that sets out to endorse the status quo.

Woman in a Dressing Gown was very popular with contemporary audiences, making £450,000 on its first release, according to Ted Willis, and featuring in *Kinematograph Weekly*'s list of the top money-makers of the year.[18] Janet Thumim's retrospective analysis of the most popular films in Britain in 1957, taking into account evidence from *Picturegoer* as well as *Kine Weekly*, places the film in the top twelve. This seems all the more remarkable for a 'woman's picture' in a period of rapidly declining female cinema attendance, suggesting an interesting dynamic: women who are not getting out of the house very often *do* go out to see a film about a woman who doesn't get out of the house very often.[19] *Woman in a Dressing Gown*'s popularity is the strongest argument that it struck a chord in the public psyche. One could argue, as Geraghty does of other popular fifties British films, that its success comes from 'giving audiences a rest from the stress of being citizens in the grip of modernisation', but this does not really fit *Woman in a Dressing Gown*, a film far from being restful or conciliatory.[20] The elements of the film I have described above are not the result of reading 'against the grain': you do not have to look very hard for its cracks and contradictions.

Ted Willis, talking about a stage adaptation of *Woman in a Dressing Gown*, emphasises that the keystone of the piece is being able to identify with the characters, and explains how the character of Amy has meant something to women all over the world: 'Argentinian, German, Swedish, Dutch and British women have told me that they "know Amy", that a woman like this lives "next door" or "along the road".'[21] However, the women's recognition of Amy is not *personal* identification but *outward* identification; she is not like them but someone they know. If we compare this to the reaction to Betty Friedan's work, the difference is startling: '"I've got tears in my eyes that my inner turmoil is shared with other women", a young Connecticut mother wrote me when I first began to put this problem into words.'[22] In the radical feminist text, collective recognition of the feminine mystique is the first step in doing something about the problem. Instead, in *Woman in a Dressing Gown*, the problems articulated about housewifery are all projected onto a misfit character who is painted as a freak, albeit a sympathetic one. However, *Woman in a Dressing Gown* remains an eloquent presentation of 'the problem with no name' when it still has no name and no widespread acknowledgement – when, in Brandon French's phrase, women were 'on the verge of revolt'.[23] Being the product of a national cinema so frequently maligned for its lack of social awareness during the 1950s, especially when it came to women, it is all the more remarkable.

Notes

1 Simon Hattenstone, 'A Very British View', *Guardian* (2 September 1995), p. 30.
2 Raymond Durgnat, *A Mirror for England* (Faber & Faber, 1970), p. 181.
3 Christine Geraghty, *British Cinema in the Fifties: Gender, Genre and the 'New Look'* (Routledge, 2000), pp. 156–60.
4 Marcia Landy, *British Genres* (Princeton University Press, 1991), p. 235.
5 Derek Hill, 'Life Is More Than Burnt Toast', *Tribune* (18 October 1986), p. 98.
6 Ted Willis, *Evening All: Fifty Years over a Hot Typewriter* (Macmillan, 1991), p. 138. For the play, see Willis's *Woman in a Dressing Gown: A Play in Two Acts* (Evans, 1964).
7 Jean-Luc Godard, *Godard on Godard*, trans. Tom Milne (Secker & Warburg, 1972), p. 86.
8 Durgnat, *A Mirror for England*, p. 181.
9 John Hill, *Sex, Class and Realism: British Cinema 1956–1963* (British Film Institute, 1986), p. 30.
10 Thomas Elsaesser, 'Tales of Sound and Fury: Observations on the Family Melodrama', in

Christine Gledhill (ed.), *Home Is Where the Heart Is: Studies in Melodrama and the Woman's Film* ([1972] British Film Institute, 1987).

11 John Gillett, 'Woman in a Dressing Gown', *Sight and Sound* 27, 2 (1957), p. 92.

12 D.W. Winnicott, *The Child, the Family and the Outside World* (Harmondsworth, 1964), p. 120.

13 Betty Friedan, *The Feminine Mystique*, ([1963] Gollancz, 1971), p. 9.

14 Durgnat, *A Mirror for England*, p. 181.

15 See Barbara Klinger, *Melodrama and Meaning: History, Culture and the Films of Douglas Sirk* (Indiana University Press, 1994), p. 76.

16 Gillett, 'Woman in a Dressing Gown', p. 92.

17 Hill, *Sex, Class and Realism*, p. 100.

18 Willis, *Evening All*, p. 141.

19 Sue Harper and Vincent Porter, 'Cinema Audience Tastes in 1950s Britain', *Journal of Popular British Cinema* 2 (1999), p. 67.

20 Geraghty, *British Cinema in the Fifties*, p. 37.

21 Willis, *Evening All*, p. 6.

22 Friedan, *The Feminine Mystique*, p. 33.

23 See Brandon French, *On the Verge of Revolt: Women in American Films of the Fifties* (Ungar, 1978).

Adaptibility

Too theatrical by half?
The Admirable Crichton and *Look Back in Anger*

STEPHEN LACEY

THERE IS NO doubt that British theatre has been very important to the development of British cinema, and – the input of television in general and Channel 4 in particular notwithstanding – it remains so, as a quick glance at the number of film adaptations from stage plays from the 1980s and early 1990s testifies. This is clearly the case in the 1950s, not least because a great many films have their origins in the theatre. I estimate that of the 1,033 British films of the 1950s listed in David Quinlan's *British Sound Films*, some 152 were based on stage plays.[1] However, the provision of source texts is not the only issue, and this figure should be set alongside the 330 films in the decade that were based on novels and short stories, the 18 that came from radio and the 22 adapted from television. If theatre seems more important than other media to the cinema of the 1950s, then it is partly because there are deeper connections, and it is worth reminding ourselves of some of these.

The institutions of theatre and cinema were, by the 1950s, bound to each other. Many of the dominant personnel of the cinema – actors, directors, technicians and writers – had backgrounds in the theatre. Even such luminaries of the period as Kenneth More and Dirk Bogarde began as stage actors. (More began in variety before moving into films via the legitimate theatre and Bogarde worked in both provincial repertory theatre as well as the West End before becoming a screen actor.) However, it was not a relationship between equals. Theatre occupied a higher cultural status than film, lending it a credibility and legitimacy that was needed by a medium conscious of its inferior status. This was particularly apparent in the attitude of many stage actors towards their screen work (the physical proximity of

I am a Principal Lecturer in the Department of Contemporary Arts at Manchester Metropolitan University. I have written on British theatre in the 1950s and 1960s, notably *British Realist Theatre: The New Wave in its Context, 1956–1965* (Routledge, 1995). Given an abiding academic and personal interest in cinema, it was a short step to writing about film in the 1950s, too. *Stephen Lacey*

the major film studios to the West End meant that it was possible to film during the day and still be on stage in time for an evening performance), and a certain opportunism was tolerated, even encouraged. As David Thomson has noted, 'for eminent actors of the English stage, some films are allowed like holidays. Lord Olivier can appear in clinkers so that his little ones can be provided for.'[2] In addition, theatre and its products functioned as signs for 'Englishness' in a post-war culture pervaded by a deep unease about an encroaching 'Americanisation'.

There are also interesting parallels between the institutions of cinema and theatre in the decade and there is a way of relating the history of both media that emphasises this. The production of both plays and films, for example, derives from a tension between the 'mainstream' and the 'independents', who, whilst not being free from commercial pressures and compromises, sought to create room for manoeuvre within their respective industries: Rank and ABC have their equivalent in Stoll-Moss, and Woodfall and Bryanston have theirs in the English Stage Company at the Royal Court Theatre and Theatre Workshop at the Theatre Royal, Stratford East. Some of the leading figures in the new theatre often emerge at the centre of independent cinema; for example, the director Tony Richardson (see below) is central to both 'New Waves', was one of the key figures in Woodfall Films and directed both stage and film versions of John Osborne's *Look Back in Anger* (in 1956 and 1959 respectively) and the film of Shelagh Delaney's *A Taste of Honey* (1961).

Running alongside these parallel institutional histories are converging histories of forms once, but perhaps no longer, dominant, in which realism is foregrounded. In these histories, theatre and cinema occupied a kind of wasteland for most of the 1950s, limited in their artistic ambition and social reach, confined to the lower-middle-class parochialism of Ealing comedy on the one hand and the torpor of upper-middle-class country-house drama on the other. In this version, rescue came in the form of working-class realism (though earlier in the decade for theatre than for film), which extended the social basis of both media, whilst at the same time challenging staging and filming orthodoxies. Against this, there is now a revisionist history (currently stronger in film studies than in theatre studies, though perhaps not for much longer) that has sought to re-evaluate hitherto marginalised genres, texts and practitioners. In film history, this is evident in the recent interest in melodrama and fantasy shown by Pam Cook and others and in the current high status of the work of Powell and Pressburger.[3] In theatre history, this has been paralleled by a reconsideration of the once despised Terence Rattigan (of interest because of the gay sub-text to his plays) and a re-evaluation of the crucial 'moment' of 1956; here, there is a sense that the real 'turning point' in post-war theatre was the first production of Samuel Beckett's *Waiting for Godot* in 1955 rather than of John Osborne's *Look Back in Anger* a year later, and that the once denigrated drama of the late 1940s and early 1950s was of much more aesthetic and social value than the post-Osborne generation allowed.[4]

However, despite these important aesthetic and institutional connec-tions, the relationship between film and theatre in the period – and beyond it – is not without its paradoxes and tensions. To explore this it is necessary, for a while, to go outside the 1950s, and away from film history, for film criticism and theory has been churlish about the theatrical in cinema; indeed, the inferiority felt by the film industry towards the theatre noted earlier is markedly absent. In theatre criticism, to note that a play is 'cinematic' is often to find something interesting in it, to point towards its ambitions, especially in the narrative (where 'cinematic' sometimes refers to disruptions to the causal chain of conventional naturalist plotting, or a more overt use of montage) or use of space (where it may denote a more fluid use of multiple fictional locations). 'Cinematic' may also refer to overt theatrical references to film genres (see, for example, the plays of David Hare).[5] In film criticism, however, 'theatrical' is nearly always a term of abuse. The need of film theorists to slough off the associations with the theatre has been an essential aspect of some versions of cinema's history; as Susan Sontag has observed, 'the history of cinema is often treated as the history of its emancipation from theatrical models'.[6] This has led to some curious and untenable judgments about the 'essential' differences between theatre and film (many of which Sontag has usefully and thoroughly demolished) and to the term 'theatrical' acquiring largely negative associations.

The resistance to the 'theatrical' is evident in the case of stage-to-film adaptations, where a refusal to reshape spatial and narrative structures, to move the camera through the door of the box set/studio out into the world beyond, is usually considered stagey and too reliant on the limitations of the time/space conventions of theatre. However, criticism of theatricality in cinema goes beyond this. To be 'theatrical' on the screen might mean (in no particular order) all or some of the following attributes. It often suggests an over-reliance on the 'word', the residue of the literary text, which is privileged over the visual image. 'Theatricality' may connote a style of acting that seems scaled towards the open spaces of a theatre auditorium rather than the enforced intimacy of the camera; more generally, it suggests an 'artificiality' in performance (judged against the criteria of realism, that is), which is largely unconscious and the result of bad habits rather than a self-reflexive intention (although, at a tangent to this discussion, it is interesting to note how artifice, the potential for self-reflexivity in theatre, has defined the theatrical in a more positive sense in much postmodern cultural theory, and in a way that is not restricted by the literary bias of the well-made play).[7] 'Theatrical' may also mean 'flatness' in the depiction and construction of space, as if the camera is afraid to move through the fourth wall and interrupt an established environment. Connected to this, 'theatrical' is sometimes used to describe the lack of an integrated *mise-en-scène*; that is, a *mise-en-scène* where location is merely a backdrop to the action, rather than being pulled into, and motivated by, the character and narrative (although why this should be considered 'theatrical' is not clear, as the activation and integration of the theatrical environment is as essential to a successful theatre performance as it is to a film, even if the means by which it is achieved are different). Finally, 'theatrical' also connotes a preference for studio over location, and a reliance on a shooting system that is dominated by the mid-shot and discrete and minimal editing.

That these attributes of a theatricalised cinema are always to be avoided is open to debate, as is the corollary that the shedding of all connections to a theatrical aesthetic will somehow allow a 'pure' cinema to emerge.[8] Clearly, there is a great deal that might be said about this use of the theatrical, not least that it seems to refer to the text-based, illusionist/naturalist well-made play, performed behind a proscenium arch. (It is ironic that such a conception of the theatrical should be mobilised in film theory when theatre practice since the mid–1950s has resolutely moved away from the dominance of the literary text, has frequently jettisoned verisimilitude in theatre design, even in the staging of naturalist plays, and has often abandoned the proscenium – and indeed the entire theatre auditorium – entirely.)

Although there is no space here to develop these arguments further, it is worth pointing out that, although 'theatrical' in this usage refers primarily to aspects of film style, the term is also complicated by contextual factors. By the 1950s, theatrical habits are in reality a dominant form of studio filming, and it is a moot point whether the kind of practices outlined above are to be thought of as theatrical at all. Also, in a transposition of the term from the aesthetic to the social and cultural planes, 'theatrical' also connotes a particular kind of middle-class, socially restricted film, carrying the same kind of associations that 'well-made play' or 'West End' have in the theatre. To reject this sort of theatricality, like rejecting naturalism in the theatre, was often to make a gesture towards realism. Whether on the formal or cultural level, it is often around realism that the theatrical seems the most problematic.

The issue of theatricality, then, cannot be separated from questions of context, convention and genre. Yet, despite the low status of the theatrical in film, it will form an important part of the argument that follows that while the theatrical, in its many senses, may be damaging to the ambitions of one kind of film, it can be acknowledged and celebrated in another kind of film. It is best to explore these matters in relation to particular examples, and we shall turn now to two film adaptations, conceived in different genres, from the latter part of the decade: *The Admirable Crichton* (US: *Paradise Lagoon*), directed by Lewis Gilbert in 1957 from the play by J.M. Barrie written in 1902, and *Look Back in Anger* directed by Tony Richardson in 1959 from John Osborne's play of 1956.

The Admirable Crichton is about the family and servants of a nondescript aristocrat with democratic pretensions, Lord Loam (Cecil Parker), who find themselves shipwrecked on a desert island, at which point the eponymous Crichton (Kenneth More), being the only member of the party with any practical know-how, becomes the ruler of the community. Both play and film are, therefore, comedies of social reversal; Crichton, the butler, champions the established social order, whilst his employer, the aristocrat, pontificates about the coming egalitarian society. On the island, the status quo is undermined, and Crichton, 'the guv'nor', almost marries Lord Loam's eldest daughter. However, the social order is rapidly restored when, as the wedding service is about to take place, they are predictably rescued. Crichton becomes the butler once more, leaving the family to assume the glory for ensuring their communal survival.

In what ways, then, might *The Admirable Crichton* be considered theatrical? The casting provides some evidence, especially in the film's use of character actors such as Cecil Parker and Martita Hunt (Lady Brockenhurst) familiar from both stage and screen (Kenneth More was by this time already an established film star.) There is also the issue of fidelity to the play text. Lewis Gilbert remarked in interview that the film was 'freely adapted' from Barrie's original, largely as 'a vehicle for Kenny More'.[9] By the standards of the period, the film is a fairly free adaptation, with the island sequences shot on location. However, the film keeps, to a large extent, the main events of the play's narrative, many of its jokes and much of its important dialogue. The main alterations to the narrative are to do with an explicit recognition of its star's particular talents and an implicit acknowledgement of the film's new social and generic context.

The action is transposed to 1905, presumably to allow for a little fun at the expense of suffragettes, with whom one of Loam's daughters becomes unwittingly involved. Also, the narrative is given an altogether sunnier ending (in recognition of the film's status as a comedy with an unambiguously happy resolution), in which Crichton, having found some pearls on the island, settles for a maid (Diane Cilento) and goes off to get married and start a business and a family. There is no such magical resolution in the play, which concludes with an uncomfortable impasse: Crichton, still the mouthpiece of conservatism, faces the young woman he almost married across the gulf of privilege and social difference.

These differences notwithstanding, the similarity between the two narratives might also be considered part of the film's theatricality and it is interesting to note that the film reproduces the main locations of the play with only minor additions; it centres on Lord Loam's stately home (interior shots, staged in a studio) and the island (shot on location). In one sense, the film does what films often do with a stage play, which is to 'open out' the action, representing on screen what can only be retold in dialogue on stage (the shipwreck) and suggested indexically (the stockade standing in for the whole island). Certainly, the island sequences seem the more 'filmic', relying on flexible and varied shooting strategies: there is, for example, plentiful use of close-up, mid-shot and long shot, and the camera moves in and around the location, creating a sense of fictional space that reflects the castaway's growing sense of the island as a South Sea idyll.

Lewis Gilbert was primarily a director of action films such as *Reach for the Sky* (1956), *Carve her Name with Pride* (1958) and *Sink the Bismarck* (1960), and it is not surprising that the island scenes seem the furthest away from the theatricality that characterises the interior sequences. It is in the scenes in Loam Hall that we can see the deadening effect of theatrical habit refracted through dominant studio practices. Typically, the interiors are shot front-on, with the camera positioned at one (fixed) side of the space. When the camera moves, it is normally only on a line parallel to the 'back wall', simulating the fourth wall so integral to proscenium-arch theatre. There is a scene early on in the film (and the theatrical term 'scene' seems particularly appropriate, since it comes from the play) in which Lord Loam organises a tea party in order to ensure that his servants, his daughters and their suitors can meet on equal terms. The scene is shot on a flat plane, and the camera seems reluctant to cut into the space, to enter these interior spaces and reshape them. The actors are similarly filmed from the front, often in mid-shot and in small groups, with the camera moving only minimally to focus and select what it wants us to pay attention to. The acting styles seem to match this reproduction of a theatre staging technique. In one vignette, Lord Brockenhurst, a would-be suitor to Mary, is seated on a settee alongside a maid, having been instructed to converse with her 'as equals'. The scene is shot from the front in a single take, the embarrassment of both characters projected as if to the back of the Drury Lane theatre (this is, in fact, an example of an inappropriate acting style combining with a characteristic 1950s tendency to see working-class characters as comic grotesques).

However, these interior sequences reveal another kind of theatricality, which is more conscious in the film, and which is offered as a source of knowing pleasure to the audience. The film is aware of its status as a 'film of a play', and it is not too fanciful to suggest that this awareness is part of the film's appeal to a popular audience. *The Admirable Crichton* has an interesting relationship to another, earlier film based on a stage play from about the same historical period, Oscar Wilde's *The Importance of Being Earnest* (directed by Anthony Asquith in 1952). *The Admirable Crichton* does not signify 'theatre' in the way that Asquith's film does in its opening sequence, but it offers an interesting intertextual reference to one of Wilde's most famous characters. In Barrie's play, Lady Brockenhurst, Mary's prospective mother-in-law, appears only in the last act, where she is brought in to interrogate the castaways about their conduct on the island. In Gilbert's film, she is in many of the scenes set in England, including the tea party. As played by Martita Hunt, Lady Brockenhurst's dress, vocal and gestural mannerisms and her effect on other characters all refer us to Wilde's Lady Bracknell, immortalised by Edith Evans five years previously. Martita Hunt's performance undoubtedly gains from this cross-referencing to a theatrical and now cinematic icon, and, through the lingering gaze of the camera, which allows her to dominate the frame, the film seems to ask its audience to take pleasure in the recognition.

An awareness – indeed celebration – of the theatrical in *The Admirable Crichton* also governs the design of the interiors. Lord Loam's house, and especially the hall and the ballroom, are composed rather like stage sets. This is partly because the filming strategies ensure that we only see three walls, which in the case of the hall are 'opened out' into an approximate V-shape, as it might be on stage. However, it is also (taking the hall as our example again) because the walls are obviously painted, in two senses: they are covered with paintings and murals, which have the effect of connoting an artifice that seems at odds with most representations of Edwardian stately homes, and they are clearly 'painted', often with exaggerated detail and with the use of colours that catch the eye. These scenes have several layers of connotation: we are being referred, on the one hand, to a theatrical genre, the country-house play, familiar in the 1950s as it had been half a century earlier; on the other, we are being asked to enjoy the idea of the theatrical-as-artifice, which in turn helps to locate the play as a comedy, something which the dominant acting style clearly indicates. The credit sequence (which has no counterpart in the play) brings both the theatricalised comedy acting and the use of setting together in a wordless pantomime, in which the audience follow the servants as they move, under Crichton's stern supervision, from the kitchen to Lord Loam's bedroom via the hall, bringing the lord his morning tea.

At the end of the decade, with realism once more on the agenda, we can trace a rather different and antagonistic attitude towards the theatrical in film. The repression of theatricality is evident in our second example, Tony Richardson's film of *Look Back in Anger*, and this is an essential part of its claim to realism. There is a paradox here: on the one hand, Richardson – and others – were attempting to create the same kind of appeal (and success) that the new realism had achieved in the theatre, and, as was indicated earlier, many of the source texts for New Wave cinema were stage plays. 'It is absolutely vital', Richardson argued, 'to get into British films the same sort of impact and sense of life that … the Angry Young Man cult has had in the theatre and literary worlds.'[10] However, this was achieved by an active, if only partly successful, removal of any sense of the theatrical in the film versions of Osborne plays in the name of cinematic realism. This was particularly apparent in Richardson's version of *The Entertainer* (1960) in which a highly theatrical device (playing the music-hall routines of the central character, Archie Rice, 'out front' and treating the theatre audience as if it were the audience at one of Archie's second-rate variety shows) is ignored, the songs and gags being naturalised into a seamless realist fiction.

Look Back in Anger was not conceived as the 'film of the play' in a simple sense, and this is indicated by the fact that the screenplay was by Nigel Kneale (although Osborne is credited with supplying additional dialogue). The avoidance of signifiers of the theatrical was not, however, simply a matter of film 'style' (just as realism is never simply a matter of technique in film or theatre), but was connected to the film's awareness that it was essential to acknowledge a new social and cultural context.

Richardson's film adopts the usual strategy of opening-out the narrative in a highly systematic way. The play is famously set in a single playing-space, a drab Midlands garret, and focuses on a narrow set of characters and their interaction (Jimmy Porter, his wife Alison, their lodger Cliff, Alison's friend – and Jimmy's temporary lover – Helena and, briefly, Alison's father). However, little of the film's action remains within the Porter's seedy bed-sit. The film opens, not in the flat, but in a jazz club/pub. As the narrative progresses, locations only mentioned in the play are represented directly on screen; we follow Jimmy and Cliff to the street market where they run a sweet stall; we see Jimmy attend the funeral of Mrs Tanner, the mother of his oldest friend; we accompany Jimmy on a visit to the run-down repertory theatre where Helena, an actress, is currently performing; the narrative concludes in a railway station.

One effect of Richardson's narrative strategy is that we see a lot more of the society that Jimmy famously rails against, and which remains offstage in the play. Indeed, there is an almost documentary impulse in the film (and in most other films of the New Wave), indicated in the way in which the camera frequently dwells on the environments before introducing the characters and picking up the narrative. The street market, for example, is filmed as if it were of interest in its own right, rather than being the location for the next development in the plot. These sequences carry a particular weight in the film, acting as guarantors of the truth of its depiction of social reality. This is the epistemology of naturalism, in which reality is 'captured' rather than created on screen, its mere presence serving to authenticate the veracity of the fiction that surrounds it. In the theatre, naturalism often relies on the same epistemology – that what is observed and plausibly recreated must necessarily be real and 'true' – yet is unable to observe or recreate very much of the society it engages with. In professing a freedom from the limitations of stage naturalism, the film of *Look Back in Anger* exercises the right of the cinema to show, as well as refer to, the contemporary world in which it is located, a right, which this film – like other New Wave films – wears like a medal.

There is another effect of this kind of cinematic realism that is important to this argument. Opening out the narrative has the effect of diffusing the claustrophobia of the play. *Look Back in Anger* sits easily within the dominant conventions of the European naturalist tradition, its single playing space (albeit a lower-class bed-sit rather than a bourgeois drawing-room) functioning as an embodiment of the forces of determinism that constrain the characters that inhabit it. The room becomes a trap, as Raymond Williams suggested, for Jimmy Porter just as surely as it did for Ibsen's Nora in *A Doll's House*.[11] Claustrophobia is both a tangible aspect of the immediate events of a naturalist drama of this sort and a metaphor for social and moral constraints. The restless prowling of Jimmy Porter around his room, hemmed in by a life that he does not know how to change, is all but gone from the film; inaction is turned into action.

Certainly, Jimmy as played by Richard Burton is a much more active hero than is suggested by the play. In this sense, the casting of Burton in the lead role, which was much criticised at the time, is entirely appropriate.

There is little of the Angry Young Man about Burton's performance. He is instead much more of a 1960s liberal intellectual hero, with an appeal to a market beyond the United Kingdom. The reconceptualising of Jimmy Porter evident in Burton's portrayal was not an unplanned consequence of the film's rejection of its theatrical roots, but an indication of the makers' awareness of a new audience and a new social context. There is a deliberate internationalising of the play's essentially provincial British atmosphere in the casting of Burton, who had been familiar as a Hollywood movie star since *The Robe* (1953). Internationalisation is indicated by the introduction of a 'race' theme, absent from the play. In the film, Jimmy and Cliff unsuccessfully defend an Asian stallholder, who is forced off the market by the racism of the other traders. This is recognition of racial intolerance as an issue for Britain, in the wake of the first waves of post-war immigration (the first so-called post-war 'race riots' had occurred in Notting Hill in 1958). It was a theme that also echoed abroad, especially in the USA in the context of the emerging civil rights movement. The film has, in addition, a more deliberate appeal to the idea of an international 'youth' – and it was in the hands of the new, young audience (in its late teens and twenties) that the fate of British cinema was said to reside. This is evident in the prominence given to Jimmy's jazz trumpet playing which is not seen in the play and the sequence in a jazz club with which the films begins: it is crowded with young people, male, female, black and white. The strategy is particularly apparent in the overt sexuality of both Burton's Jimmy and Gary Raymond's Cliff. The latter is a 'cuddly bear' of a character in the play, whose friendship with Alison is non-sexual. In Richardson's film, he is more recognisably a late 1950s/early 1960s type, a single, sexually active (and sexually attractive) refugee from the provinces (Wales), who has pictures of women on his bedroom walls and boasts of his sexual conquests.

There is an interesting addendum to our main argument that is worth considering here. The play is full of the kind of camp linguistic by-play that, as Michael Billington has pointed out, is part of the sub-culture of the provincial actor to which the young Osborne belonged. Jimmy and Cliff swap music-hall jokes, charged with sexual innuendo, and indulge in the opening of a 'front-cloth' comedy routine.[12] Camp, whatever else it may be, is self-consciously artificial and 'theatrical', connoting both 'performance' and the feminine/homosexual. After his death in 1994, Osborne's one-time collaborator, Anthony Creighton, 'outed' him as a closet bisexual; if true, it might make the relationship between Jimmy and Cliff the central one of the play. However, this simply does not emerge as an issue in the film, since the dialogue removes much of the play's theatrical jokiness, and the conjunction of the theatrical and the homosexual is effaced by the overt – almost aggressive – heterosexuality of both Burton and Raymond.

The suppression of the theatrical was an essential part, therefore, of the realism of the New Wave in cinema (although this was for social and historical reasons as much as aesthetic ones). However, the confident embrace of a new realism allowed for the return of artifice in another form and the documentary/naturalist intention referred to above was accompanied by an aesthetic/poetic one. 'Poetic realism' became the dominant form of the realist New Wave, although it did not, significantly, mean a reappropriation of the theatrical. 'Poetic' meant in this context a style of shooting that 'aestheticised' the object of attention, that drew attention to itself as 'cinematic', and which also allowed a personal signature. There was a 'poetic realism' in the new theatre, too, notably in performance, which signified the emergence of a new kind of 'theatricality', especially in theatre design.[13] Yet, as the example of *The Admirable Crichton* shows, the realist aesthetic, however it is qualified, should not be allowed to monopolise the cinema's relationship to the theatrical. Perhaps the first step towards remedying this would be recognition that the theatre need not be a leaden weight dragging film away from its destiny; that in certain circumstances theatricality can be creatively appropriated.

Notes

1　David Quinlan, *British Sound Films: The Studio Years, 1928–1959* (Batsford, 1984).
2　David Thomson, 'Acting English', *Film Comment* 18, 3 (May–June 1982), p. 8.
3　See, for example, Pam Cook (ed.), *Gainsborough Pictures* (Cassell, 1997).
4　See Dan Rebellatto, *1956 and All That: The Making of Modern British Drama* (Routledge, 1999). The introduction contains a very useful summary of the main aspects of this revisionist position.
5　See Stephen Lacey, 'Public Spaces and Private Narratives: The Plays and Films of David Hare' in J. Bignell (ed.), *Writing and Cinema* (Longman, 1999).
6　Susan Sontag, 'Film and Theatre' in Gerald Mast, Marshall Cohen and Leo Braudy (eds), *Film Theory and Criticism: Introductory Readings* (Oxford University Press, 1992), p. 362.
7　See, for example, Steven Connor, *Postmodernist Culture: An Introduction to Theories of the Contemporary* (Blackwell, 1996).
8　This is also Sontag's conclusion; see 'Film and Theatre'.
9　Interview with Lewis Gilbert in Brian McFarlane (ed.), *An Autobiography of British Cinema* (Methuen, 1997), p. 222.
10　Quoted in John Hill, *Sex, Class, Realism: British Cinema 1956–1963* (British Film Institute, 1986), p. 40.
11　See Raymond Williams, 'Forms', in *Culture* (Fontana, 1981).
12　Michael Billington, *The Modern Actor* (Hamish Hamilton, 1973).
13　For further discussion of poetic realism in both theatre and film, see Stephen Lacey, *British Realist Theatre: The New Wave in its Context, 1956–1965* (Routledge, 1995) and Andrew Higson, 'Space, Place and Spectacle' in *Screen* 4–5 (1984), pp. 2–21.

A Tale of Two Cities and the Cold War

ROBERT GIDDINGS

There was probably never a book by a great humorist, and an artist so prolific in the conception of character, with so little humour and so few rememberable figures. Its merits lie elsewhere. (John Forster, *The Life of Charles Dickens* (1872))

RALPH THOMAS'S *A Tale of Two Cities* of 1958 occupies a secure if modest place among that bunch of 1950s British releases based on novels by Dickens, including Brian Desmond Hurst's *Scrooge* (1951) and Noel Langley's *The Pickwick Papers* (1952).[1] When all the arguments about successfully filming Dickens are considered it must be conceded that his fiction offers significant qualities that appeal to film-makers: strong and contrasting characters, fascinating plots and frequent confrontations and collisions of personality. In unsuspected ways, Ralph Thomas's film is indeed one of the best film versions of a Dickens novel and part of this rests upon the fact that, as Dickens's novels go, *A Tale of Two Cities* is unusual. Dickens elaborately works up material in this novel which must have been marinating in his imagination. Two themes stand out: the dual personality, the *doppelgänger* or alter ego; and mob behaviour when public order collapses. Several strands come together. Dickens had voluminously researched the Gordon Riots which were, up to then, the worst public riots in British history. Charles Mackay's *Popular Delusions and the Madness of Crowds* (1845)

I am Professor Emeritus in the School of Media Arts, Bournemouth University. My schooling was interrupted by polio, but I was very well educated by wireless, cinema and second-hand books. As an undergraduate in Bristol in the 1950s I spent more time in film societies and flea-pits than in class. This cultural irresponsibility has continued and been complicated by TV and video. I have written for *New Society*, *Tribune*, *The Listener* and *New Statesman and Society* on film and media, and published *The Changing World of Charles Dickens* (Vision Press, 1984); with Chris Wensley and Keith Selby, *Screening the Novel* (Palgrave, 1992); *The War Poets* (Bloomsbury, 1998); and with Keith Selby, *The Classic Serial on Television and Radio* (Palgrave, 2001). I am a devout and practising Dickensian: my *Student Guide to Charles Dickens* was published in 2002 by Greenwich Exchange. *Robert Giddings*

was in his library at Gad's Hill. Dickens was a young parliamentary reporter when one of the most dreadful political riots took place during Reform agitation in Bristol in 1831. Reading Thomas Carlyle's *History of the French Revolution* (1837) kindled his interest in mob violence. He read it constantly and carried it in his pocket. According to John Forster, his first biographer, Dickens claimed to have read it five hundred times. He heard Carlyle lecture in 1840 and was deeply impressed.[2] The violence implicit in Chartist agitation caused much anxiety. As the economy deteriorated, the Chartist challenge became more pressing and public order became an issue, Dickens found the manifestation of the mob an ever more fascinating subject. The Anti-Corn Law League was formed in 1838; in 1839 there were Chartist riots in Birmingham during July where force was used against the imported Metropolitan Police and again at Newport in November. Britain had survived the Chartist threat. (Dickens himself had served as a 'Special Constable' (a volunteer policeman) during the height of Chartist agitation in 1848.) The British now read about revolutions in Paris, Berlin, Budapest, Vienna. Dickens had been an eye-witness of the Genevese revolution in 1846. In January 1858 there was an assassination attempt on Napoleon III in which ten people were killed and 150 injured. As France assisted the attempts to free Italy from Austrian domination, revolutions occurred in Tuscany, Modena, Parma, Bologna, Ferrara and Ravenna. Abroad was a dangerous place to British eyes.

These events were the stuff of headlines during the publication of *A Tale of Two Cities*. It posed an ideal: a quiet industrious life in England in contrast to the violence, injustice and insecurity of France. This was shadowed forth in the wrapper to the monthly serial parts of *A Tale of Two Cities*. Hablot Browne's engraving shows prosperous, mercantile London at the top (ships, merchandise, peaceful panoramic cityscape) and French revolutionary violence at the bottom of the page (guillotine, tumbril, agitators, crowds, revolutionary caps); these were the very different 'Two Cities'.

A Tale of Two Cities certainly has its weaknesses, including the notorious Dickensian melodrama, sentimentality and theatricality of dialogue. It offers few well-drawn locations or striking characters. Apart from the obvious fear of public violence, it has little to say in terms of social comment. The tedious nature of the plot is further rendered unattractive by the fact that it is very difficult to identify with any of the leading characters. Its narrative is simple. Charles is a good-looking young French aristocrat living in England, from a family held in particular loathing for its brutal treatment of social inferiors before the Revolution. His family in Paris is attacked and their tax and rent collector, Gabelle, writes to England begging his help.

Charles returns to France, is arrested and sentenced to death. His life is saved by Sydney Carton, a drunken and dissolute young lawyer, whom physically he resembles. Charles and Sydney are both in love with Lucie Manette, daughter of a French aristocrat long incarcerated in the Bastille. Carton smuggles Charles out of prison and dies in his stead at the guillotine. He goes to his death with the words, 'It is a far, far better thing that I do, than I have ever done; it is a far, far better rest that I go to than I have ever known.'

The novel leaves a major impression of an elemental sweep of mob violence. Despite the passages inserted about the abuse of power by the aristocracy to justify the rising of the French people, Dickens's revolution is totally devoid of any political idealism. Sydney Carton martyrs himself to save the skin of an aristocrat. The most memorable of the revolutionaries is Madame Defarge, whose zeal is motivated more by vengeance than the wish to make the world a better place. By the time we reach the sections where Monsieur Defarge and his followers at the wine shop are plotting to rebel, adding names to the list of people to be revenged upon, it is all pure Tappertit and personal vendetta. It is only in the crowd scenes that *A Tale of Two Cities* really comes to life.

The reception of Charles Dickens's *A Tale of Two Cities* was mixed. It was not critically acclaimed. It was serialised weekly in *All the Year Round*, but Dickens came up with what he called the 'rather original and bold idea' to publish at the end of each month a shilling monthly part in a green cover with two illustrations.[3] Sales were good. By March 1859 monthly instalments totalled 35,000. Nevertheless the general feeling seems to have been that while *Hard Times* and *Little Dorrit* showed signs of Dickens's magic beginning to fade, *A Tale of Two Cities* was frankly dull to the readership which had greedily lapped up *David Copperfield* and the earlier novels. But the novel did subsequently enjoy a vigorous life of its own as play, film, radio, television and opera, an enduring vitality shared by very few novels, possibly only rivalled by *War and Peace*.[4]

A Tale of Two Cities was filmed several times, in silent and talkie versions, and frequently serialised on BBC radio and television. Arthur Benjamin's opera *A Tale of Two Cities* was premièred in 1950 and broadcast by BBC television in 1958.[5] CBS produced a TV movie version in 1980 in which Chris Sarandon played both roles of Darnay and Carton. *Variety* praised the 'impressive costumes and plenty of candles'. Indeed, interest in the novel has to a considerable extent been maintained by the media which find melodrama the very stuff of entertainment.

We are used to radio, film and TV dramatisations of the classics, the media's continuation of literature by other means. The Victorians were well used to stage versions of novels of the day, not only *East Lynne*, *Lily of Killarney* and *Lady Audley's Secret* but more serious books as well. Dickens was sometimes a willing collaborator. *A Tale of Two Cities* had a long theatrical life which extended well into the twentieth century, and served to turn Carton into the star of the show. The influence of *A Tale of Two Cities* on film-makers was clear and is very marked in D.W. Griffith's *Orphans of the Storm* of 1921. The crowd scenes are still impressive. The novel was filmed again in 1926 with Maurice Costello and John Martin-Harvey as *The Only Way*. A famous version with Ronald Colman came out in 1935. Film-makers may endeavour to be faithful in rendering past classics, but dramatisations of classic novels always carry the fingerprints of their own time. Dickens viewed the French Revolution as an *arriviste* of mid-Victorian genteel society, trying to come to terms with the impact of a major political upheaval not so very long before his own time. He had the heart of a socialist, but some instincts of a conservative. He sympathised with the plight of the poor and the dispossessed, but feared what would happen if the masses got together to right social wrongs. This accounts for the suspicion of trade unions in *Hard Times* and the swirling mobs in *Barnaby Rudge* and *A Tale of Two Cities*. When he writes of late eighteenth-century French history there is Chartist agitation at home at the back of his mind. Similarly, Ralph Thomas's film of *A Tale of Two Cities* was released in the tense atmosphere of the Cold War. And it shows.

Ten years previously the United Kingdom, France, Belgium, Luxembourg and the Netherlands signed the Brussels Treaty, allying themselves against armed attack in Europe. Three days after the Treaty was signed, the USSR delegates walked out of the Allied Control Commission for Germany. The Berlin air lift began on 24 June 1948. As the free world and the eastern-bloc countries stockpiled arms and suspiciously faced each other, the Rosenbergs were executed for spying for the Reds, the Korean War broke out, Alger Hiss was found guilty of perjury in concealing his Communist Party membership, the atom spy Klaus Fuchs was exposed, Senator Joseph McCarthy investigated the State Department, and Burgess and MacLean fled to the USSR. The atomic bomb overshadowed the decade. There were claims and counter-claims between the powers about espionage. The Hungarian crisis dominated the news in 1956. Anxiety seeped into the way the age explored its values and expressed itself. The division of our world into two opposing power blocs produced a pressure for social and political conformity. Conformism and 'belongingness' replaced Protestant individualism, the theme of Herman Wouk's novel *The Caine Mutiny* (1951), a key work of the decade. In it the crew of a US minesweeper are led by Steve

Maryk, the executive officer, to mutiny against the paranoid and incompetent Captain Queeg. In the subsequent court martial Maryk is acquitted and Queeg exonerated because the survival of 'corporate management' is judged as more important than satisfaction of individual conscience. This theme was very strongly represented in Wouk's stage play, *The Caine Mutiny Court-Martial* (1954), on which the film version of the same year, with Bogart as Queeg, was based.

The massive nation state of Soviet Russia was believed to pose an active threat to the western world. Russia had, of course, gone down the road of revolution whereas the free world had taken the more careful democratic route. Its cautious consensual progress was consolidated in the post-war settlement, its modest optimism maintaining a fragile balance which typified the British 'tone' of the 1950s. In 1955 the American Edward Shils observed Britain's security curiously in *Encounter*:

> Who criticizes Britain now in any fundamental sense, except for a few Communists and a few Bevanite irreconcilables? There are complaints here and there and on many specific issues, but – in the main – scarcely anyone in Britain seems any longer to feel that there is anything fundamentally wrong. On the contrary, Great Britain on the whole, and especially in comparison with other countries, seems to the British intellectual of the mid-1950s to be all right and even much more than that.

What were the tastes and values which had so reconciled the readership of *Encounter* at this period (in which Shils was writing) to the 'Englishness of English life'? Shils may not have got it right, but his perception was that it was 'continental holidays, the connoisseurship of wine and food, the knowledge of wild flowers and birds, acquaintance with the writings of Jane Austen, a knowing indulgence for the worthies of the English past, an appreciation of the more leisurely epochs, doing one's job dutifully and reliably, the cultivation of personal relations – these are the elements in the ethos of the emerging British intellectual class'. So it seemed, and the seemings of nations are significant. When the English looked abroad, or around them on a 'continental holiday', they saw little national concord.[6] France seemed unable to achieve stable government and had serious trouble in Algeria. Germany was divided. The European nations under communism were kept in place by repression. Across the Atlantic there was the wealthy but materialistic United States, a nation who had bought 'civilisation' at the price of 'culture'. The British watched wryly and were aware of tears in the fabric of world stability. The Cold War was therefore the backdrop for many anxious mystery stories and thrillers. Ian Fleming's novels (the novels rather than the later jovially fatuous features films) dominated popular fiction lists in the

1950s: *Casino Royale* (1953), *Moonraker* (1955), *Diamonds Are Forever* (1956), *Doctor No* (1958), *Goldfinger* (1959). There were the Graham Greene fictions of espionage: *The Quiet American* (1955) and *Our Man in Havana* (1958). The Cold War as subject for film was initiated by the film which Arthur Marwick calls 'the film of Post-War Europe', that is, Carol Reed's and Greene's *The Third Man* (1949). Cinema audiences consumed such treatments of the Cold War as *The Big Lift* (1950), *The Red Danube* (1950), *I Was a Communist for the FBI* (1951), *Diplomatic Courier* (1952) and *The Man Between* (1953).

Ralph Thomas said that he was mainly interested in making films which expressed contemporary sentiments and ideas whatever their subject. 'Generally speaking, I look for a story that is a reflection of the modes and manners of the times.'[7] To see *A Tale of Two Cities* in this context is to recognise British calm, an inner stability in a troubled world. Thomas revelled in 'us versus them' structures. In 1955 he had directed *Above Us the Waves*, a naval war picture starring John Mills which bodied forth the struggle between a midget submarine and the might of Nazi sea power. In 1958 he directed an adaptation of Richard Mason's romantic wartime novel *The Wind Cannot Read*, with Dirk Bogarde as a naive British officer who falls in love with a young Japanese interpreter with terminal brain disease.[8] The doomed romance is enacted in a threatening and exotic (and confusing) Raj setting. It has one extraordinary sequence, usually cut for transmission on British television, in which Bogarde is captured by the Japanese, who are played as robotic martinets. They command Bogarde's loyal Sikh fellow officer to spit on him. Under duress, he does so, and then makes a dash for it. The Japanese officer shoots him in the back.

It is Dirk Bogarde who stars as Sydney Carton in Ralph Thomas's *A Tale of Two Cities*. He remembered it as a well-dressed failure.

> We had a most impressive cast of (mainly) theatre actors; enormous care was lavished on the authenticity of the sets and costumes; we went all the way to Bourges in France and shot the film there. But even though it was a faithful 'reproduction' of Dickens, even though we spoke his words and delivered his rather preposterous plot perfectly to the screen, the film failed. My contention is that (a) they wanted Ronald Colman, and (b) we cut costs and made it in black and white ... As a 'classic' adaptation, it could not be faulted, but it did not transfer to the screen of the late fifties. It was not of its time.[9]

Nevertheless, *A Tale of Two Cities* has the fingerprints of the 1950s all over it and the film sits comfortably in its historical moment. The film's main action is placed in the context of threatening revolutionary change, but its narrative style – vigorously eschewing the characteristically Dickensian grotesque and opting for rather humdrum cinematic historical realism – is timidly conformist. This manner is established at the outset in the opening credits. Thomas deploys old prints to give a straightforward sense of the past. British stability, good common sense and, at bottom, guts and courage, are represented in the sturdy person of Cecil Parker as Jarvis Lorry, manager of Tellson's bank. Parker was a familiar figure to cinema-goers: *The Man in the White Suit* (1951), *I Believe In You* (1952), *Isn't Life Wonderful* and *Father Brown* (both 1954), *The Constant Husband* and *The Ladykillers* (both 1955). His physique, plummy voice and controlled fussiness enabled him to play both warm-hearted characters and management types. As Jarvis Lorry he projects the decent paternalism required to safeguard such vulnerable fugitives from political chaos in France as Lucy Manette and her father. He is counterbalanced across the Channel by Christopher Lee as the evil aristo-crat who indifferently runs his horses over peasant lads and or rogers the chateau servants. Memories are invoked of his sinister presence in *Moby Dick* (1956), *Ill Met by Moonlight* (1956), *The Traitor* (1957) and above all Lee's Frankenstein's monster, which he first played on screen in 1956. His definitive impersonation of Dracula was also on release at the same time as *A Tale of Two Cities*. With such dark tones, no screen performer could so credibly project casual menace. The fragile Lucy Manette was radiantly presented by Dorothy Tutin in a performance which drew on her experience as Gwendolen in *The Importance of Being Earnest* (1952) and Polly in Peter Brook's *The Beggar's Opera* (1952), as well as stage roles such as Rose in Graham Greene's *The Living Room* (1953), Sally in John Van Druten's *I am a Camera* (1954), St Joan in Jean Anouilh's *The Lark* and Hedvig in Ibsen's *The Wild Duck* (both in 1955). When *A Tale of Two Cities* was in the cinemas, she was a brilliant success in three Shakespearean leads, Viola, Ophelia and Juliet. Tutin was well able to convey both vulnerable innocence and sexual magnetism. On the big screen 1950s audiences were delighted to see her with the eyes seen by Bogarde's Sydney Carton who sacrificed himself for her and them. The role of Carton's double, Charles Darnay, was played by Paul Guers, who only vaguely resembled Bogarde. The cinematic trick of having both parts played by the same actor was resisted. The theme of the *doppelgänger* which so fascinated the gothic romantics (Hoffmann, Heine, Poe) was given only subdued treatment by Dickens and Thomas, who were not to be drawn into phantasmagoric excess. Donald Pleasance as the spy Barsad represented the materialist, non-idealist agent with neither relish for nor loyalty to the profession of espionage. 'I admit that I am a spy, and that it is considered a discreditable station – though it must be filled by somebody.' He offers his services in typically 1950s style by telling Bogarde and his companions, 'I could be a very useful comrade.'

The tragic love entanglements of the plot are played out against a very cursorily sketched French Revolution which in this film appears to have been ignited by little more than a couple of broken barrels of wine and some careless driving on the part of a single aristocrat. Just as Dickens's readers could enjoy the adventures in safety while the raging battle between good and bad took place safely on the other side of the Channel, so the 1950s could relish the contest between well-spoken Englishmen and treacherous East Europeans in the Cold War. Britain in the 1950s may have had its drab side, but it afforded a safe view of European intensities.

Notes

1   My epigraph is taken from Book IX, Chapter 2 of Forster's *Life*. For film adaptations of Dickens, see David Parossien, 'Dickens and the Cinema', *Dickens Studies Annual* 7 (Southern Illinois Press, 1978) and Robert Giddings, 'Great Misrepresentations: Dickens and Film', *Critical Survey* (1991), pp. 305–12.

2   John Forster, *The Life of Charles Dickens*, 1872, Book IX, Chapter 2 (Chapman and Hall, Fireside edition), p. 796.

3   William Oddie, *Dickens and Carlyle: The Question of Influence* (Century Press, 1972), p. 61.

4   *War and Peace* was filmed by Vitagraph in 1911. It is frequently claimed that D.W Griffith's French Revolutionary film *Orphans of the Storm* (1921) borrows from the novel: see Kevin Brownlow, *The Parade's Gone By* (Secker & Warburg, 1968) pp. 14–16, 84–85. *War and Peace* was notably filmed by King Vidor (1956) and Serge Bondarchuk (1964). It was adapted for the stage, and a television version by R.D. MacDonald, transmitted by Granada in 1963, won an Emmy Award. It was the subject of an opera by Prokofiev, first performed 1946 (revised and extended 1955). Jack Pulman's magisterial serial dramatisation for television was transmitted by BBC2 in 1972. The novel has been well served by BBC radio as a classic serial; the last version was broadcast in 1997.

5   The television production, by Rudolph Cartier, utilised three studios, a cast of 120 and the Royal Philharmonic Orchestra conducted by Leon Lovett. It was the most spectacular musical production undertaken by British television that decade.

6   Edward Shils is quoted by Robert Hewison in *In Anger: Culture and the Cold War, 1945–1960* (Methuen, 1981), p. 72. Shils was a sociologist who taught at the London School of Economics and at Manchester University.

7   Ralph Thomas, quoted by Ronald Bergan in obituary of Thomas (1915–2001), *Guardian* (20 March 2001).

8   *The Wind Cannot Read* was to have been directed by David Lean, but the producer, Korda, was not satisfied with Lean's approach to the subject. It was sold to Rank and landed on Ralph Thomas's desk.

9   Dirk Bogarde in 'Books Are Better', *Literary Review* (July 1994), reprinted in *For The Time Being* (Penguin, 1998).

Value for money: Baker and Berman, and Tempean Films

BRIAN MCFARLANE

You don't need to be as fond of British 'B' movies of the 1950s as I am to feel that there is something to be said for the production team of Bob Baker and Monty Berman and their production company, Tempean.[1] The second features that emerged from this partnership are generally speaking fast-moving, unpretentious, lively and characterful, and, within their modest budgets, well enough staged to look more expensive than they were. However, it is not my primary intention to offer elaborate analyses of these films, or to make unsustainable claims for their being long-buried, unsung treasures of auteurist film-making. It is worth looking at the Tempean phenomenon for a number of reasons in a book devoted to 1950s British cinema. First, it relates significantly to the exhibition procedures of the period, when audiences typically expected a 'double bill', with a main feature and a supporting film, which might be designated either a co-feature or a second feature according to the lavishness of its casting and budget. If a major film ran to over two hours, say, it was likely to be supported by 'shorts' (often designated 'selected featurettes') rather than by another feature film of the kind made by Tempean. In any case, a three-hour programme was the norm, and as long as this persisted, there was a steady demand for the sort of supporting film Tempean made until the late 1950s.

Thus, second, Tempean sums up a prolific area of 1950s production, fuelled by these exhibition patterns. To riffle through the pages of Denis Gifford's *British Film Catalogue* is to be aware of how much activity at this level there was from the late 1940s through until the mid-1960s.[2] If it has been the focus for so little critical attention, this may be the result of several factors, including the unforgiving approach to the 'quota quickies' of the 1930s, films

I am Honorary Associate Professor of the School of Literary, Visual and Cultural Studies, Monash University, Melbourne. My recent books include *Novel to Film: An Introduction to the Theory of Adaptation* (1996), *An Autobiography of British Cinema* (1997), *The Oxford Companion to Australian Film* (co-editor) (1999) and *Lance Comfort* (1999). I am currently compiling *The Encyclopedia of British Film. Brian McFarlane*

made in the expectation of swift oblivion and to satisfy quota requirements for British films, with no reference to aesthetic criteria. Another reason for so little notice having been taken of so vast an area of film-making (much of it certainly deserved no more) may be that reviewers almost never saw or reviewed these films. They were both prolific and disregarded. They made their way direct to the public without the intervention of quality-minded middle-brow critics.

Third, Tempean turned out 'B' movies at a more sustained level of competence and enjoyment than perhaps any other of the companies regularly occupied with filling the bottom half of the double bill. Baker and Berman relied on the services of personnel they could trust and built up a roster of actors and others who knew their job and could be relied on to get it done in the required time and within the allotted budget. This was a company that knew exactly what it wanted to achieve and did so; and what they achieved is worth looking at nearly half a century later.

Who were Baker and Berman? Both had been involved in film-making before World War II. Monty Berman (born in London, 1913), not to be confused with the costumier of the same name, entered films in 1930 as a camera assistant at Twickenham Studios, and during the 1930s worked as camera operator at Teddington (1934–8) and Ealing (1938–40) Studios. Michael Powell described him as 'a young cameraman who had done outstanding work on my two films at Warner Brothers' Teddington Studios', at the time of appointing him lighting cameraman for *The Edge of the World*, and he went into the army as a camera operator.[3] Robert S. Baker (born in London, 1916) entered films in 1937 as assistant director 'on a film called *Night in Havana*, which was basically a musical that ran for about 20 minutes'.[4] He had been a keen amateur director before this and had even won prizes for short documentaries. Baker and Berman met in the African desert during the war, when both were army sergeants and were transferred to the army film unit, both having had significant experience as cameramen covering military action. Their memories of this was later to feed into their 'A' film, *Sea of Sand* (1958). As Baker recalled in 1995, they decided that

> when we got out of the army we were going to make our own pictures. We were demobbed at roughly the same time and we begged, borrowed and stole to get finance together to make a picture called *A Date with a Dream* (1948). That was our first break, as it were, into the movie business. We were pretty green at that time, so we used our own money, which we probably would have been forced to do, because, coming out of the army, we had no reputation to fall back on. So we financed it ourselves; I think the film cost about just under £10,000.[4]

Like many film-makers whose careers had been disrupted by the war, they were determined to make their way in what was still far and away the most popular entertainment form available. What they did was to set up Tempean as their production company. It was possible then to set up a company for £100 but, in order to make it look more than a fly-by-night enterprise, they felt that they needed to finance it to the tune of £1,000, thereby creating a thousand £1 shares which could be allocated as they chose. The 'board' consisted of Baker and Berman, Baker's father Morris, and Dicky Leeman who was also their contract director, though he made only one film for them before leaving to work in television variety.[5] Their contract screenwriter was Carl Nystrom, who wrote three screenplays for them: *Date with a Dream*, *Melody Club* (1949) and *Impulse* (1955). The studio at which they made their first film was Viking, a tiny studio in Kensington, with some interiors shot at Collins Music Hall, Islington, neither of which survives. It was one thing to set up a production company, even to make a film as Baker and Berman had done, but the effort would have been wasted without effective distribution. According to Baker in 2000, they 'didn't go to a distributor to get a deal to make the film [*A Date with a Dream*] ... we showed it to a company called Eros who ... liked the picture and decided to finance us on our next pictures, so we then had a distribution deal with them. We were coming in on budget with presentable pictures and they were happy with them. We must have made twenty to thirty pictures with Eros.'[6] Having steady distribution arrangements was an indicator of Tempean's businesslike approach from the start. Eros was primarily the concern of two brothers, Phil and Sydney Hyams. Phil Hyams, chairman in its key period, and his brother Syd Hyams, managing director, entered the industry in 1912 as cinema owners, forming Eros post-World War II. In the mid-1950s, Eros also became involved in the production of such independently produced 'A' films as *The Man Who Watched Trains Go By* (1952) and *The Sea Shall Not Have Them* (1954), but it was essentially a distribution outfit. It went into liquidation in 1961. Bob Baker recalled that Eros would buy American films outright for showing in the United Kingdom, then take a British film as a co-feature and distribute the double bill, an arrangement which was clearly to the advantage of Tempean.

Tempean finally wound up in the early 1960s, having by this time produced several 'A' films, including the war film *Sea of Sand* (1958), the horror films *Blood of the Vampire* (1958), *The Flesh and the Fiends* (1959) and *Jack the Ripper* (1959), an unusual tale of pre-World War I anarchists in London, *The Siege of Sidney Street* (1960), and *The Count of Monte Cristo* (1961). These last two, in fact, appear under the company name of Mid-Century, but, as Baker explained, this was just an arm of Tempean, deriving from a loss-making company he and Berman had bought up as a legitimate tax manoeuvre. They bought loss companies such as Mid-Century, Kenilworth and New World so that they could write off any profits Tempean made against that loss. All the 'B' films bearing the Kenilworth/Mid-Century logo were distributed by GFD. The other company whose name appears on some of Baker–Berman's second features (e.g. *Barbados Quest* (1955), *Breakaway* (1956) and *High Terrace* (1957) is CIPA, 'a company with some other people [including Emmett Dalton] involved in it, and which made films for RKO Radio Pictures as it was then' (Baker in 2000). (They also made four films in Eire for Dalton, a friend of Michael Collins during 'The Troubles', who had tried to start a film industry in Ireland, and Baker and Berman made *Professor Tim* (1957), the first film at Dublin's Bray Studios. These Irish-based films had nothing to do with Tempean.) As for the others, they are Tempean under other names. A list of the full Baker and Berman output, under various company names, can be found below, on pp. 188–9.

The details of the organisation of Tempean Films and the other companies are interesting not so much in themselves as for what they reveal of Baker and Berman's business acumen, which, along with an ear to the ground for judging what was acceptable to audiences, perhaps accounts for their sustained success. They had a sure grasp of film financing, and knew how to make best use of the National Film Finance Corporation's processes, especially as they related to cross-collateralisation. In Baker's own words:

> For instance, if you had a picture that was successful and you wanted to borrow money, from the National Film Service, they often asked you to cross-collateralise your successful film with the film that you wanted to make. Consequently, if the film that you wanted to make didn't make any money within a certain period of time, then they could take the profits from the successful film to set off against it. It was just a way of the National Film Finance Corporation securing their loan ... What happened was you went to a distributor and he gave you a distribution contract. A distribution contract covered 75% of the budget. Then you took the distribution contract to a bank who would advance you the money against the distribution contract. You are left with 25% to find in order to finance a picture, so what we used to do invariably was we would defer our fees, which would pay a certain percentage of the 25%, and the National Film Finance Corporation put up the rest of the money.

The remarks show business acumen, an ear to the ground – and also a genuine feel for the game. This was not immediately apparent from their first two films. *A Date with a Dream* has some engaging moments, some of them provided by the often insufferably cute, but here poised and confident

Jeannie Carson, and with 'turns' by Terry-Thomas (paid £50 per week) and Norman Wisdom each in his first film, and the likeable comic team of Len and Bill Lowe. This is basically a low-key, domestic version of the US musical staple of the kids' saying, 'Let's put on a show', and of course finally doing it – in production circumstances considerably more restrained than, say, Mickey Rooney and Judy Garland would have had to contend with at MGM. It is an ingenuous piece of work, which just about gets by on the basis of the inherent talent of its cast and a kind of amateur's enthusiasm it would be surly to abuse. Tempean didn't make any money out of *A Date with a Dream*, partly because its distributor – Grand National – was a very small company and perhaps, as Baker says, 'their bookkeeping wasn't strictly accurate either' (Baker in 2000). They began with Eros as distributor on their next film, *Melody Club*, starring again the Lowe brothers and Terry-Thomas. Directed by Baker himself, it seems no longer to exist, about which he is glad, calling it 'terrible'. It has been described as a 'collection of well-worn jokes stitched together to make a plot'.[7]

These were not the sort of films that would account for Tempean's prolific output in the 1950s. In 1950 they began to turn out the kind of efficient crime thrillers that would be their staple for most of the decade. The first five are wholly indigenous in flavour, with British stars, generally of the second rank, supported by sturdy character actors who became a sort of Tempean repertory company. I have not been able to see *Blackout* (1950) for this study – it is the second film in this category and features Dinah Sheridan, before she became a major star, and Maxwell Reed, who never did become one – but the other four are more than adequate second features. *No Trace* (1950) stars Hugh Sinclair and Dinah Sheridan again, here pluckily unmasking a murderous employer and reminding us never to trust men in smoking jackets; *The Quiet Woman* (1951), set and filmed on the Romney Marshes, starring the excellent and undervalued Jane Hylton, and Derek Bond, refreshingly combines smuggling, fractured personal relationships and postwar malaise; *13 East Street* (1952) involves an undercover detective and rackets in luxury items like nylon stockings; and *The Frightened Man* (1952), with Charles Victor and Dermot Walsh, quite grippingly mixes father–son conflict with robbery. These are the films that made me Tempean's devoted follower. They are entirely without pretension; they tell their stories neatly and suspensefully; they make excellent use of location and studio shooting; and they are already establishing that reputation for dependable character work that makes them still so enjoyable to watch. Michael Balfour, who first appears for Tempean in *Melody Club*, John Horsley, who may have arrested more felons than any other British actor (or possibly most

British policemen), Thora Hird, Dora Bryan, Michael Ward and Michael Brennan all appear in these and other Tempean films, so that it is not so surprising if the films seem to have a richer texture than might be expected, given their modest budgets.

With an eye on the US markets, Baker and Berman very often secured the services of American actors. These were not major stars at the height of their fame, of course; they were people who had enjoyed palpable if not first-league stardom, like Mark Stevens – the first of Tempean's imports – in *The Lost Hours* (1952), or Scott Brady, or Arthur Kennedy, names big enough still to mean something in the mid-West, even if not huge draws. Some had been 'B' movie leads in Hollywood: actors like Rod Cameron, Mary Castle and Forrest Tucker; and there was the sad serendipity of blacklisted Larry Parks, briefly a big star after *The Jolson Story* (1946), but destroyed by McCarthy, and finding asylum in the politically more tolerant climate of England. Baker and Berman knew exactly what they were doing in signing these Americans. It wasn't just a matter of their minor or faded stellar status; it was because they gave a touch of international gloss to the modest programmers. As Baker said, 'They [American actors] gave a lift to British co-features – plus the different accent helped to make the picture more universal', and he praised them for their efficiency, which he believed came from their training in the art of film-making. '[They] knew the camera and consequently their performances were very, very smooth ... The result was a bit like a professionally made pullover compared to a well-meant hand-knitted job.'[8]

To acquire this American connection, Tempean worked through a man called Bob Goldstein who had been a casting director for many years at Universal and who then 'came over here and established a co-production organisation. He was able to get quite big names; we would make a deal together whereby he would supply the actor and a certain amount of the finance and we would supply the rest.' They would commission a script with an American lead, meet with Eros and Goldstein, and go through a list of names that he could supply. Baker and Berman would choose who they thought was the right person and Goldstein would do a deal with the American. This arrangement relieved the pair of a lot of responsibility and saved the time it would have taken to do the deal in America. The whole negotiation was conducted in Britain, and Goldstein was happy with his percentage of the American market.

Whatever the quality of second or co-features, there was little chance of their being critically noticed. There was no British critic with the eye for a 'sleeper' on the bottom half of the double bill in the way that James Agee had spotted them in the US in the 1940s. The pictures would be noticed in the trade papers, such as *Kinematograph Weekly*, and might get very brief notices in *Picturegoer* and *Picture Show*, but the daily and weekend newspapers virtually never reviewed – possibly never saw – them. The Tempean pair accepted this and got on with the business for as long as there was a market for their product and, when this dried up, turned first to making the 'A' features referred to above and then with consummate success to television, where their Tempean experiences fitted them admirably to adjust to the length, generic conventions and tight shooting schedules of weekly episodes in such series as *The Saint* (1962–9), *Gideon's Way* (1964) and *The Persuaders* (1970–1). In 1964, Berman told a reporter, 'To produce a TV series, you must keep everything orderly; and providing the scripts are all right, then the rest of the work is selecting the right people and checking up all the time.' [9] That sounds very much like the successful recipe they had followed at Tempean.

In the end, though, audiences are not going to be moved by sheer efficiency, or by amiability, even if Brian Worth said at the time of Tempean's silver jubilee (that is, the celebration of their twenty-fifth film completed since the company was founded), 'I have never worked with two nicer blokes.' [10] It matters nothing to filmgoers that films were made on time or within budget, however impressive such virtues may be in the industry – and however important they may be in accounting for the productivity and continuity of the company. It is one thing for the article just quoted to claim that 'A company which uses its resources so competently deserves to succeed' (and remember, we are talking of films made in about three weeks for between £12,000 and £20,000), but the time comes when one asks: What was the production output like?

In terms of genre, Tempean and its associated companies produced mainly thrillers. This was largely a matter of market demand. As Baker said: 'The public appetite was in favour of thrillers ... You could make a comedy or a thriller. Anything in between was very dubious! ... It's easy to hook an audience with a thriller, not so easy to hook them on a soft romantic plot.' [11] It may be that in relation to romantic films, audiences expect major stars as a focus for their attention and empathy. For whatever reason, none of Tempean's second features fall into this category. There is usually a romantic action proceeding in parallel with the thriller plot, as was the case with most crime films, but the romance was never the centre of attention; it provided a means of winding up the film on a more or less upbeat note, though the films do not follow this pattern slavishly. *The Voice of Merrill* (1952), a strong co-feature with a significant star in Valerie Hobson, and *The Frightened Man*

(1952) both end with one of the romantic pair dead while the other walks off into the night. There is also in some of the thrillers a touch of American *film noir*, quite deliberate according to Baker, who admired this moody style.

Of the more than thirty second features that Baker and Berman produced for Tempean (including Mid-Century, Kenilworth and CIPA) and one for Butchers (*Blind Spot*, 1958), and not including the Irish-set and -financed films they made for Emmett Dalton's own company (for example, *Professor Tim* (1957), *Sally's Irish Rogue* (1958), *Home Is the Hero* (1959) and *Boyd's Shop* (1960)), only six belong to non-thriller genres, and none is among the pair's best. The first two – musicals – are referred to above, and no one would have expected much of the makers; there are two mild comedies – *Love in Pawn* (1953) and *The Reluctant Bride* (1955), the latter given some zing by two second-league Hollywood stars, Virginia Bruce and John Carroll; *No Smoking* (1955), described by David Quinlan as a 'potty comedy'; and the science-fiction piece, *The Trollenberg Terror* (1958), the last of their 'B' films. The last-named has some scary moments though the special effects, for those who care about such matters, today look inevitably meagre, but the Swiss Alps are the real thing – shot by Berman while he and Baker and their families were on holiday there.

This last point about locations is worth noting. One of the besetting faults of British 'B' movies is their airless look, as if they were made entirely in some very confined studios, as indeed many of them were. The Tempean pair made a point of using actual locations whenever possible, believing it 'gave another dimension to the picture … But Britain has never been geared to location shooting like America has. You had to get police permission and there were all sorts of problems.'[12] This complaint has been borne out by other film-makers, working on a more ambitious scale than Baker and Berman, who were also motivated by the fact that, if carefully planned, location work could be cheaper than building lavish sets. They used back-projection when they had to, as in the case of *The Quiet Woman*, for scenes involving the smugglers' boat, but Baker felt it wasn't very efficient and they tried to avoid it whenever possible. His own account of their location shooting habits gives a vivid picture of location work at these budget levels:

> Since we would select our locations before production we would make quite sure that they were feasible and they weren't going to be too expensive and that the hire cost wasn't going to be too high. We were shooting on locations before it was the popular thing to do as it is now. Nowadays, if they go on location they have all sorts of wagons, eating wagons, food wagons, cars or trailers for the stars and so forth. We had none of that. We just went in two or three cars and the location manager would go to the nearest cafe at lunchtime and get some

sandwiches and an urn of tea or coffee or something and we would sit quite often
at the kerb sometimes having our lunch during shooting. We'd never thought of
taking a caravan for an actor. We used to go somewhere and go into a pub and
hire a couple of rooms so the actors could get changed if they had to. We'd make
do on a day-to-day basis. It was planned, but it was planned very economically.
(Baker in 2000)

Another aspect of their efficiency was no doubt in using personnel they
could rely on. They had Michael Craig and the Canadian actress Dianne
Foster briefly under contract, but in general people such as those character
players named above worked for them again and again and understood the
constraints of filming on tight budgets and schedules. Apart from actors,
they also used the same director, John Gilling, on a dozen second features,
Gilling often being responsible for the screenplay as well. Some actors,
including Craig and Diana Dors (replaced, owing to 'illness', after a couple
of days on *The Quiet Woman* by Tempean regular Dora Bryan), thought
Gilling was abrasive, but the producers found him wholly reliable, and, after
he had gone off to direct a series of mixed-genre pieces for Warwick Films
starting with *The Gamma People* (1955), he returned to Tempean to direct
The Flesh and the Fiends, the horror calling-card that took him to Hammer
for the final stage of his prolific career. Much of Tempean's most enjoyable
output is directed by Gilling, but others such as Baker himself, former editor
Charles Saunders, former theatre producer Henry Cass and cinematographer C. Pennington-Richards each directed several for the company.
Apart from Gilling, though, the chief continuity was in the Baker–Berman
production team itself and in having Berman as the cinematographer. As
Berman said: 'Because I'm co-producer with Robert, I can take far more
chances than an ordinary cameraman. I don't have to worry about where my
next job is coming from.' [13] Tempean was nothing if not pragmatic.

All these elements which characterise the Tempean enterprise – continuity
of personnel, the use of locations outside the studio when feasible and desir-
able, the ensuring that the money spent on the films (on casting, on settings)
would be up there on the screen, the clear sense of what would work with
audiences, the long background of varied experience amassed by the partners
– help to account for a sustained level of achievement not common in the
British second feature. (It is worth noting that this corner of production is
not as barren of interest as has been assumed: directors such as Ken Hughes,
Lance Comfort, Montgomery Tully, Peter Graham Scott and Francis Searle
all made second features that repay closer attention.) I want, before conclud-
ing, to look briefly at several paradigmatic second features that derive from
Tempean in one or other of its mutations, to suggest how a more or less

conventional framework has been worked on to provide more than conventional interest.

The Frightened Man, The Voice of Merrill and *Impulse* will do as well as any to suggest the Tempean virtues in action. The first is a thriller based on a jewel robbery masterminded by Alec Stone (the ever-oleaginous Martin Benson in a smoking jacket) and involving the son of Stone's gang's usual fence. The son, Julius (Dermot Walsh, whose 'A' film career had petered out by now), has been sent down from Oxford and his father, antique dealer Rosselli (Charles Victor), is desperate to keep him out of the robbery. In a rooftop chase, very well filmed by director Gilling, Julius falls to his death as his father tries to save him, and Rosselli's wife (Barbara Murray) walks off into the night. On to this bare outline are grafted several strands which give the film more than usual texture. The relationship between father and son is given more interest than the plot strictly needs: the idea of the son educated above his father's aspirations and having been corrupted in the process makes some unobtrusive points about class in 1950s Britain, points reinforced by the casting of Walsh, who projects an insolent superiority, and Victor, so resonant of working-class decency, even if here he is a notch or two higher socially as keeper of an antiques shop. There is a brief touch suggestive of Rosselli's Roman Catholic background in the saying of grace at meals in the house which takes in lodgers, one of whom is an undercover policeman, played of course by John Horsley, and presided over by housekeeper Thora Hird. This only matters insofar as it suggests the kind of trouble taken to imbue the film with a touch of what Henry James might have called 'felt life'. The same might be said of Julius's homophobic reaction to his father's shop assistant, Cornelius, played by the inveterately camp actor, Michael Ward, but here given a chance to do more than his usual prissy cameo. Again, this interaction between Julius and Cornelius is not a major plot point, but it works as an individuating touch: the film merely notes, and doesn't need to explain, why Julius reacts as he does; and Cornelius is allowed the dignity of being seriously good at his work.

In this unobtrusive way, second features sometimes wear better than 'A' films because they are not so *consciously* commenting on the age, but simply (and unconsciously?) build perceptions into the fabric of events: in hindsight, a film such as this can suggest a range of social connotations which probably didn't bother Tempean at the time, in a way that, if they had been, say, Basil Dearden, they would have been bothered at the forefront of their minds.

Baker was very clear on the differences between second features and co-features. You could tell it by the billing – half-and-half for co-features and roughly 80–20 ratio for second features – on the posters. *The Voice of Merrill* is distinctly a co-feature. Valerie Hobson, though near the end of her career, didn't come as cheaply as, say, Barbara Murray, the female lead in *The Frightened Man*, and the money was well spent. She had been a major star and came trailing associations of class and classiness that one wouldn't expect of the usual 'B' movie leading lady. Her elegance, the subtle sexiness alongside a certain chilliness, and her intelligence make her very good casting as the erring wife of a famous writer (James Robertson Justice). Her persona generates the right degree of interest without evoking a tone-destroying sympathy. The more than usually complicated plot concerns the murder of a blackmailer, the suspects James Robertson Justice, Valerie Hobson and a another writer loved by Hobson (Edward Underdown). It ends badly for everyone. One wonders why Hobson was ever sufficiently attracted to the vituperative Justice to marry him, but their difficult marriage does provide a starting point for her interest in Underdown. The film makes neat use of radio as plot device; the plot has enough twists and turns, made more provocative by the casting; and there are convincing sexual sparks between Hobson and Underdown. The murder which initiates the film is shot with a properly mystifying sense as the camera picks out legs moving down a dark, wet street, entering a building with back still to the camera; a woman turns around; a shot rings out and she collapses. Again and again, the Tempean films succeed in hooking the view with provocative opening episodes which have an element of ambiguity that one doesn't expect in budget film-making. Gilling, working again from his own screenplay, maintains a degree of tension between event and consequence, and between event and character, impressive enough to lift the film well clear of second-feature obloquy. In fact, it played co-feature dates and was sometimes the main film on a double bill, the distributors finding they had bought more than they had expected.

One of the most interesting films in the Tempean output is *Impulse* (1955). Though the credits list Charles de Lautour (a.k.a. de La Tour) as director, the actual director was blacklisted American Cy Endfield. According to Baker, 'in order to overcome the problem of Cy Endfield – if his name was on the screen they wouldn't take the film in America – we just had this stand-by director who was actually a documentary film maker, Charles de Lautour, who just sat on the set all day long whilst Endfield directed and he [de Lautour] just sat there and did nothing' (Baker in 2000). *Impulse* is much influenced by noir narrative tendencies: the hero, Alan Curtis (Arthur Kennedy), an American lawyer in an English provincial town, presumably having stayed on after the war (though this is not spelled out), is vaguely dissatisfied with his life. He is caught in a domestic and social routine which offers little prospect of excitement, when an attractive woman, Lila (Constance Smith), enters his life and, in the absence of his wife (Joy Shelton), on impulse he lies to the police about Lila's whereabouts. She is a nightclub singer, a very noir job for a dangerous woman, and she lures Curtis to London where he becomes involved with the shifty club owner, falls easily for Lila's sexual allure, and is caught up in crimes including diamond theft and murder. The London scenes, many at night, have the sense of big-city danger associated with *film noir*, whereas the provincial scenes which flank them are photographed in a way which flattens out distinctions. The film has marked similarities to the 1948 Hollywood thriller *Pitfall*, directed by André de Toth and starring Dick Powell and Lizabeth Scott as the straying husband and the siren. The American gloss, in the better sense of the word, which derives from the noir influences and from the complex, intense performance from Arthur Kennedy, gives *Impulse* a restless, teasing quality that works in significant opposition to the English setting and supporting cast.

There is not the space here to work one's way through the Tempean filmography, nor is it my intention. The three films briefly noted are perhaps enough to suggest ways in which these robust film-makers went about giving touches of individuality to more or less quotidian enterprises. There are plenty of others which deserve to be noted. *The Quiet Woman* (1950) makes valuable use of its rural setting and contrasts this to both the criminal activities involved and the sense of postwar restlessness that motivates its hero. *The Lost Hours* (1952), mixing romantic triangle with murder enquiry, in its use of Mark Stevens, a US pilot in England for a RAF reunion, ushers in the deliberate Tempean policy of blending Hollywood influences with the domestic. (His British co-star, Jean Kent, recalled suggesting she should initiate a kiss, but he courteously explained that this was not the American way, implying that it would compromise his masculinity and be unacceptable to US audiences.)[14] *The Embezzler* (1954) marries thriller to morality play in the style of *Passing of the Third Floor Back*, the two elements linked by another excellent performance from Charles Victor; and *Black Orchid*, *Deadly Nightshade* (both 1953), *Delayed Action* (1954), with American Robert Ayres, and *Double Exposure* (1954), all work enjoyable variations on conventional thriller plots.

No one wants to suggest that the prestige of British cinema depended on Tempean and the like. It is, however, equally true that, in their unaffected meeting of a marketplace demand, Baker and Berman made every penny work in the interest of the film-goer. Their aim was to entertain, and in providing films that found ready acceptance with audiences for a decade they are often revealing about the nature of public taste, not just in films but in a wider sense culturally. The lure of Americanisation, albeit in a setting cosily recognisable, is but one example.

Tempean Films

This list includes films made under the company names Kenilworth and Mid-Century. Those made as CIPA are asterisked. Directors' names are in brackets.

1948	*A Date with a Dream* (Dicky Leeman)
1949	*Melody Club* (John Gilling)
1950	*No Trace* (Gilling)
	Blackout (Robert S. Baker)
1951	*The Quiet Woman* (Gilling)
1952	*The Frightened Man* (Gilling)
	The Lost Hours (Gilling)
	The Voice of Merill (Gilling)
	13 East Street (Baker)
1953	*The Steel Key* (Gilling)
	Recoil (Gilling)
	Three Steps to the Gallows (Gilling)
	Deadly Nightshade (Gilling)
	Black Orchid (Charles Saunders)
	Love in Pawn (Saunders)
1954	*Escape by Night* (Gilling)
	Double Exposure (Gilling)
	The Embezzler (Gilling)
	Delayed Action (John Harlow)
1955	*The Gilded Cage* (Gilling)
	Tiger by the Tail (Gilling)
	The Reluctant Bride (Henry Cass)
	No Smoking (Cass)
	Impulse (Cy Endfield, as Charles de Lautour)
	Barbados Quest (Bernard Knowles)*
1956	*Passport to Treason* (Baker)
	Breakaway (Cass)*
1957	*Hour of Decision* (C. Pennington-Richards)
	Stranger in Town (George Pollock)
	High Terrace (Cass)
1958	*Stormy Crossing* (Pennington-Richards)
	The Trollenberg Terror (Quentin Lawrence)
	Blind Spot (Peter Maxwell, for Butcher's)
	Blood of the Vampire (Cass)
	Sea of Sand (Guy Green)
1959	*Jack the Ripper* (Baker)
	The Flesh and the Fiends (Baker)

1960	*The Siege of Sidney Street* (Baker)
1961	*The Hellfire Club* (Baker)
	The Treasure of Monte Cristo (Baker)
1962	*What a Carve Up!* (Pat Jackson)

Baker and Berman made for Emmett Dalton's Irish company:

1957	*Professor Tim* (Cass)
1958	*Sally's Irish Rogue* (Pollock)
1959	*Home is the Hero* (Fielder Cook)
1960	*Boyd's Shop* (Cass)

Notes

1 Bob Baker can no longer remember the origin of the company's name, except perhaps that, recalling the Vale of Tempe, it suggested a touch of class, borne out in the classical pillars of the Tempean logo.

2 Denis Gifford, *The British Film Catalogue, 1895–1970* (David & Charles, 1973).

3 Michael Powell, *A Life in Movies* (Heinemann, 1986), p. 242. It is not clear which 'two films' Powell means; Berman is certainly listed as co-cinematographer with Basil Emmott on *Someday* (1935), but the inadequate credits available for Powell's other Warner films offer no clue.

4 All further unattributed comments from Robert S. Baker come from my interviews with him in either 1995 or 2000. Some of the earlier interviews were published in my *An Autobiography of British Cinema* (Methuen and British Film Institute, 1997).

5 See Peter Noble (ed.), *British Film Yearbook 1949–50* (Skelton Robinson, 1949), p. 272.

6 McFarlane, *Autobiography*, p. 43.

7 David Quinlan, *British Sound Films. The Studio Years 1929–1959* (B. T. Batsford, 1984), p. 230.

8 McFarlane, *Autobiography*, p. 44.

9 Quoted in Tony Gruner, 'Baker and Berman's 'Saint' goes marching on – and on', *Kinematograph Weekly* (13 August 1964), p. 15.

10 Quoted in Tom Hutchinson, 'Tempean Films to Make Bigger Pictures', *Kinematograph Weekly* (21 April 1955), p. 37.

11 McFarlane, *Autobiography*, p. 46.

12 McFarlane, *Autobiography*, pp. 44–5.

13 Quoted in Hutchinson, 'Tempean Films to Make Bigger Pictures', p. 37.

14 In conversation with the author, UK (September 2000).

Adaptable Terence Rattigan: *Separate Tables*, separate entities?

DOMINIC SHELLARD

TERENCE RATTIGAN'S REPUTATION has essentially been that of a theatre writer, and a conservative one, who is supposed to have avoided the darker themes that invaded the British stage after (roughly) the arrival of *Look Back in Anger* in 1956. This view of Rattigan is by now surely on its way out. His relation to the theatre and the so-called New Wave is undoubtedly more complex. However, his track record as a screenwriter, sometimes but not always adapting his own plays, should not be forgotten. In 1939 we have *French Without Tears*, then *Quiet Wedding* (1940), *The Day Will Dawn* (1942), *Uncensored* (1942), *English Without Tears* (1944), *Journey Together* (1945), *The Way to the Stars* (1945), *While the Sun Shines* (1947), *Brighton Rock* (1947, from Greene's novel), *Bond Street* (1948), and then a wonderful version of his own play *The Winslow Boy* (1948). In the 1950s he wrote *The Browning Version* (1951), *The Sound Barrier* (1952), *The Final Test* (1953), then disappointingly *The Man Who Loved Redheads* (1954), but triumphantly another adaptation of his own play *The Deep Blue Sea* (1955). *The Prince and the Showgirl* (1957), starring Marilyn Monroe and Laurence Olivier, who also directed, is often seen as the end of his film career. (It was an unsatisfactory, though intermittently charming, tardy revival of his Festival of Britain stage play that celebrated nation and the Oliviers – Vivien Leigh had the Monroe role – called *The Sleeping Prince*.) But actually his last film was much more distinguished: *Separate Tables* (1959), an American adaptation by Rattigan himself – but see below – of his own play (or rather two one-acters) of the same name. In it the work of the 'West End dramatist' (the cliché view of Rattigan) was brought to the screen by director Delbert Mann

My interest in the 1950s was sparked by my father giving up smoking on the death from emphysema of Kenneth Tynan, his schoolboy hero, in 1980. I subsequently wrote a study of Harold Hobson (*Harold Hobson: Witness and Judge*, 1995) and a survey of post-war theatre (*British Theatre Since the War*, 1999), and I am working on a book about Tynan and theatre criticism for Yale University Press. I am Head of Drama in the Department of English Literature at Sheffield University. *Dominic Shellard*

who was at the heart of New York realism in his earlier films, with versions of Paddy Chayevsky's brilliant, working-class TV dramas *Marty* (1955) and *The Bachelor Party* (1957).

In this essay I am going to explore the 'separate entities' that are Rattigan's play and Rattigan's screenplay, first by distinguishing the strength of the theatre *Separate Tables* (1954), and then by trying to locate the distinction and peculiarity of the film, which earned two Oscars in 1959. On the way we will see how some interesting problems of censorship and homosexuality arose in Rattigan's time. The theatrical *Separate Tables* is a double-hander consisting of 'Table by the Window' and 'Table Number Seven'. It was first produced at the St James's Theatre, London, on 22 September 1954, two years before the frequently trumpeted theatrical watershed of 1956, when post-war drama allegedly came of age.[1] The film which conflated the two plays was released in 1958, directed by Mann, produced by Harold Hecht and starring the very English David Niven, Wendy Hiller and Gladys Cooper as well as the very American Rita Hayworth and Burt Lancaster.

'Table by the Window' and 'Table Number Seven' are both set in the Beauregard Private Hotel (a deliberately significant name), near Bournemouth, the south-coast resort that was notable then and now for its large retirement population.[2] The action of the two plays occurs within eighteen months. The atmosphere is one of stasis, the outside world a disconcerting presence for the majority of residents, mediated by television, gossip in the dining room or the expression of prejudice in the residents' lounge.

The well-spring of *Separate Tables* is isolation from one's fellow human beings, and there are few plays that manage so effectively to convey the debilitating effects of loneliness. In the opening scene of 'Table by the Window' the frigidity of the hotel is disrupted by the arrival of the glamorous Anne Shankland. This upsets John Malcolm, the dyspeptic, pub-frequenting resident in his forties, because they share an uncomfortable past. By piecing together snippets of biography from a tense conversation across the tables ('separate'), the audience can work out the play's pre-history. John and Anne had been married for three years; eight have elapsed since John attacked her and was jailed for domestic violence and assault on a police officer; her subsequent marriage ended in divorce on grounds of cruelty. John now earns his living by writing for a left-wing journal, *New Outlook*, and has been attempting to rebuild his life. The fragile equanimity of their conversation disintegrates when Anne hints that she is prepared to forgive him ('Eight years will cure most scars') and John rushes out into the night to seek solace at 'The Feathers'. The wise, realistic hotel manager, Miss Cooper (Pat), who remarks that superficial conversation is an obligatory part her job, observes pertinently to Anne, 'People are sometimes so odd about not talking to newcomers, I don't know why, and I hate any of my guests to feel lonely. [*Conversationally*] Loneliness is a terrible thing, don't you agree?'

Later the theme of loneliness and incompatibility is developed through a series of vignettes in a delicacy of characterisation which could earn Rattigan the title of 'the Jane Austen of British theatre'. The youngest guests, Charles and Jean, disagree about marriage. Interestingly, he wants respectability while she is eager to maintain her independence. An elder resident, Lady Railton-Bell, reveals to a tipsy John Malcolm her revulsion at the leftist slant of his *New Outlook* pieces and confesses she would rather die than vote for the Labour Party; and Miss Cooper and John, now ashamed of his 'sordid little piece of alcoholic self-assertion', discuss whether he could ever go back to his old career which was (a surprise to most audiences) as junior minister in the 1945 Labour government, before his prison term. Cut off from this previous life by his own *hamatia*, he has no way back, though he has found some quiet happiness with Miss Cooper, who is naturally destabilised by the arrival of Anne. In *Separate Tables* romantic closure and the false reassurance of a neatly congenial relationship is always avoided.

> JOHN: [*Simply*] Do you know, Pat, that I love you very sincerely?
> MISS COOPER: [*With a smile*] Sincerely? That sounds a little like what a brother says to a sister.
> JOHN: [*With an answering smile*] You have surely reason enough to know that my feelings for you can transcend the fraternal.
> [MISS COOPER *rises and moves to* JOHN, *who puts his hand on her arm*]

But 'they move apart, not in alarm, but as if from long practice'. This physical 'separation' is emblematic of 'Table by the Window's' poignant yearning for union.

A second conversation between Anne and John ends in disaster. They cannot agree why they broke up. He stresses their different backgrounds, her refusal to have children and impatience with his (lack of) social graces. She counters with her career as a model and his delusion that she never really loved him. As they talk they become gentler. Anne confesses she is in 'a bad way' and cannot bear her loneliness, dreading a life 'in a few years' time at one of those separate tables'. Relaxed by intimacy, their sexual attraction is reawakened and Anne proposes they go to her room, but she is called to the telephone by Miss Cooper – who corrects John's belief that the meeting with his wife was a true coincidence. Anne was on the phone that very minute to his publisher, Wilder. John realises she had tracked him down and, angry at seemingly being trapped into 'unconditional surrender', he melodramatically '*slips his hand on to her throat*', but instead of injuring her he pushes her to the floor and leaves.

There is a short final scene to this one-act play which introduces a motif common to both one-acters that make up *Separate Tables*: *abnegation*. In spite of loving John, Miss Cooper, we learn, sat up all night with Anne, while John paced the seafront. In her kind, cautious way, she established that Anne was addicted to sleeping pills and drugs; she now says – incredibly – that she feels it necessary to give John up for Anne's sake:

> She didn't win me over, for heaven's sake! Feeling the way I do, do you think she could? Anyway, to do her justice, she didn't even try… She didn't give me an act, and I could see her as she is all right. I think all you've ever told me about her is probably true. She *is* vain and spoiled and selfish and deceitful. Of course, with you being in love with her, you look at all those faults like in a kind of distorting mirror, so they seem like monstrous sins and drive you to – well – the sort of thing that happened last night. Well, I just see them as ordinary human faults, that's all – the sort of faults a lot of people have – mostly women, I grant, but some men, too. I don't like them, but they don't stop me feeling sorry for a woman who's unhappy and desperate and ill and needing help more than anyone I have ever known.

Miss Cooper's quiescence was soon to become outdated in the blast of angry rhetoric that swept through parts of the British theatre in the late 1950s, but its calm stoicism has a renewed resonance today in an era in which grandiloquent gestures are viewed with more suspicion. With quiet fervour, Miss Cooper is articulating a world view every bit as passionate as Jimmy Porter's outbursts, but in a lower key and a more equable tone. Her universal plea for greater understanding and tolerance of human frailty and her pointed emphasis on 'ordinary human faults' foreshadows 'Table Number Seven', the second play in *Separate Tables*, in which we see Rattigan's involvement with questions of sexual identity.

'Table Number Seven' is a play which represents a significant shift in Rattigan's dramaturgy. In his introduction to the second volume of his *Collected Plays* in 1953, Rattigan disastrously defined his ideal audience member by proclaiming the 'simple truth' that the theatre could not afford to offend a 'nice, respectable, middle-class, middle-aged, maiden lady with time on her hands and the money to help her pass it', whom he chose to call 'Aunt Edna'.[3] But 'Table by the Window' deliberately subverted Aunt Edna's respectable expectations by an ending that stressed incompatibility and a lack of clarity. John's belief that they 'haven't very much hope together' is matched by Anne's questioning of whether they have very much hope apart. Instead of leaving the hotel, perhaps in a sunset together, they merely agree to share a table for lunch, a downbeat ending that might disappoint Aunt Edna.

'Table by the Window' cleverly uses bathos. It is tense, dispassionate and equivocal, but it is overshadowed by 'Table Number Seven' which has the most famous character in *Separate Tables*, Major Pollock. Absent in the first play ('away visiting friends') his presence in the second which takes place eighteen months later provides the dramatic focus. There seems something slightly bogus about this major from the beginning. His posh voice and locutions ('Lovely day, what?') are anachronistic in the postwar period. He says he was at Sandhurst, but gives a shaky response when asked if he was awarded the Sword of Honour. He embarrassingly confuses a Latin phrase for a Greek one which shocks the retired schoolmaster, Mr Fowler, and makes him doubt that the Major really was at Wellington.

It soon emerges that the Major has reason to be evasive about his recent past. He becomes suspiciously anxious to hide a copy of the local newspaper from his fellow residents and it is soon revealed that the paper has a report of the Major being bound over by the magistrates' court for committing a criminal offence. What does Major Pollock have to hide?

When he was writing 'Table Number Seven', Rattigan was very sure that he wanted the Major to be involved with something close to his own life: homosexuality.

> The play as I had originally conceived it concerned the effect on a collection of highly conventional people of the discovery that one of their number was a sexual deviant, and that deviation I had naturally imagined as the one most likely to cause a dramatic shock, the one most likely to be outside the sphere of their sympathetic understanding: the one which the Major would be most ashamed of their finding out and the one for which the whole of the part of the character of the Major was originally conceived: obviously homosexuality.[4]

He himself felt obliged to conceal his sexuality, but he also wanted to show not only a version of the love (or sexuality) that dared not speak its name, but the tolerance of this love by ordinary people. This had been recently demonstrated after the actor John Gielgud's conviction in 1953 for propositioning a man in a public lavatory ('cottaging'). Rattigan was impressed by the fact that when Gielgud (bravely) went on stage after his court appearance, he was greeted by a standing ovation and empathetic warmth. It seemed that the audience had the good sense Rattigan portrayed in Miss Cooper in *Separate Tables*. But he soon acknowledged that the Lord Chamberlain would not allow the Major's offence to be related to homosexuality: "I realized that, if I were to get the play done in the West End at all, I would have to find a way round the Lord Chamberlain's present objection to any mention of this particular subject."[5] The term actually used by the Lord Chamberlain's office was the 'forbidden' subject.[6] Rattigan altered his plot and the Major's offence. Now the Major was in court for indecent behaviour in a cinema. He 'persistently nudged' one woman in the arm and later 'attempted to take other liberties. She subsequently vacated her seat, and complained to an usherette.' The censor had no difficulty with this and the reader's report for 'Table Number Seven' termed it 'a little masterpiece'. *Separate Tables* duly opened on 22 September 1954 and ran for 726 performances. Soon a Broadway transfer was organised. Perhaps because of the liberalising of attitudes seemingly announced by the arrival of *Look Back in Anger* in 1956, Rattigan was now eager to return to his original conception of the Major's offence. There had after all been two important American plays concerned with homosexuality: Arthur Miller's *A View from the Bridge* (1955) and Robert Anderson's *Tea and Sympathy* performed on the London stage in 1953 and filmed by Vincente Minnelli in 1956. Paddy Chayevsky, the television writer, author of *Marty* and collaborator with Delbert Mann, had written interestingly on the subject of homosexuality in the preface to *Marty* in his collected *Television Plays* (1955), though it was only published in America. Rattigan therefore rewrote the magistrates' court material more boldly and more interestingly than his rather anodyne segment on the Major nudging an arm in a cinema. This was how the charge was now framed.

A Mr. William Osborne, 38, of 4 Studland Row, giving evidence, said that about 11.15 p.m. on July the 18th Pollock had approached him on the Esplanade, and had asked him for a light. He had obliged and Pollock had thereupon offered him a cigarette, which he had accepted. A few words were exchanged, following which Pollock made a certain suggestion. He (Mr. Osborne) walked away and issued a complaint to the first policeman he saw. Under cross-examination by L. P. Crowther, the defendant's counsel, Mr. Osborne admitted that he had twice previously given evidence in Bournemouth, in similar cases, but refused to admit that he had acted as a 'stooge' for the police. Counsel then observed that it was indeed a remarkable coincidence. Inspector Franklin, giving evidence, said that following Mr. Osborne's complaint a watch was kept on Pollock for roughly an hour. During this time he was seen to approach no less than four persons, on each occasion with an unlighted cigarette in his mouth. There was quite a heavy drizzle that night and the Inspector noted that on at least two occasions the cigarette would not light, and Pollock had had to throw it away. None of them, he admitted, had seemed particularly disturbed or shocked by what was said to them by the defendant, but of course this was not unusual in cases of this kind. At 1 a.m. Pollock was arrested and, after being charged and cautioned, stated, 'You have made a terrible mistake. You have the wrong man. I was only walking home and wanted a light for my cigarette, I am a Colonel in the Scots Guards.' Later he made a statement. A petrol lighter, in perfect working order, was found in his pocket. Mr. Crowther, in his plea for the defendant, stated that his client had had a momentary aberration. He was extremely sorry and ashamed of himself and would undertake never to behave in so stupid and improper a manner in future. He asked that his client's blameless record should be taken into account. He had enlisted in the army in 1925 and in 1939 was granted a commission as a second lieutenant in the Royal Army Service Corps ...[7]

However, American producer Bob Whitehead was horrified by the fore-grounding of this theme; 'in being so specific about his "offence" I feel the play becomes smaller', he wrote in September 1956. Rattigan therefore reluctantly shelved the new version.[8]

Arguably it does not matter too much what the Major did because the emotional centre of the play is the residents' reactions to *some* act outside their experience. The central segment is really a 'trial scene', a meeting called by the bully Mrs Railton-Bell who wants the Major expelled from the Beauregard Hotel. However, she is confronted with some surprising responses: the gentle Lady Matheson and Mr Fowler are discomforted by Mrs Railton-Bell's vehement bigotry; the female half of the 'nice young couple' in the previous play, Jean (now married to Charles), from whom tolerance might be expected, declares herself disgusted by the Major's sexuality. But Charles makes a rousingly positive speech:

> My dislike of the Major's offence is emotional and not logical. My lack of understanding of it is probably a shortcoming in me. The Major presumably understands my form of love-making. I should therefore understand his. But I don't. So I am plainly in a state of prejudice against him, and must be wary of any moral judgements I may pass in this matter. It's only fair to approach it from the purely logical standpoint of practical Christian ethics, and ask myself the question: 'What harm has the man done?' Well, apart from possibly bruising the arm of a certain lady, ... and apart from telling a few rather pathetic lies about his past life, which most of us do from time to time, I really can't see he's done anything to justify us chucking him out into the street.

In this plea for the appreciation of difference, Charles appears to be acting as Rattigan's mouthpiece and underlines, in his measured, insightful appeal, the difference between the strident polemic of the 'angry young men' and the plaintive, diplomatic persuasion of this representative of the old guard.

Not everybody is as magnanimous as Charles. Mrs Railton-Bell has a down-trodden, nervy daughter Sybil (beautifully played by Deborah Kerr), who had been drawn to the Major through a mutual insecurity. She is devastated by his offence. Her pitiful plea to the Major ('Why have you told so many awful lies?') provokes a moving moment of anagnorisis on his part: 'I don't like myself as I am, I suppose, so I've had to invent another person. It's not so harmful, really. We've all got daydreams. Mine have gone a step further than most people's – that's all. Quite often I've even managed to believe in the Major myself.' This is the key point about the two plays in *Separate Tables*. The characters suffer from loneliness and disappointment, against which they quietly battle, and we realise that their struggle might be alleviated if they opened themselves up to the understanding of others rather than rely on an isolating stoicism. Rattigan is saying that the stiff upper lip can cause disastrous emotional constriction – not a view that his detractors, then and now, are keen to acknowledge, just as they will not admit that he is a more multivalent writer than is usually believed. The climax of the plays occurs when the inhibited, now distraught, Sybil opens up, surely for the first time, about her real feelings to Miss Cooper: 'The Major says that we're both scared of life and people and sex. There – I've said the word. He says I hate saying it even, and he's right – I do. What's the matter with me? There must be something the matter with me – I'm a freak, aren't I?' Miss Cooper, embodiment of Rattiganesque (and British, postwar?) good sense, makes the core speech of the play about 'freaks'.

> I never know what that word means. If you mean you're different from other people, then, I suppose, you are a freak. But all human beings are a bit different from each other, aren't they? What a dull world it would be if they weren't. You see, I've never met an ordinary person. To me all people are extraordinary. I meet all sorts here, you know, in my job, and the one thing I've learnt in five years is that the word normal, applied to any human being, is utterly meaningless. In a sort of way its an insult to our Maker, don't you think, to suppose that He could possibly work to any set pattern?

This open celebration of diversity makes *Separate Tables* a very forward-looking work and the beautiful simplicity of its final scene makes it a heartening one, too. It is believed that the Major will 'slink away', but finally he has the courage to make a quiet arrival which is electrifying. One by one the residents, to the mortification of the detestable Mrs Railton-Bell, engage in minimal but gently cordial pleasantries with him. We learn that he is no longer to call himself 'Major'; he tells the waitress he no longer says things like 'mea culpa'; and crucially he indicates that he is yet to make a decision as to how long he will be staying at the Beauregard. (In this we know he has the support of Miss Cooper.) There is no easy closure to the episode in his life, or the play. The acceptance of *Mr* Pollock is not guaranteed and his re-assimilation is far from complete, but the unsentimental humanity of the other residents is an encouraging start, brought about by his own honesty.

Mrs Railton-Bell, however, isolates herself by attempting to stage a dramatic walk-out from the dining room – and Sybil refuses to follow her, on the edge of emancipation. Mrs Railton-Bell retreats to the sound of Sybil engaging in conversation with her friend, *Mr* Pollock, and Rattigan takes great pains to avoid any facile symmetry at the end of 'Table by the Window'. The final stage direction is '*A decorous silence, broken only by the renewed murmur of the casuals, reigns once more, and the dining-room of the Beauregard Private Hotel no longer gives any sign of the battle that has just been fought and won between its four, bare walls.*'

The Broadway production of *Separate Tables* was a smash-hit, opening on 25 October 1956 and running for 322 performances, followed by a six-month tour. Harold Freedman sold the film rights to Ben Hecht and his new partner, Burt Lancaster, for $175,000, rising to a maximum of $300,000. Rattigan was to be paid $50,000 for a script to be delivered by 1 June 1957. It was to be a United Artists production.

The production company insisted on significant changes. The film con-flated the two one-act plays. On the stage the same actor (Eric Portman) played the disgraced politician and the Major, but for the film Burt Lancaster was John and David Niven took the part of Major Pollock. The film played up a hint of romance between the Major and Sybil Railton-Bell, suggesting at least a potential heterosexuality for the military man. Rattigan never wanted this, however, thinking it would be a 'bowdlerisation of the original'.[9] So the studio covertly employed a second screenwriter, John Gay, to deliver its wishes. Rattigan was furious, but partly because of personal exhaustion, partly because he realised the change was commercially sensible, he agreed to a jointly devised screenplay so long as he had first place in the credits.

It would be completely wrong to see Hecht, Lancaster and Delbert Mann's *Separate Tables* as a watered-down version of the play. The conflation of the two plots adds intensity and there is a deeper characterisation of several of the residents, like the eccentric Miss Meacham (enthusiastic billiards player and committed student of racing form) and Jean Stratton, the antithesis of the passive 1950s wife, wearing slacks, refusing to dress for dinner and confidently stating that she intends to 'produce paintings and not children'.

The casting of the stars Burt Lancaster as John Malcolm, the leftist fire-brand, and Rita Hayworth as Anne Shankland (his ex-wife, the model), necessarily imparted different significance to their characters. Hayworth gives glamour to Anne's arrival in the dowdy hotel. Beautiful, distant and discon-certing, she claims that she has come down to Bournemouth to help John having heard he was in difficulties: skilfully little time is left to consider the plausibility of this, as the crisis of the Major's court case swiftly envelops the Beauregard. Although the references to British party politics are removed and John is transformed into a reclusive American writer, he is still depicted as a class warrior who enjoys taunting the snobbish Mrs Railton-Bell. It is quite apparent that in this English-American film there is still latitude to consider the issue of class division, and there is, if anything, a greater sense of class consciousness than in the play. Lancaster and Hayworth are self-evident Americans, a fresh national presence which catalytically highlights the antiquated nature of the class codes by which the English residents appear to operate.

One crucial alteration in the film is the presence of John at the residents' meeting to discuss Major Pollock's future. He is refreshingly flippant about the number of nudges the Major is alleged to have made in the darkness of the cinema and Burt Lancaster obviously enjoys the rhetorical flourishes that this repointing of John's character allows.

After the drama of the residents' meeting, Anne and John retire to the verandah where their physical attraction for each other is made much more explicit than in the play. A very passionate embrace is interrupted by Miss Cooper – and this is, perhaps, the weakest moment of the film. The ambiguous nature of their relationship in 'Table by the Window' now becomes a more calculating, less open-ended affair which descends into a violence that seems more appropriate for *A Streetcar Named Desire* than a Rattigan drama. (Though elsewhere, in Hayworth's performance, the film is able to rise to *Streetcar*-like intensities, as we shall see.) But if the drama of the violence itself is heavy-handed, its consequence is one of the subtle touches which elevates the film. It is Miss Meacham who confirms that Anne is not seriously hurt by revealing that she is going to leave. 'She's not the alone type,' Miss Meacham concludes, and then, with a wistfulness that confirms the pervasive nature of the residents' isolation, observes that 'people have always scared me'. Sybil Railton-Bell, too, is afraid of human contact: she begs the Major not to 'pretend anymore' but when he explains, in the key moment of the film, that 'I'm made in a certain way and I can't change it', she is less distressed by this revelation than by his accurate diagnosis of their shared misfortune: 'You're so scared of life ... We're awfully alike.' In a tender new scene, it is to the wounded Anne and not to Miss Cooper that Sybil confides her fear of sex. This allows Miss Cooper to become Anne's confidante after John's violence. In a highly effective set-piece, Miss Cooper explains to John that Anne takes three times the recommended dose of sleeping pills and in her palpable vulnerability is as similar to John as the Major is to Sybil. There is 'not much to choose between the two of you', she adds, and in a moment of poignant self-abnegation that must have contributed to Wendy Hiller's securing her Oscar as Best Supporting Actress, she urges John to go to her again because it is quite clear that 'you love her'.

The themes of *Separate Tables* come together in the final dining-room scene. John enters having spent the night walking on the seafront and sits at a separate table from Anne. She apologises to him for lying about how she had tracked him down and admits that he is all the things that she is not ('honest, true and dependable'). With simple symbolism, John joins her table. At this point, Major Pollock enters. Uncertain as to how to react, the fellow residents are nervously silent: a truly thrilling moment of cinema. After a long pause, the camera enquiring (as it were) of several characters, it is John who is first to address him with a simple 'Good morning', an affirmation of friendship.

The film *Separate Tables* was as much a box-office success as its stage counterpart. Its opening in Britain on 13 February 1959 was swiftly followed by the award of Oscars to David Niven (Best Actor) and Wendy Hiller (Best Supporting Actress). What is most striking today is how skilfully the film manages to convey the stifling claustrophobia of the Beauregard Hotel. Rita Hayworth, in one of her very few powerful mature roles, invites comparison with Vivien Leigh in *A Streetcar Named Desire*. Burt Lancaster has emerged as an actor of subtlety, having come far from the flamboyant heroics and circus skills of his early films like *The Flame and the Arrow* (1950). He is a real rebel in the dusty chintz. David Niven's bluster as the Major embarrassingly jars, a parody of his 'decent chap' screen selves. Gladys Cooper (Mrs Railton-Bell) is a beguiling mixture of the stern and the sinister, prowling the hotel with haughty elegance. The American factors in the film (the stars Lancaster and Hayworth and the noir-ish melodrama) heighten the Englishness of the theme and of the other performers, leading and supporting. And at the heart of this success is Rattigan, the discreet, adaptable, morally thoughtful dramatist. But for all Rattigan's success as writer in *Separate Tables*, the shift in the tectonic plates of British theatre after the *Look Back in Anger* watershed of 1956 swiftly cast him to the sidelines.

Notes

1 It was first published as *Separate Tables* by Hamish Hamilton in 1955; a second impression appeared in July 1955 and a third in January 1957.
2 The 1955 Samuel French 'Acting Edition' of *Separate Tables* renamed the two plays as 'Table No. 1' and 'Table No. 2', 'according to the Author's wishes', p. iv. I have retained the unamended titles of the third Hamish Hamilton impression of the play, since this was published two years later in 1957.
3 Terence Rattigan, 'Introduction', *Collected Plays: Volume Two* (Hamish Hamilton, 1953), p. iv.
4 Geoffrey Wansell, *Terence Rattigan* (Fourth Estate, 1995), p. 252.
5 Wansell, *Rattigan*, p. 253.
6 This was the term given to the theme of homosexuality by the Lord Chamberlain, who retained powers of censorship over British drama until 1968. There was a complete ban on any reference to the topic until 1958 when the Lord Chamberlain issued a secret memor-

andum to his readers that reluctantly explained his reasons for a relaxation of the edict. See Dominic Shellard, *British Theatre Since the War* (Yale University Press, 2000).

7 The altered version is in the Terence Rattigan Archive, Department of Literary Manuscripts, British Library.

8 Bob Whitehead, letter to Terence Rattigan (5 September 1956), British Library.

9 Wansell, *Rattigan*, pp. 256, 56–9.

Personal views

Archiving the 1950s

BRYONY DIXON

$\mathbf{A}$ NUMBER OF factors have contributed to the relative neglect of the 1950s as a decade in British cinema history. It was a complex and unhappy decade in England and its films appear to have little contiguity or popular profile. The conventional back-of-a-postage-stamp view of British cinema history takes a strange skip and a jump when it comes to the 1950s. Much is made of the so-called 'golden age' of British cinema in the 1940s, but we tend go straight on to the 1960s and its 'New Wave' films. There is a vague sense of cosiness about the 1950s commercial films which were produced by the Rank machine or lacklustre government-sponsored ventures. A sense of mounting irrelevance resulted in the Angry Young Men/Free Cinema backlash, which is often strangely attributed to the 1960s despite clearly having originated in the mid-1950s.

A major reason for this neglect of the 1950s is that there has been no authoritative, dedicated history of the period of the Rachael Low type. Her *History of British Film* (1948–71) went up to the end of the 1930s and no one has since attempted to cover the later decades in the same fashion. As a period of cinema history the 1950s suffers from the auteur and genre models of examining film, neither of which methods really brings out the best in it. Another contributory factor to the lack of 'visibility' of its films is the fact that so few prints are available for researchers or filmgoers. If film programmers or lecturers want to show more than the classics from these years, they are hard pressed to find enough prints in screenable condition. As an archivist at the British Film Institute, I'll try to explain what survives and why, and some of the really awkward technical, preservation and access problems.

I must start with the nature of the collections relating to this period of film history, how they came to be where they are, and what was going on at that time in the international archiving world. The 1950s is a particularly

---

Bryony Dixon is the Archival Bookings Officer for the British Film Institute in London. Here she writes about the physical existence of film of the 1950s and the complex relationship between preservation and access.

fascinating decade for the film archivist. Technically speaking there was a lot going on: the end of the nitrate era, the development of wide-screen and novelty formats, the increasing use of colour, advances in sound recording technology, lighter more portable 16mm camera equipment, the coming of television. I am concentrating on the holdings of the British Film Institute's National Film and TV Archive (hereafter NFTVA). Appropriately for this story the name 'National Film Archive' *not* 'National Film Library' came into existence in 1955, with the word 'Television' added in 1993. It is the largest collection of 1950s films in the UK, but I am also going to refer to other large collections and to some related, non-film archives. I'm going to make some general comments on the relationship between academia and the archives which I think will be relevant to readers of this book.

Films physically survive for a variety of reasons, mainly economic, but sometimes technical. Film is, as Penelope Houston put it in her examination of British film archives, 'fragile, expensive and dangerous'. (See her excellent guide *Keepers of the Frame* published by the British Film Institute in 1997.) Film companies may not want to store films once they have finished their run of commercial exploitation. Technological change contributed to a higher survival rate for films of the 1950s than those of the silent era, 70–80 per cent of which have been lost. The move from nitrate to acetate 'safety' film stock was a big factor in improving the longevity of films, but it was the development of the film archives themselves which has done most to save our film heritage.

To assess the survival rate of the films of the 1950s means a complex calculation due to the way in which films have been categorised in the BFI's records, as fiction or non-fiction rather than as features, shorts, documentary television, newsreel and so on. This makes it impossible to run off a list from a database of 1950s British titles, but the following figures indicate that the majority of productions are extant. In addition very considerable holdings are still held in the major film libraries in this country for post–1951–2 titles. The number of feature films produced for the period 1950–9 according to figures given in the BFI *Handbook* (figures compiled by *Screen Digest*, *Screen Finance* and the BFI) is as follows:

Year	Number of feature films
1950	125
1951	114
1952	117
1953	138
1954	150

1955	110
1956	108
1957	138
1958	121
1959	122

The total for the decade is 1,243. For the same years the 1985 edition of Gifford's *British Film Catalogue* (published by David and Charles) gives a total of between 964 and approximately 1,000 films, depending on your definition of a 'feature film'. (His figure of 964 is for any fiction production over 60 minutes.) Discrepancies may also occur, of course, depending on what is meant by 'British', although in this period the definition was at least reasonably clear.

The NFTVA holds 5,493 titles for the years 1950–9. Of these, 1,184 are listed as fiction titles (i.e. features, shorts, serials, television dramas, animation, trailers, etc.) and 371 are listed as being government-sponsored films. These figures have to be viewed with a certain amount of caution because, as with any archive, cataloguing tends to lag behind acquisition and there is probably a number of titles which have not been categorised on the computer record. The figures suggest that the bulk of the film industry's output is covered in terms of preservation. Recent acquisitions of British 'B' pictures, too, have filled some gaps in the collection and may not appear in these figures as yet.

Of course, for the film critic, historian or scholar the key issue is accessibility. Of the total number of titles held in the archive 1,184 have viewing copies, meaning that the archive has several copies so one or more can be made available for viewing or screening. As a percentage of 5,493, this is 22 per cent. At first sight this looks an astonishingly low proportion, especially when compared with the silent period for which we have viewing copies of about 80 per cent of the available films, or the 1990s for which we have an excellent 97 per cent.

But this is not the full story. There are other film collections in the UK, but very few of these are equipped to run full preservation programmes and commercial companies are not obliged to provide access to their prints outside their business activities. I will come back to the availability of materials on other collections, but for the moment let's look at the technological reasons for the survival of film elements.

Nitrate

There are good historical and technical reasons why the 1950s scores so low on the accessibility scale. All archives tend to concentrate on their nitrate holdings, which broadly speaking covers the pre-cinema years up to 1951–2 when the switch to safety stock was made. Nitrate film stock not only decays, but is also highly flammable. The NFTVA is one of very few locations in the UK allowed by law to keep nitrate. Not only does this mean that the archive has acquired huge amounts of nitrate film from the studios no longer able to store it, but also, due to nitrate's in-built decay mechanisms, the archive has had to duplicate it on to safety stock in order to preserve images for as long as possible. (Of course, a kind of archivists' Sod's Law has dictated that we now discover that 'safety' acetate stocks *also* decay from the so-called 'vinegar syndrome'.) The result of necessary concentration on nitrate copying is that the earlier material is being duplicated first as a priority. Time and resources will always limit the amount of copying done by the archive resulting from an access request rather than a preservation imperative. As it happens, a slight change of emphasis has occurred recently as archives have come to realise that predictions made about the longevity of nitrate may have been exaggerated. Partly, no doubt, the dangers were exaggerated in the past, in order to persuade government departments to fund preservation (the government only funded the programme after an accident at a chemical plant brought to the fore the dangerous substances legislation: it was never very concerned with arguments about preserving film as such) but it also led to the archive being a slave to the nitrate copying programme for many years. Recent rethinking has led to a shift towards a more access-led policy.

Colour

Other technical issues impact on the accessibility of 1950s film material. By the early 1950s colour was being used increasingly to differentiate film and television, and colour in particular had an enormous effect on the problems and costs of preserving and restoring film. The NFTVA has specialised in the past years on restoring Technicolor, including some classics of the 1950s: *Gone to Earth* (1950), *The Importance of Being Earnest* (1952), *Oh, Rosalinda!* (1955), *The Tales of Hoffman* (1953). The BFI is currently attempting restoration of the 1951 production *The Magic Box*. A full-scale restoration of titles such as these can cost tens of thousands of pounds and really does require special funding or sponsorship. However, you can get magnificent results with Technicolor, which also has the advantage that it is possible to preserve the three separate film elements on black and white film stock thereby avoiding the fading problems of later colour systems. This is because 3-strip Technicolor is shot, as the name implies, on three separate rolls of film stock, each through a different-coloured filter. Restoration problems can arise if the film has shrunk at different rates so that the three images are difficult to register. In 1950, the development of Eastman color negative film stock was to have a major impact on the production of colour film, making the 3-strip Technicolor camera unnecessary as a monopack negative containing all three primary colours made this step obsolete. After the mid–1950s nearly all colour film was shot on this stock and printed using one of a variety of processes including Technicolor, Deluxe, Warnercolor and Metrocolor. Improvements to colour grading came at the end of the decade.

Formats

The proliferation of formats in the 1950s engendered by the new competition from television brought with it its own set of restoration and preservation problems. Wide-screen and large formats, anamorphic systems and non-standard geometry such as VistaVision need specialised equipment to print and also to screen which means there can only be limited access to these films in performance. Specialised projection facilities and trained projection staff in Britain's remaining art-house cinemas become rarer year by year. Commercial cinemas are not geared to cope with alternative formats. This can limit access to film on film and we are likely to see much of this type of material only available on video and DVD in the future. (The exception to this may be the few remaining cinémathèques such as the National Film Theatre in London and a few of the larger regional film theatres.) The projection of film is likely to become a museum activity as the digital age replaces celluloid with electronic means of delivery to cinemas. At the same time it is also possible that transferring film into the digital domain may assist us, once the complex restoration and transfer process has been done, in delivering unusual formats with greater ease. (One successful gimmick of the 1950s was the development of 3-D for the commercial cinema. Requiring specialised equipment to project and polarised or colour-filtered glasses to be worn by the public, this was enormously popular as an occasional spectacle – and still is. In this country a few stereoscopic films were made as exhibits for the Festival of Britain in 1951, an occasion when interestingly much of the government-financed film culture infrastructure came in by the back door.) 'Gimmicky' formats still have the power to attract audiences.

Wide-screen format, of course, is now the norm, but it is worth remembering that there is a whole generation of movie-literate youngsters who have never had a chance to see a 3-D film at the cinema. New formats which were launched in the 1950s such as CinemaScope, Cinerama, Techniscope, VistaVision and Todd A-O were developed specifically to be bigger and better than television, but smaller formats were also developed in response to a huge growth in amateur film-making and non-theatrical distribution and, of course, telerecording of TV on 16mm film. Eight mm took over from 9.5mm as the amateur small gauge of choice for home movies. One small but noteworthy experiment funded by the BFI was Glenn H. Alvey Junior's 'Dynamic Frame' film process, used in the short film *Door in the Wall* (1956), which used masking in the printing stage to heighten dramatic effects. One example shows a character coming out of an alleyway with the picture masked to a thin vertical strip, and as the character emerges the picture widens out to its full horizontal width. But this was only an experiment, never to be repeated.

Sound

Magnetic sound recording began to be used in the film industry by the beginning of the 1950s with improved methods of synchronisation, issued in 1959. This had an enormous effect on documentary film-making styles which were already emerging (like Free Cinema). Wide-screen formats using any available film area for more picture availed themselves of the possibilities offered by magnetic tracks and several processes had sound on up to six tracks striped on to the show-prints. Again, in terms of presenting these films today, this poses a projection problem to all but the best-equipped cinemas.

Travelling mattes and the jump cut

These were further developed from 1940s blue-screen processes, but using the new Eastman color negative stock and blue light. Some print-through of the original image seemed to be inevitable, as can be seen in productions such as *The Ladykillers* (1955). It is generally agreed that in the 1950s directors could not resist the jump cut. Various productions in the decade used the jump cut and shock edits as a stylistic device (as in *The Elusive Pimpernel* (1950), *Somebody Up There Likes Me* (1956), *Woman in a Dressing Gown* (1957)). Barry Salt notes that such devices were much criticised by French critics until Truffaut adopted some of them himself.

A case in point: *Women of Twilight*

Women of Twilight (1952) is a relatively little-known film of considerable social/historical interest, famous today for being one of the earliest films to get an 'X' certificate. This is, of course, the kind of film for which the British Film Institute should have materials in its collections. There is indeed a 16mm print available for research or screenings and a back-up 16mm master, but we would hope to have good, original-format, 35mm preservation and viewing material. In fact, the Romulus collection, now administered by Carlton plc, does have an available 35mm print. In this case the private sector and the public archives have it covered, but it is still important that the national archive has preservation material in the long term. In these days of frequent mergers and de-mergers a sympathetic company attitude to archiving cannot be assumed.

As it happens *Women of Twilight* is not in particularly good shape, but the cost of restoring would be very high. If the BFI were to borrow original negative elements for duplication it would have to make inter-positive material, then duplicate sound and picture negatives (which would be the preservation master copies) and prints. This would cost at minimum (and this is just black and white!) £16,000. This is *without* 'restoration' work, i.e. repairs, grading, examination, testing, research, etc. The hopes of recouping any of this cost in film-hire charges is minimal as charges are £50 at most and likely frequency of booking is a couple of screenings a year. At these prices it becomes more understandable why certain films are only ever seen on television or video. The art-works of film and television history, the basic data for critics and scholars, can indeed be elusive. Let us go back to the search for these phantoms.

There has always been a close if sometimes prickly relationship between academics and archivists. Film historians with limited time and resources for research can dislike the laborious and expensive processes of getting access to materials. Archivists can dislike the tetchy demands of students and researchers as they struggle against the clock just to rescue the films from decomposing for ever – and having to persuade successive uninterested government departments and funders to keep the money coming in. Despite the proliferation of courses in film studies and media studies, the funding of access to the source materials has not increased *at all*.

There can be surprisingly simple misunderstandings about what a film archive is. People who understand perfectly that they can't walk in and browse around manuscript collections of the British Library are illogically outraged when a film archive refuses them access to original masters, the film archival equivalent of the Gutenberg Bible.

I'll make, from the archivist's angle, a comparison.

Our National Film and TV Archive can be seen as a hospital for sick film. Films come to us in all sorts of conditions, battered and bruised and with their in-built decay processes eroding them steadily from within. Sometimes they have only a scratch or two and can be left for the moment. We deal with the emergencies first, and the others when we can. Most of an archivist's job will be a race against time to deal with the emergencies, 'A and E', if you like. Other cases are diagnosed for treatment in the longer term and are sent up to the various 'wards'. Access policy is a way of prioritising the non-urgent cases for 'preservation' (keeping them alive as long as possible) and 'restoration' (patching them up and sending out into the world). Hospitals are complex, totally essential, and sometimes exasperating. So with the film archival hospital: thank goodness it is not a hospice.

Being a film reviewer in the 1950s

ISABEL QUIGLY

'THE PAST IS a foreign country.' This magical first sentence from *The Go-Between* (1953) was the opening line of the first novel I was ever sent to review. The *Manchester Guardian*, as it was then, had sent me a parcel of books and after reading L. P. Hartley's masterly tale of love and snobbery and guile and much else I felt that if this was reviewing, it was a wonderful way of earning, not perhaps a living, but at least a crust. Soon afterwards I was asked, out of the blue, to be film critic of the *Spectator*, and entered what now seems a very foreign country indeed, the film world of the 1950s, in which I stayed for ten years. It was a past separated from us today not just by the changes in films and film-making, but by the social upheavals between then and now; its climate altogether different from ours, with attitudes and behaviour unrecognisable now, a past closer to the world of *The Go-Between* (which was set at the turn of the nineteenth century, just a hundred years ago) than to our world today. Foreign, even exotic, that 1950s world now seems.

My time in the film world spanned the crucial decade of change, from the mid-1950s to the mid-1960s (so that some of the films and events I mention will go a little beyond the 1950s). I said I was asked out of the blue by the *Spectator*, and this was the amateurish way things were done in those days. It would never happen now. All they knew of my tastes and interests and knowledge came from an article I had sent in (again out of the blue), which

Isabel Quigly was born in Spain and has lived in Sussex for many years. She has published a novel, *The Eye of Heaven* (Collins), called *The Exchange of Joy* in America (Harcourt Brace), and several books of criticism and social history; including *The Heirs of Tom Brown: The English School Story* (Chatto & Windus; in paperback, OUP). She edited the Penguin Shelley, still in print after 45 years, introduced and edited *Stalky & Co* in the World's Classics (OUP), and has translated about 100 books, mostly from Italian, some from Spanish and French. For a decade she was the *Spectator*'s film critic and wrote *Charlie Chaplin: The Early Comedies* (Studio Vista; in USA, Dutton). Until recently, for 12 years, she was literary adviser to *The Tablet*. She is a Fellow of the Royal Society of Literature, and has served on its Council.

had nothing to do with the cinema, and perhaps a novel I had published, which had no film connections either. How could they know (well, of course they didn't) that for years I had been carrying on a secret love affair with the cinema, that my favourite films were seen over and over again, nine or ten times, that my copy of Roger Manvell's *Film* (the only easily available manual) was covered in underlinings and scrawls, that the Everyman and the Curzon and the Academy were familiar haunts of mine and film society shows in louche fleapits my idea of evening heaven? For all the *Spectator* knew, I might never have seen a film in my life. Today, a film critic would be expected to have years of experience, an education in the cinema, a knowledge far beyond any I had in those early days of ignorant enthusiasm. But none of this occurred to them or me, and I was simply flung in, displacing, rather to my shame and for no good reason, a gifted lady, my predecessor Virginia Graham.

The cinema, like the society around it, was then on what is sometimes called a cusp. This is taken to mean a time of change, a wave about to break. But it has a more literal meaning. It is the point at which two lines meet, similarly curved like the point of a spear or a trefoil. Push the image a bit further and it becomes one of lines coming together, overlapping, one side taking over from the other. Throughout the 1950s something like this was happening in the film world. Noticeably and fast, the cinema was being pushed from its central position in people's recreational lives by the advent and then the quick growth of television. Something similar was happening in society in general – also, to some extent, because of television.

Anyone who was not around in those days must find it hard to imagine the scale of these changes. In outlook, opinions, culture, everything was shifting. In society the changes took time to break through, to become visible, to overcome reluctance to alter the safe, familiar ways. But in the cinema the changes could be quantified. Film audiences in Britain had slipped from over 30 million a week to about 8 million by the 1960s. People sometimes asked me if it wasn't depressing to be involved in something so obviously in decline. They even wondered if the film was on its way out altogether, if its audience would dwindle to zero and within a few years would be sitting at home in front of a television set.

As we know, this didn't happen. The cinema ceased to be the *only* form of national entertainment, but it survived and flourished in a different way, learning new tricks and throwing up new talents. Before, a visit to the cinema had been a twice-weekly ritual for the majority of the British, a long, dogged session, perhaps sometimes almost a chore: three hours long, with two films shown, the 'big picture' and the 'B' picture, the occasional documentary or nature film, the advertisements (not just of films 'coming shortly' but of all kinds of local doings), the ice creams, and, in the big cinemas, the Wurlitzer organ that rose majestically from the depths to play to an audience of chatter and laughs. Shorter performances, a single film at a time, and slicker presentation took over. With so much more to do outside the cinema, people made filmgoing a special occasion rather than a habit, a more careful, sophisticated choice. With flagging attendances, cinemas closed all over the country; small towns no longer had them, so filmgoing became more deliberate, more metropolitan, a treat. As film critics, we had the concentrated experience of seeing a film without the trimmings. We arrived at one of the big West End cinemas at 10.30 a.m., an emotionally unsuitable hour for filmgoing, clutching our tickets and sometimes a friend (it made us more popular than we might have been), and at 2.30 p.m. did much the same. Between the two there was often a party or an interview. Drinks flowed. If some arrived bleary-eyed at the morning shows, some arrived in the early afternoon a little the worse for those midday drinks. We were not a drunken lot, far from it, but a few looked slightly askew, slumped in their seats, or walked rather carefully. Meeting the same people two or three times a week made for familiarity and on the whole friendliness, though with this went a certain wariness, even caution, in discussing the films we saw.

As I remember it, we thought it bad form to ask anyone, 'What did you think of that?' or even to mention unasked what we thought of this or that film. People wanted time for it to sink in, to come to a decision, perhaps to revise the initial reaction a little. To say something was great, then modify this in writing a day or two later, was to invite suspicion, even ill-will. So, when we met afterwards, most of us kept diplomatically silent on the film just seen and talked about almost anything else. In a world persuaded that critics were venal creatures likely to be in a conspiracy of some sort together, bribed by those drinks and modest treats, this was a necessary precaution. But suspicion of bribery and collusion was certainly misplaced. I remember Dilys Powell telling me that, as she and C. A. Lejeune, on respectively the *Sunday Times* and the *Observer*, were considered by some to be cinematic twins, a duo of some sort, people thought they got together to decide what they were going to say, splitting their views down the middle, as it were: an absurd belief, of course, but hard to dislodge if they ever happened to agree.

Of course there were treats and to outsiders ours seemed an enviable job, a round of parties with film stars where we were flattered into praising them. And of course there was real excitement and pleasure over the best films, the surprises, the breakthroughs, the arrival (in those insular days) of films from abroad, new trends, new expectations. But with four or five films to see each week, much of our time was spent plodding through the mediocre or the plain awful. There were moments of absurdity in our filmgoing, mostly connected with late arrivals or large hats (which women still wore). My brush with absurdity came when I was selling raffle tickets. In those simple days, we held raffles in our village to raise money for this or that, and the top prize was often a live pig. Film parties were ideal for the sale of tickets: a captive group of varied people, better off than the average villager, would generally buy without fuss, and whether it was pigs or chocolates to be won no one much cared. But one Hollywood tycoon became seriously worried when he thought he might win a pig. How would he get it to America? What about quarantine, transport, vets and jabs, insurance?

Ructions and rows occasionally turned up as well: C. A. Lejeune storming out of *Psycho* (1960) after the murder in the shower, a dramatic moment made all the more so by the fact that Hitchcock was known to be a friend of hers; an elderly Jewish critic offended almost to tears and then to weeks of coldness and complaint by a scene in Kevin Brownlow's *It Happened Here* (1963), in which a National Front member – a 'real' person, not an actor – spewed out his own passionately anti-Semitic opinions; newspapers shutting down without warning, as the *News Chronicle* did, leaving its well-liked film man Paul Dehn high and dry (though not for long), to our passionate indignation and sympathy; a piece I had written about a particularly filthy film blown up hugely and jubilantly displayed outside the cinema where it was showing (it wasn't sexually filthy: it used physical handicaps for sensational effect, and taught me that such protests, as I should have known, excited nasty reactions).

Film stars in the flesh – perhaps our most envied perk – were nearly always a disappointment, shorter, older, less pretty and certainly less friendly than one had imagined or perhaps hoped. But what did we hope for? To them we were all church mice, dull outsiders they had to be polite to, just in case. Of the many actors I met in those days only three stand out in my memory as real people rather than well-drilled automata: John Cassavetes, Sophia Loren and Tom Courtenay. All of them I met and came to know a little, as it were, privately, outside the usual run of publicity parties. Cassavetes was as human as his films, as responsive as one could hope for. He sent a friend to see me when he got back to America, who terrified my baby-sitter by telephoning with (not surprisingly) an American accent. I came home to find two small children and the sitter clutching one another in terror on a sofa, convinced that a gangster had rung up and was going to pop round at any moment. (Village girls in Sussex were then a lot less knowledgeable and cool than they are now.) Sophia Loren was friendlier than anyone might have expected, and remembered two visitors to her day's filming well enough to ask me, years later, with what seemed like real interest, what had become of the beautiful Italian au pair girl I had brought with me (everyone who saw her at the studio took her for a star). Tom Courtenay was hardly famous when I met him but he too had no 'side'. He was in training for *The Loneliness of the Long Distance Runner* (1962) and we ran over Waterloo Bridge together as part of the practice.

The big treats and extras, which came even to church-mice critics like me, depended a good deal on how much time you could spare for them. My first film festival was in Berlin in 1958, a city then divided between the West and the Soviets, the Western side gleaming with affluence and modernity, the Soviet side a desert of bomb sites, ragged streets and gloomy citizens, about which we made nervous jokes concerning salt mines and gulags. I was so naive about newspaper practice that I had arranged to write for no less than five national newspapers (*Times, Financial Times, Manchester Guardian*, the *Tablet* and my own *Spectator* – surely a criminal offence in journalistic terms). This seemed to me perfectly in order so long as I wrote quite discrete pieces for each one of them (a challenge? a nonsense?) and amazingly nobody questioned it (perhaps nobody read more than one of them). An unexpected spin-off was almost an entire evening spent talking to Willy Brandt, then at the height of his fame and prestige. Because I was introduced as the representative of *The Times*, he clearly thought me a lot more important than I was.

The whole festival was something of an eye-opener, its scale, its luxury after what was still a fairly drab London, the proliferation of stars, directors and film moguls (Walt Disney!), the sight of heroic figures like Giulietta Masina, the friendliness of the members of the international jury I was serving on, our cosy meals together and the chance, across the fortnight, to make new friends. Bjorn Rasmussen, a leading figure in the Danish film world, was on our jury – its chairman, if I remember rightly – a large, burly and entirely delightful man with seven young children at home in Copenhagen and a face recognised in the street there from his television appearances, so that his anonymity in Berlin was a relief. A very practising Catholic, he stood at the end of our long table and said grace without self-consciousness before each meal, like the abbot of his little flock. He liked everything English, spoke the language almost perfectly, and knew all about us, which was flattering and funny: the only mistake I ever caught him out in was when he mentioned 'Spencer and Marks'. He had a gripe about the Germans' determination to suggest they had all been heroic plotters against Hitler. This riled him so much that he sometimes lost some of his natural cordiality and sweetness. Alas, he died not long afterwards of a heart attack, alone in a hotel in Rome without family or friends; but in Berlin he was the centre of all our doings and is still affectionately remembered.

Another festival I went to was in Acapulco, where the Critics Circle in London was invited to send a member to serve on another jury. Ten London people wanted to go so we put our names in a hat and I (who still find myself declaring I never win raffles) was amazingly picked. This was an even more exotic affair, hot in early December beside a transparent blue sea and swarming with starlets and paparazzi. A famous English couple was there on a well-publicised bolt from spouses at home and as they spoke no Spanish, I, who did speak it, occasionally had to get between them and aggressive Mexican journalists. Another visitor was Josef von Sternberg, old, saturnine, impressive. For some reason I saw a good deal of him. My most vivid memory of the great man was his expression when a young starlet asked him, in the tone that might be used to an Alzheimer's patient in a home, 'Did you ever work in the cinema, Mr von Sternberg?'

As in Berlin, our jury became a friendly band and we went about together. One was a Dutchman 6 foot 10 inches tall, and wherever we went we were followed by an exclaiming, even shrieking crowd of mostly squat Mexicans. Was he monster or superman? Whether to be proud or embarrassed was a constant problem. When he wore a hat, which the hot sun often demanded, our Dutchman touched at least 7 foot, and a little of his exotic quality seemed to spread to the rest of us.

But these were the frills of the job. Day-to-day work was much more sober, often a hassle to get things fitted in and copy delivered on time. Sometimes we were at the mercy of outside events: transport strikes or parking rules, minor illnesses or extremes in the weather. My filmgoing days covered the winter when Britain froze for three months (again, no-one who wasn't there will credit what it was like): hard thick ice on every road, mountainous snow-drifts, impossibly dangerous driving, all combined to keep country film critics snug at home instead of in slushy London. So how did we manage? I remember missing a broadcast I was to make and an alarming announcement being put out to explain my absence, but films somehow got seen and somehow written about. Before faxes and e-mails this of course meant post (which might be lost in a snow-drift), or the telephone, which marvellously survived.

And all the while, across the decade, things were moving on as movements came and sometimes went, fashions rose and always fell, and, at a deeper level, society shook itself and decided that it would never be the same again: Pandora's box, the genie in the bottle, the end, fifty years after its official ending, of the nineteenth century. The British cinema had by then moved far from its recent past of Ealing comedies and familiar cliché. Influenced by kitchen-sink theatre and the new aspects of life around it, it was turning out vigorous, outspoken films that reflected the new atmosphere, whereas Italian cinema had gone in an almost opposite direction, changing radically from its postwar realism to the smoothest of modern fantasies, a kind of mannerist style and a newer realism of luxury. The American cinema continued to send us its daily diet, which, for all the developments in life and film-making, seemed more familiar than any other and still gave the screens a high percentage of their protein. From the rest of the world new arrivals meant new riches: they came in from India and Japan, Scandinavia and Australia, from Czechoslovakia and Poland and the USSR, South America and the Middle East and other places here and there, and were seen not just by specialised audiences, as in the past.

Technical innovations were supposed to save the cinema from extinction but most of them proved to be gimmicks soon forgotten – Cinerama, 3-D, CinemaScope, Technirama, VistaVision, Panavision, Todd-AO, with hugely wide screens and sometimes special spectacles to wear with them – and the cinema survived without or even despite them. The great rival and bogeyman, television, was ironically spreading knowledge of films by showing them in large numbers on the small screen, in private, very different conditions from those for which they were made. Film watching was no longer a communal experience, but something more intimate, whatever the original large subject. Yet it became easier to be a film buff, to study the history of the cinema from way back, than it had been in the days of specialised performances in those hard-to-find fleapits.

Alongside these cinematic changes the world was making its great social shifts throughout the 1950s, and early in the 1960s – quite suddenly, it seemed to many, as it did in Philip Larkin's poem 'High Windows' – it was another place, with other customs that again to many seemed unrecognisable. Taboos in sexual matters and much else counted for less and the new openness and freedom had their champions but also their disconcerted critics. One example of the kind of thing that was happening came in 1956 when a Czech film actress, Eva Bartok, had an illegitimate child. Of course there had been plenty of illegitimate children around but not openly, without apology, born to someone well known and apparently not in hiding. At the end of that year a well-known cartoonist published a drawing summarising the big political and social events of the year, the things people had been talking about around the world (it was the year of Suez, cataclysmic and alarming). In the corner of his picture, among the great events, stood (as if she mattered uniquely and everyone was agog to see her) a recognisable but waif-like figure with a shawl round her shoulders, and in her arms what in the novel *Cold Comfort Farm* (1932) they called a shameful bundle. To me, that seems to sum up the attitudes of the time as memorably as anything. A foreign country indeed. Ten years later, such a phrase and such a cartoon would have seemed grotesque.

Michael Redgrave and *The Mountebank's Tale*

CORIN REDGRAVE

In 1958 MICHAEL REDGRAVE was appearing for the third and last time at Stratford-upon-Avon. The parts he played that year were Hamlet and Benedick in *Much Ado about Nothing*. Hamlet was a brave choice. My father was by then 50. In an age less fearful than ours of growing old, great actors like Sir John Martin Harvey had been able to make a lifetime's work out of a part like Sidney Carton in *A Tale of Two Cities*. Sir John performed it 4,004 times and gave his farewell performance in the role at 74 and audiences hardly seemed to mind. But by 1958, to play Hamlet at 50 was a risky thing to do and on the whole I think that Michael managed it with great skill. No, I'll go further: I think it was the best Hamlet he ever gave.

Stratford then, as I think it still does, had a summer festival to which scholars, historians and artists came from all over the world. My father was invited, as he had been twice before, to give a lecture. He was a good lecturer. He had given four Rockefeller lectures at Bristol University in 1953, which then became one of the most suggestive, illuminating books about acting, *The Actor's Ways and Means* (1953). Other lectures were brought together in a book called *Mask or Face* (1958).

But on this occasion he must have felt that he had said all he wanted to say about acting in lecture form and he chose instead to write a long short story or novella, *The Mountebank's Tale* (1959). I think that this was a shrewd choice. In fiction he was able to say more about himself, his acting, more about his understanding of theatre than he had yet been able to say in the more conventional form of lecture or essay.

Corin Redgrave is an actor, director and author. Since his debut in 1962 his work has been divided almost evenly between theatre, film and television. He is the author of *Michael Redgrave: My Father* (RCB, Fourth Estate, 1995) and *Julius Caesar and the English Revolution* (Faber & Faber, 2002). As a playwright he has written *Roy and Daisy* (1998), *Fool for the Rest of his Life* (2000), *Blunt Speaking* (2001) and *Not Half the Man I Used to Be* (2002?), all plays commissioned for BBC radio. He has been the editor of *The Marxist*, a bi-monthly journal, since 1987, and is an occasional freelance journalist.

The Mountebank's Tale was published by Heinemann, but is now a rarity, a collector's item. It is a tale of two actors, or rather an actor and his double. Joseph Charles is a supremely gifted, cultivated, classical actor in the Austrian theatre. His double, Paul Hammer, is a young man ten or fifteen years his junior but otherwise identical to himself in every outward respect. Charles has taught his young double to speak elegant German. He has also taught him how to act. He discovers that his pupil has a natural gift almost the equal of his own.

Joseph Charles is preparing a light comedy whose plot relies on the presence of a pair of identical twins. The play was written for himself, as virtuoso, to double both parts, but for a joke he allows his protégé one evening to play the other twin, without announcing the substitution in the programme. The audience is completely taken in. The performance is a success. Charles decides to continue with the experiment.

At first the younger man is quite content to play the second twin without acknowledgement. He is head-over-heels stage-struck, and it is enough for him to be acting before a large audience, sharing the stage with the greatest actor of the day. But after a while he starts to pine for more independence and the chance to make a reputation for himself out of the shadows of his great master. And seeing this, Charles decides on an even more daring substitution. There is a one-act comedy about an old man and his servant and the young man plays the older man, the part normally played by Charles himself, while Charles plays the servant.

Again the audience is not informed in advance and is completely unaware of the substitution. It is delighted with the performance and Paul, the young actor, becomes more and more confident as he hears the response to his daring moments of improvisation, his unexpected gags. Emboldened by the applause, he invents more and more. The performance is undoubtedly the most successful of that light comedy ever given on the Viennese stage. And then suddenly in mid-performance Joseph Charles does something that he has never done: he forgets his lines. He 'dries'.

My father was a friend and a disciple of the Danish writer and novelist Isak Dinesen. Today more people know her as Karen Blixen because a film, *Out of Africa*, was made about her. My father borrowed from Isak Dinesen a very gothic method of story-telling with much deflection and sleight of hand to build up suspense and atmosphere. All these are in evidence in *The Mountebank's Tale*.

At first one thinks it is obvious that the narrator, a successful man of the theatre approaching middle age must be my father. We find him in his club in Covent Garden, which is unmistakably modelled on the Garrick Club.

He is given a photograph of two men, one of whom he recognises as his late friend, a historian called St John Fielding. The two men are pictured in front of a seventeenth-century Cotswold stone farmhouse, although the presence of a giant eucalyptus tree in the background suggests California rather than the Cotswolds.

The narrator is curious to know who the other figure in the photograph might be. He finds amongst his late friend's scrapbooks and letters a type-script. It tells the story of Fielding's encounter in Santa Barbara with the legendary Viennese actor Joseph Charles. As the story progresses one realises that each new person we are introduced to bears some resemblance to my father, but is in fact only a decoy. The actor has discarded each disguise, as if flinging off pieces of costume as he runs from the stage to his dressing room. We follow the trail – cloak, jacket, vest – but when we reach the dressing room, the actor is not there.

Through this story my father tells more about the art of acting than I think one can learn from him anywhere else. As I read *The Mountebank's Tale* I can see my father signalling to me, beckoning me on, saying, 'This is who I am, this is why I act.' Why, for example, did Joseph Charles forget his lines? Because he was astonished and somewhat shocked to find that the audience was applauding his young double for doing things that he would never had dreamed of doing.

My father had a very strict contract with himself as a performer and he kept to its terms all his life. He suffered under it, somewhat. By comparison with his great contemporary Laurence Olivier, who was the consummate showman, my father very rarely allowed that necessary side of an actor's personality to dominate his work. Joseph Charles forgets his lines because he is appalled to see that the audience prefers his young double's decoration of the part to the more chaste, pure, classical performance which he is accustomed to giving.

There are other things in this novella that are very reminiscent of my father. In particular, the description of a hellish dress rehearsal in which the slightest unexpected event, such as an actor wearing a different costume or wearing it in a different way, would cause Charles to forget his lines. As a boy of 13 I saw my father in such a dress rehearsal, of *Antony and Cleopatra* at Stratford, stop over and over again to ask for a prompt. He was wearing his costume, of course, wig, beard, make-up and so on, and yet he hardly seemed to be there.

And then there is his nightmare. My father had a recurring nightmare, in which he found himself looking at his reflection in a mirror in his dressing room having applied a rather heavy make-up. He was a great specialist in make-up, something which we actors today have almost lost the art of. In fact we hardly make up for the stage at all. In his nightmare he looks at first approvingly in the mirror at this make-up. And then the make-up begins to slip down his face and the entire face which he has adopted slides down on to his chest, so that what is left behind is not his real face but a blank.

Finally, Joseph Charles decides that he has had enough. He says good-bye to acting and in mid-production he asks his young double into his dressing room and he says, 'I am never going to appear in this part again or in any other. Will you please now take over all my parts?' The young double does so. And thus it turns out that the man whom Fielding meets in Hollywood is not the legendary Joseph Charles after all but his double, Paul Hammer, who has assumed his personality, his name and his career. Charles himself has disappeared.

My father disappeared, too. He suffered from Parkinson's Disease, one of the worst afflictions that can befall a performer because it robs him of all those things which he most relies upon: his voice, which becomes feeble; his plasticity of movement. Worst of all, it robs him of his facial expression – the characteristic symptom of Parkinsonism is what is called the mask, a rigidity of expression that begins to overtake a person's face.

I am very aware of this in what I think of as his farewell to the cinema, *The Go-Between* (1971), directed by Joseph Losey. I can't watch it because I find it unbearably poignant. His face has already, to a small extent, surrendered to the mask of Parkinsonism. Diagnostic techniques have improved since those days, I expect. My father's illness was not diagnosed until 1972. But I can see it quite clearly with the help of hindsight, in *The Go-Between*, shot in 1970.

And yet, for every physical loss we can, given a fair wind, compensate, and my father compensated astonishingly. His eyes in this film are more eloquent than I have ever seen them in any other performance, and though his face hardly moves you can see his eyes signalling his emotions. Harold Pinter wrote the screenplay, in which there are comparatively few words. Pinter was a great admirer of my father; he described something I had never quite been able to place before, what he called my father's 'gawky grace', and I think that when you watch his body language in films you will agree that is very apt. We get to know actors if we see them often enough on the screen by their body language, by their walk. If you think, for example, of Henry Fonda you think of a characteristic set of the shoulders, a way of walking towards you or across the screen that is both modest and yet deter-mined; it appears in all his roles. My father's body language is composed of this 'gawky grace', in which sometimes the gawkiness is predominant, sometimes the grace, throughout all his film appearances. Pinter wrote the screenplay knowing that it might be my father's farewell to the cinema. Not literally his farewell, by the way. For archival reference there are two later ones: *Connecting Rooms* (1971) with a great friend of his, Bette Davis and *The Last Target* (1972). But I don't think they stand comparison with *The Go-Between* and I don't think Michael would have considered them as anything other than the sort of encore which sometimes we are obliged to give after a farewell performance.

Pinter also directed his final appearance on the London stage which was in a play by Simon Gray, *Close of Play* in 1979, when, of course, he couldn't remember any lines at all and so Simon wrote for him and Pinter directed for him a part in which he would be on stage throughout, but silently because the character had been afflicted by a stroke. And so he had to watch the proceedings through this mask, but with these extraordinarily expressive eyes. Finally, he had to say, if I remember, one line at the end of the performance: 'The door ... is open.'

He left a legacy of fifty performances in full-length feature films – I am not counting narrations and there are some famous ones such as *A Diary for Timothy* – which, in a span of work from 1938 to 1972 or 1973, is a remarkable achievement, especially when you consider that he was also a leading actor in the theatre throughout that period. It amounts to two feature films a year, though naturally it wasn't quite spread out in that way.

A few years ago I made a documentary film for the BBC *Omnibus* series. It was directed by Roger Michell and was based on a book which I wrote, *Michael Redgrave: My Father*. Preparing for that film we had to watch a very large number of Michael's films, many of which I had never seen before. His film career for me was to a large extent his biography. I watched his entire life unfolding through his film performances and I think therefore that I am a rather partial and maybe awkward critic of his work.

I tend to think that every great actor and every great dramatist is writing his or her autobiography. Even Shakespeare. No, especially Shakespeare, supposedly the most 'impersonal' of dramatists. I think it is certainly true of my father. The question that you always have to ask yourself about acting, particularly about acting in the cinema, is to what extent does the actor move towards the character that he or she is portraying, and to what extent do they take that character and adapt it to themselves?

Most of my father's favourite actors took the latter course: Spencer Tracy, for example, who over and over again takes a part and superbly moulds it around his own personality; Robert Ryan; Arthur Kennedy; Van Heflin – all Americans. You will see all of these had this great ability, an ability I think is superbly exemplified today in Tom Hanks, to mould a part around themselves and yet to contain within themselves so much that it does not seem that the part is thereby impoverished. That dialectic – how much of themselves? how much of the author's original intention? – is one of the most exciting problems of acting and it is one which I think my father's career probably addresses and answers in a number of very interesting ways.

When I was writing my book *Michael Redgrave: My Father* I looked through his diaries and I found in 1939 an entry which was clearly troubled because his writing, which was normally a neat and rather pleasing script, was awkward and jagged. He may have been drunk or distressed, probably both. He said:

> The artist as a man of character. It has been said that the two are incompatible. This agrees with the theory of artistic temperament as a disease. Particularly it is true of actors whose nature demands that they should lose themselves, or rather find themselves in other characters. The extent to which characterization alters my private life is frightening and at times ridiculous. To live happily it would seem that I must concentrate on the portrayal of romantic upright simple men, which anyway next to the childishness of Baron Tusenbach [in Chekhov's *Three Sisters*] or Sir Andrew Aguecheek is what I do best.

His first four films present us precisely with this romantic upright simple man, though sometimes with a touch of the childishness of Tusenbach or Sir Andrew. The first was *The Lady Vanishes*, directed by Hitchcock, in which he has to appear with the almost obligatory Ronald Colman moustache. He also has to do something which is a nightmare for an actor coming from the theatre to the cinema. In his first scene with Margaret Lockwood he has to perform about seventeen different physical actions: he has to come into her bedroom; stand in the door; greet her (she, of course, is upset, offended at finding this young man bursting into her bedroom); he then has to take off his coat and his knapsack and deposit them, along with a walking stick, in different parts of the room. He then has to come over; confidently sit on her bed and unpack a suitcase; and finally exit from the room, tipping his hat as he does so, saying, 'Confidentially I think you're a bit of a stinker.' And all in *one* camera set-up.

It looks a wonderful first take, but it is a nightmare for an actor, even if you're experienced. If you're inexperienced it is a triple nightmare. Film is an extraordinarily technical medium for an actor compared to theatre. Occasionally in the theatre, when working with great theatre magicians like Robert Wilson, we will be asked to hit a mark very precisely, and to raise a hand on a particular word, and the lighting will be organized in such a way that we must do so. But that degree of precision is rarely needed in the theatre. Cinema, however, is a very precise medium and so to do all that in his first shot (although the film was not shot in chronological story sequence, that was in fact the first scene he shot) was quite an achievement. It is delightfully brash and has all the arrogance of youth. It is something he probably couldn't have done three films later when he had started to take stock of the difficulties.

That simple upright romantic young man continues somewhat into the next film. It is called *Stolen Life* (1939), with the great Elizabeth Bergner. The third is a very good light comedy called *Climbing High* (1939) with Jessie Matthews, a very popular actress then. (This was the first of three films my father made which were directed by Carol Reed.) Again he displays an extraordinarily assured touch for a daft, light, romantic comedy of the kind we associate with the name of Cary Grant.

In the fourth film also the same upright, simple romantic young man appears; I think this is one of his finest performances. *The Stars Look Down* (1940), from a story by A. J. Cronin, again directed by Carol Reed, is not a light comedy; it's a serious film about a mining disaster. Michael plays a young miner, David Fenwick. He hadn't played many working-class men before so he wore his film clothes every day in the street, to see whether people behaved differently towards him when he was dressed in a cloth cap and heavy boots – a workman's clothes – and of course he found that they did.

He found, as Oscar Wilde said, that the poor are wiser, more charitable, kinder, more generous than we are, and he used some of that in his performance. It wouldn't stand the test now in terms of the authenticity of his accent. Funnily enough actors were not particularly bothered about that kind of authenticity then, and didn't have the help of experts such as Joan Washington, experts who have made a study of phonetics, like Professor Higgins in Shaw's *Pygmalion*, and in the sociology of accent. But in all other respects, it's a very authentic performance of a young working-class hero.

As I go on through his film biography I see that that upright simple young man gives way, as he grows older, to a much more troubled person in which the warning he gave himself in that 1939 diary extract about the possibility that the part can take you over is brilliantly and unexpectedly illuminated. Cavalcanti's *Dead of Night* (1945) is, I think, a remarkable film. Cavalcanti didn't make many films in this country. (He directed *Went the Day Well?* for Ealing Studios.) *Dead of Night* is a sextet of ghost stories and in the last of them my father plays Maxwell Frere, a ventriloquist who becomes possessed by his dummy. It is an extraordinary performance. The dummy, by the way, was Archie Andrews, used by Peter Brough for his radio show *Educating Archie*. (It never ceases to amaze me that in post-war

Britain the star of one of the most popular *radio* shows was a ventriloquist.)

My own personal selection of my father's three best performances are from the 1950s. One is *The Dam Busters* (1955), very well directed by Michael Anderson. There are some excellent scenes on a beach where men from the ministry in black coats and homburg hats arrive to watch the success or failure of Barnes Wallis's attempts to build the dam buster bomb. It was made in 1955. You are astounded by how nice everyone is to everyone else, how polite everyone is, how utterly deferential and how orders are given without a flicker of doubt that they will be obeyed instantly, admired, liked and thoroughly agreed with because an order from a superior, like the umpire's decision, was final. This is interesting sociologically because you're clearly moving into a time when precisely those assumptions about class and about rank and about people keeping in their place were being challenged in society. It seems that our films at that time were trying to reassert modes of behaviour which had more or less disappeared. Michael's performance as Barnes Wallis is very fine. It was based on very close observation of Wallis himself, with whom Michael spent several days. They agreed from the outset that he would not try to impersonate Wallis. Physically they were very dissimilar. But I know, because Wallis told me so himself, that he thought my father's performance 'disturbingly' accurate. That's my third favourite.

My second choice of best performance is *The Quiet American* (1958). It was directed by Joseph Mankiewicz, from the Graham Greene novel, but because it was made in 1957 when the cinema was still haunted, even after the death of the senator from Wisconsin, by McCarthyism, Mankiewicz did an unforgivable thing. Much to Graham Greene's dismay, he altered the story. Instead of the young, eponymous, quiet American being the man who, out of the very superfluity of decency and naivety, qualities which Greene records so well and detests so much, actually sends people to their deaths, it becomes the desperate, weary, cynical figure of Fowler who does so.

My father had reason himself to be afraid of McCarthyism. He'd been banned from broadcasting on the BBC during the war because of his sympathies with the Communist Party. He was, I think, mistakenly led by his fear to support Mankiewicz in making his decision. I believe that if he'd stuck out and insisted that Graham Greene's story be followed he might have succeeded. However that may be, the performance of Fowler is very fine. It makes me think that Michael should have acted in *The Heart of the Matter* or *A Burnt-Out Case*.

My first choice of best performance is when my father played Andrew Crocker-Harris in *The Browning Version* (1951). In the climactic scene my father is really crying. That's not such a difficult thing as it may sound – it's not really difficult to cry on stage – but to cry again and again, and to be so clearly distraught, I mean really *physically* distraught as this long film scene required him to be, called for real artistry. I remember my father coming back that afternoon from the studio and I said, 'How are you?' He said 'I've got a headache,' and I said 'Why?', and he said, 'I had to cry so much.' I didn't think anything more about it.

This essay began began life as a lecture at the British Library 'British Cinema of the 1950s' study day in 1998. After it there were questions. Some of these, along with Corin Redgrave's answers, follow.

What part would you say best characterised Michael Redgrave? That is, the one closest to the father you knew?

That's very difficult because, you see, probably the one that was closest to the father that I knew for a long period of time was a film called *Thunder Rock* (1943). It's from a play by an American writer, Robert Ardrey, and it has a very interesting subject. The young James Mason appears briefly in it and very well. It's an enormously veiled performance by my father: very dark, very brooding, very hollow-cheeked, rather remote and inaccessible, entirely suitable to the character, who is a lighthouse keeper who has decided to cut himself off from the rest of society, and that was the father that for long periods of time I knew. However, that does not give a fair portrait of him as a man because there were many other sides to him, even if in life one only glimpsed them rarely. In the film called *The Happy Road* (1957), directed by Gene Kelly in the mid–1950s, he performs a kind of daft, idiotic, British general at NATO headquarters in Paris. It is very funny and there is a sense of play, in the double meaning of the word, which I do associate with him. There is another performance, a lesser-known film of Orson Welles, *Confidential Report* (1955) (in America it is known as *Mr. Arkardin*). This is the only time he appeared as a gay character. He played an antique dealer. He allows himself to do all kinds of things which his film parts would not often allow him to do. But I think my first answer is probably true: the father who I knew for most of my life was the Charleston of *Thunder Rock*.

You mentioned two out of the three favourite performances of your father's were in films you described as seriously flawed. Was it the case that for most of his career he was doing good work with mediocre or lesser material that was not really worthy of him?

I don't think so. As a matter of fact, I think that if you take his work as a whole he was unusually fortunate in working with a number of great directors and scriptwriters. There is undoubtedly a leavening of film that is neither memorable nor something of which he would be particularly proud. But in a career spanning thirty-five years and fifty feature films, that is hardly surprising. My father didn't often have to do that kind of work. I do remember that he returned from Stratford in 1953 nearly bankrupt. Stratford at that time wasn't subsidised and hardly paid actors a living wage. And also he had been particularly imprudent about his financial affairs. He woke up to the fact that he owed an enormous sum of money and he had to make six films, more or less back-to-back. *The Green*

Scarf was one and *The Sea Shall Not Have Them* (1954), which is perhaps the most unmemorable film of them all, is another. Then there was a film by a fine director, Michael Powell, but it's not one of Powell's best efforts, called *Oh, Rosalinda!* (1955), which is a version of *Die Fledermaus*; there is *The Night My Number Came Up* (1954) – not memorable; and *The Dam Busters* which is a well-directed film.

Hollywood burned up some of the greatest talents. When you see Fritz Lang's *Secret Beyond the Door*, made in Hollywood in 1948, you see the work of a great director whose talent is being forced through the mincer of Hollywood's machine and doesn't happily survive, but there is still enough in that film, including my father's performance, to make it of more than just academic interest, I think.

I remember your father giving poetry recitals for the Apollo Society, in the mid-fifties. Gielgud was always praised for verse speaking, but I think your father was remarkable in that way as well.

He was a very all-round artist, or rounded artist. He was a fine pianist, a very fine singer, he spoke perfect French and German, he was a good writer – though he only wrote one novel, *The Mountebank's Tale*. (I have a theory, by the way, about single novels written by artists who excel in other dimensions, that they are often very valuable as a key to the artist's work; read Arthur Miller's novel, *Focus*, and you will see what I mean.) He had a very good ear for cadence, for rhythm, and his verse speaking was, I agree, incomparable. You don't see much of that, naturally, on film. He wrote a very good scenario screenplay for *Antony and Cleopatra*. The Italian producer, Fillipo del Giudice, who produced *Hamlet* for Olivier and *Henry V*, was bringing *Antony and Cleopatra* to the screen. It proved to be just one bridge too far for del Giudice and he just couldn't accomplish it, so it remained sadly a project which never came before the camera. You might guess something of my father's verse speaking from *The Importance of Being Earnest* (1952) because Wilde's prose is very musical, very precise.

You don't see, naturally, much of it in the cinema but certainly it's there. I think it's there in the rhythm of his delivery in *The Browning Version*. It is very interesting indeed to note the pacing of that scene, and to observe how much of that scene he wanted to be shot on his back. He actually wanted the whole scene to be shot on his back. But in the final cut the early part is and then he has to turn around and take the medicine facing the camera. He didn't want to do any of that. He felt that at moments of great emotion one's shoulders are more expressive than any other part of one's body, and I think he was absolutely right. Certainly people who know about massage would tell you that that is true, that this is where the greatest tension is stressed. Alfred Lunt, the great American actor, was famous for being able to convey volumes by turning his back on the audience. I think unfortunately that you would have to have seen my father in the theatre or in recital to have the full measure of his verse speaking. Even a recording can't quite give you that.

Index

Names of actors are listed under the entry 'actors'; British films of the 1950s are mainly listed under the entry 'British films of the 1950s'. Names in brackets indicate authors of printed work. Directors' names (i.e. 'dir') are only given when there are two versions of a film of the same name.